RECLAIMING THE
GREAT COMMISSION

*A Practical Model for Transforming
Denominations and Congregations*

Bishop Claude E. Payne

Hamilton Beazley

JOSSEY-BASS
A Wiley Company
San Francisco

Jossey-Bass books and products are available through most bookstores. To contact Jossey-Bass directly, call (888) 378–2537, fax to (800) 605–2665, or visit our website at www.josseybass.com.

Substantial discounts on bulk quantities of Jossey-Bass books are available to corporations, professional associations, and other organizations. For details and discount information, contact the special sales department at Jossey-Bass.

Manufactured in the United States of America.

Library of Congress Cataloging-in-Publication Data

Payne, Claude E.
  Reclaiming the great commission : a practical model for transforming denominations and congregations / Claude E. Payne, Hamilton Beazley.— 1st ed.
    p. cm.
  Includes bibliographical references and index.
  ISBN 0-7879-5268-0 (alk. paper)
  1. Church renewal.   I. Beazley, Hamilton.   II. Title.
  BV600.2 .P396   2000
  262'.001'7—dc21   00-035737

FIRST EDITION
HB Printing   10 9 8 7 6 5 4 3

CONTENTS

PART ONE
The New Apostolic Age:
Denominational Crisis and Opportunity

PART TWO
The New Apostolic Denomination:
From Maintenance to Mission

PART THREE
Leaders in the New Apostolic Age

PART FOUR
Outreach

LIST OF TABLES, FIGURES, AND EXHIBIT

Tables

Figures

Exhibit

To Barbara, my wife and my joy; to the staff members of the Diocese of Texas, who work tirelessly to support the diocesan vision; and to my mentors, the Reverend Willis P. Gerhart, deceased, and the Right Reverend Scott Field Bailey: "I am always thanking God for you" (I Corinthians 1:3).

—C.E.P.

To my godchildren—Margaret Sherwood Binkley, Andrew Stuart Callaway, Brett Williams Hogan, and Andrew Kitteridge Peters II— with love: "Without ceasing I remember you always in my prayers" (Romans 1:9).

—H.B.

PREFACE

Think of us in this way, as servants of Christ and stewards of
God's mysteries.

—I Corinthians 4:1

THIS BOOK IS ABOUT the congregations, judicatories, and denominations of the Christian Church in the New Apostolic Age of the twenty-first century. Therefore, it is about disciples making disciples, about spiritual transformation, and about the expectation of miracles.

It is also about spiritual hunger in America, the failure of the late-twentieth-century Christian Church to satisfy that hunger, and the drastic and frightening decline in membership among the mainline Protestant denominations. But it addresses these latter topics only as background for describing a biblically based model that can restore the missionary power of first-century Christianity to twenty-first-century mainline denominations and their congregations, which means the power of the miraculous, the power to transform individual lives and, through them, to transform society in ways that are at once breathtaking and enormously satisfying. It was this power of transformation that spread the Christian Gospel from the disciples to the whole of the Roman Empire. It is this same power that must be devoutly offered and vividly communicated to the unchurched in America in order to rebuild the mainline Church in the new century.

Over the past thirty years, the mainline Protestant denominations in America have suffered severe membership declines even as emergent religious sects, independent churches, and quasi-religious philosophies have grown in size and number. Although religious scholars have identified those factors that influence the growth and decline of churches, the mainline Protestants have failed to use this knowledge effectively in their denominations and so continue to lose members. This membership loss is ironic in a nation hungry for spirituality.

Audience for the Book

This book was written for denominational leaders, members of the clergy from small and large congregations, and lay leaders of the mainline Church. It will benefit members of the Roman Catholic Church, Orthodox Churches, and independent congregations who seek a better understanding of the ecclesiastical landscape of the new century. It will also prove useful to church consultants, educators, seminary students, and others seeking to understand the death and potential resurrection of the mainline Protestant denominations in America. The purpose of the book is to propose a new model for denominations, their judicatories, and their congregations, a model that confronts the realities of the New Apostolic Age and offers potential solutions to the crisis that has enveloped the Church. More than that, it offers the tantalizing hope of a potent mainline Church recreated and energized for the new century and powerfully positioned to transform the lives of its disciples and the spiritually hungry.

How can such goals be achieved? A look at first-century Christianity provides an answer. The nature of the early Church can be understood in terms of two fundamental polarities, each of which existed in tension with the other: building community and making disciples. Then and now, these two polarities of community and mission form a dialectic: each preserves and fulfills the other. One is internally oriented; the other is externally oriented. One is directed at disciples, the other at the unchurched. In combination, they create a synergy of meaning and action through which each is reinforced and the whole is magnified.

Metaphorically, the two polarities of community and mission are represented in the actions of St. Paul and St. Peter as revealed in the Acts of the Apostles. St. Paul can be said to represent mission, an external focus of the Church on making disciples. He left Jerusalem to preach the Word of God, particularly to the Gentiles, and to found churches throughout Asia Minor and in Greece. St. Peter, by contrast, can be said to represent community, an internal focus of the Church on meeting the needs of the faithful. Although he also participated in making disciples, his focus remained primarily on the Jewish church. Although the polarities of community and mission were in tension, both were necessary to a vital Church in the first century and, twenty centuries later, are necessary to a vital contemporary Church.

Over the past decades, however, the mainline Church in America has lost its emphasis on mission, concentrating instead on its members. Without mission, community in the mainline Church has come to mean little more than maintenance of the status quo. The Great Commission of Jesus Christ to "make disciples of all nations" has been lost as an essential part of the Christian faith, impoverishing the Church, reducing its membership, and leaving it isolated from the very society it seeks to help. Without an external orientation, the Church begins to die, just as the Dead Sea, without an outlet, fills with salt and fails to support life.

Regaining the balance that the missionary polarity provides will require the mainline Church to reclaim the missionary activity of its denominations and its congregations. But how? One way to achieve this objective is to use a contemporary model of first-century Christianity. This book describes such a transformational model, developed and implemented in the Diocese of Texas, that is based on both community and mission. This model has recaptured the missionary power of the early Church in the congregations of the Episcopal Diocese of Texas.

The Missionary Model

The mainline Christian Church in America is generally considered to include the Roman Catholic Church, the Orthodox Churches, the Episcopal Church (U.S.A.), and, among Protestant denominations, the American Baptist Church, the Disciples of Christ, the Evangelical Lutheran Church of America, the Presbyterian Church (U.S.A.), the Reformed Church in America, the United Church of Christ, and United Methodist Church. Technically, the Episcopal Church (U.S.A.), the Roman Catholic Church, and the Orthodox Churches are not denominations; in this book, however, the term *denomination* will be used to include them as well. All mainline denominations are structured in three parts: the national church (referred to as the *denomination*), the regional church (referred to as the *judicatory,* which may also be called a *diocese, synod,* or *conference*), and the local church (referred to as the *congregation* or *parish*).

The missionary model developed in the Diocese of Texas has proved effective in a judicatory of the Episcopal Church (U.S.A.), but its application is not limited to that denomination. It can be applied by any mainline denomination seeking to revitalize its judicatories and congregations and reverse its membership decline. It can be applied to an entire denomination as well as to a judicatory. It can also be applied to a congregation. This triple application of the model is possible because the three structural levels of a denomination are meant to be integrated, complementary, and synergistic. Each level is but a different part of the mystical Body of Christ. The model can spread upward, from the congregations to the judicatories to the denomination, as well as downward, from the denomination to its judicatories and its congregations. The model can also be implemented across all three levels simultaneously.

The missionary model is at once evolutionary and revolutionary. It entails a dramatic shift in perspective and focus, and yet it feels familiar. The model builds on islands of health and hope within the Church, acknowledging what already works, celebrating strengths, and embracing what has proven effective across denominations. In this respect, the model is evolutionary. Yet the model is more than an enhancement of the status quo, and in this regard it is revolutionary. The model broadly implements proven components of missionary congregations, but it also introduces new components and an overarching vision. It is the combination of the proven and the innovative that creates a contemporary missionary Church designed for the New Apostolic Age.

Although *Reclaiming the Great Commission* is a book about making congregations, judicatories, and denominations more meaningful to their members and more relevant to the unchurched, it is not a mere compendium of concepts and techniques. Rather, it is a call for deep contemplation on the meaning of the phrase "one holy catholic and apostolic Church" in the new century that draws on the two-thousand-year history of the Christian Church, the eternal legacy of Christ, and the power of the Holy Spirit. What this book offers is the vision of a new missionary Church and a path to making that vision a reality. What is unique about the book is that the missionary model it describes has actually been implemented in the judicatory of a mainline denomination by its clergy and laity and has proven to be transformational.

Denominational Advantage

This book offers practical guidelines, principles, and insights for revitalizing and reforming the mainline denominations. The model described in this book and implemented in the Diocese of Texas proceeds from the premise that the mainline Church has a powerful asset in its denominationalism, an asset especially well suited to missionary work, congregational growth, and the transformation of lives in the new century. Recent studies on Church growth have focused almost exclusively on the principles used by independent churches, or by extraordinary congregations in the mainline Church, to reach the unchurched and to build membership. Even when mainline congregations are held out as a model, however, they are described as if they had no connection to other congregations in their denominations. This is a key point. The implicit assumption of such studies is that individual congregations must succeed in spite of their denominations, or at least in isolation from them, and that they must behave more like independent churches. Some authorities have even suggested that the era of denominations is over.

This book takes a different approach. We believe that the era of the twentieth-century denomination is over, but we also believe that the era of the twenty-first-century denomination is just beginning. The dawn of the new millennium can be a time of wondrous transition for the Church as the mainline denominations adapt the powerful asset of their denominationalism to the New Apostolic Age. Their structures, traditions, and established networks can be used effectively and decisively to make disciples and to increase the denominations' membership and influence in the new century. Ironically, these denominational assets have not been used effectively for many decades, even though the organizational world apart from religion is moving toward integrating structures that capitalize on holism, community, and a unifying vision. At the present time, the denominational asset is being squandered. The mainline denominations are following an obsolete model that is largely ineffectual in a world beset by rapid change. Like all organic structures, the Church must adapt to meet the challenges and imperatives of altered circumstances. For two thousand years, the Church has been able to do so. This book is about how it can continue to do so in the new century. It is about denominational change, denominational strength, and denominational growth.

Critical Role of the Laity

Because the missionary model is anchored in the congregations, its implementation can be initiated there by an individual layperson. For example, a lay leader inspired by the missionary model could involve his or her friends in studying it, form a group of laity dedicated to mission, bring the clergy to a new vision for the congregation, transform that congregation, lead another congregation to a similar transformation, form a group of congregations dedicated to community, mission, and personal transformation, and involve the judicatory in implementing the missionary model throughout the congregations. Regardless of whether laypersons initiate implementation of the missionary model, their support is essential. The missionary model is highly dependent on the role of the laity in proclaiming the Word of God, as first-century Christianity also was. The vision of living in expectation of the miraculous and of personal transformation through the power and presence of the Holy Sprit is a compelling one. Such a vision, when expressed, calls people to it, and it calls them to action.

Role of the Clergy

Implementation of the missionary model can be initiated by a single member of the clergy who shares the vision of a missionary Church with his or her congregation, judicatory, or denomination. The clergy thus may lead the laity into the missionary model, or the clergy may follow the laity in supporting it. Clergy may interact with denominational or judicatory leaders to involve multiple judicatories or congregations, may move leaders to adopt the model, or may follow leaders in implementing it. These various alternatives are made possible by the power of the model and its vision to find adherents at every level and to inspire people to follow.

Denominational Polity

Each of the mainline denominations has a different polity, or form of governance, that provides for more centralized or more decentralized decision-making authority. Denominations with episcopal polity (the Episcopal Church, the United Methodist Church, and the Evangelical Lutheran Church of America as well as the Roman Catholic Church and the Orthodox Churches) have more centralized organizational structures. Therefore, their judicatories have more direct involvement in the affairs of their congregations. By contrast, denominations with congregational polity (the American Baptists, the Disciples of Christ, the Presbyterian Church, the Reformed Church in America, and the United Church of Christ) have more decentralized structures, and so their judicatories are less able to directly coordinate and influence the activities of individual congregations.

Everything else being equal, it may be easier to apply the model in denominations with more centralized episcopal polity because bishops in those denominations can directly influence the congregations in their dioceses and more effectively coordinate their policies and activities. Nevertheless, it is possible to apply the model to denominations with congregational polity, but people in decentralized denominations may have to exert greater effort in working together through their judicatories to achieve a common purpose. Because the judicatories are already in place, however, decentralized denominations can use them for this purpose if they choose to do so.

The Episcopal Diocese of Texas is used in this book to illustrate the missionary model because it is the judicatory where the model was developed, and it was the first to implement it. To facilitate an understanding of how the model can be applied to other denominations, it may be helpful to refer to Table 0.1, which shows the terms used for judicatory units and judicatory leaders in churches of the Protestant, Catholic, and Orthodox mainline. The reader, by referring to the table, can ascertain for his or her own denomination the judicatory terminology equivalent to the use of the terms *diocese* and *bishop* in the Diocese of Texas. A Methodist applying the model, for example, would retain the *bishop* to mean the judicatory leader but would substitute the term *conference* for *diocese*. A Presbyterian would substitute *synod executive* for *bishop* and *synod* for *diocese* in order to understand their roles in his or her own church.

A Work in Progress

The missionary model for evangelism and transformation, as implemented in the Diocese of Texas, remains a work in progress. Although many changes will still occur, however, its essential elements are now in place

Table 0.1 Governance Structures of the Mainline Churches.

Denomination	Term for Judicatory Unit	Term for Judicatory Leader
Protestant/Anglican Denominations		
American Baptist	Convention	Executive minister
Disciples of Christ	Region	Regional minister
The Episcopal Church, U.S.A.	Diocese	Bishop
Evangelical Lutheran Church of America	Synod	Bishop
Presbyterian Church (U.S.A.)	Synod (composed of presbyteries)	Synod executive
Reformed Church in America (R.C.A.)	Regional synods (composed of classes)	President
United Church of Christ	Association	Moderator
United Methodist Church	Conference (composed of districts)	Bishop
Non-Protestant/Non-Anglican Denominations		
Orthodox Church	Diocese	Bishop
Roman Catholic Church	Diocese	Bishop

and understood. The Episcopal Diocese of Southern Ohio implemented the model in the fall of 1998, and the effect has been remarkable. The Right Reverend Herbert Thompson Jr., Bishop of Southern Ohio, says that in the short time since its implementation, the model "has changed the very nature of the diocese, who we are, and what we are called to be and do as God's people" (personal communication, January 28, 2000). Other dioceses and denominations, intrigued by the model's transformational potential, are also studying it. The missionary language of the model has begun to appear in Episcopal Church writings and in interviews with and talks by liberal and conservative bishops alike. It is now being considered as a model for whole denominations.

This book describes a nascent model, not a final one, a model that is still evolving, still developing. The missionary model of the Christian Church in the New Apostolic Age is still being born. How it will be applied across the spectrum of the mainline Churches is still unknown. The model presented in this book is offered by a group of pilgrims with the expectation that, in the fullness of time, other expressions will be developed and used to strengthen and enlarge the mainline Church and fulfill its potential for meeting the spiritual needs of God's people in America. We are confident that the features described in this book can be adapted by all dioceses of the Episcopal Church, by the national Episcopal Church, and by any other mainline denomination as a model for the national church, judicatories, and congregations.

Overview of the Book

This book consists of four parts. Part One explores the New Apostolic Age of the twenty-first century and the crises and opportunities it presents for the mainline denominations. It addresses the spiritual hunger in America and the church's opportunity to address that hunger. It also discusses the paradigm that has guided the Christian Church in many parts of the world since the days of the Roman Empire, and it describes the New Apostolic Age of the twenty-first century.

Part Two describes the missionary model applied to denominations, judicatories, and congregations. It also describes the development and implementation of a guiding vision, the changes in organizational alignment and culture that accompany the vision, the management of resistance to change, and congregational development. The model is described in enough detail for clergy and lay leaders in the mainline Church to be able to implement it.

Part Three explores the role of the clergy and lay leaders in the New Apostolic Age. It examines the nature of missionary congregations, the apostolate of the laity, the apostolate of the clergy, and the apostolate of judicatory leaders in the missionary Church.

Part Four examines the evangelistic focus of outreach in the New Apostolic Age, the importance of communications, the role of technology, and the nature of Christian education and youth ministry.

Throughout Christian history, the Holy Spirit has moved among the faithful when a loss of missionary focus has weakened the Body of Christ and divided its people. From such movement, a renewed commitment to the Gospel has emerged to strengthen the Church and its mission in the world. Let us pray that now is such a time.

March 2000   CLAUDE E. PAYNE
                                                          Houston, Texas

                                                       HAMILTON BEAZLEY
                                                        Washington, D.C.

ACKNOWLEDGMENTS

MANY INDIVIDUALS gave generously of their time, effort, and expertise in order to make this book possible. Although it bears our names, it is their offering as well as ours.

For their insights, contributions, and encouragement, we are especially grateful to the staff members of the Diocese of Texas, to whom this book is in part dedicated: Leo Alard, Carol Barnwell, Kathy Barrow, Robert Browne, Ronda Carman, Gordon Charlton, Eleanor Chote, Susan Cooper, Arlie Eldridge, David Galloway, Rayford High, Alice Kerr, Sherley Holden, Nancy Lennard, John Logan, Kevin Martin, Jennifer Michel, Bonnie Montgomery, Ron Null, Judy Perez, Sally Rutherford, Rebecca Seay, Joel Shannon, Noreen Statham, Bill Sterling, Gay Stricklin, David Thames, and Don Wimberly.

Rebecca Seay, Bishop Payne's administrative assistant, was tireless in keeping the two of us connected despite our travel schedules, in coordinating our times together, and in keeping track of the materials flowing between us.

The Reverend and Mrs. David Thames and the staff at Camp Allen were exceedingly gracious during our stays there for conferencing and writing, and they made Hamilton Beazley in particular feel very much at home. Father Thames also provided counsel and encouragement during the development of this book, and for that we are grateful.

Special thanks go to our editor at Jossey-Bass, Sarah Polster, who made important contributions to the book and supported its publication from the beginning. We are also thankful to Beth Gaede, a freelance editor, who caught the spirit of the book from the first draft and made valuable suggestions that significantly improved the design, concept, and effectiveness of the manuscript.

John W. Baker, D.D.S., Ph.D., M.Div., provided us with editorial support and the miracle of the catch as a metaphor for the work. He also contributed a unique spiritual perspective that enhanced several portions of the book. A number of other people read the manuscript at various stages of its development and made suggestions that were much appreciated. For these contributions we thank James J. McGee, Ph.D., spirituality and business project director at the Leavey School of Business of Santa Clara University; Canon Frederick Barbee, editor of *The Anglican Digest*; the Reverend Hugh Magers of the Office of Evangelism of the Protestant Episcopal Church in the United States; and the Right Reverend Scott Field Bailey, now retired, Sixth Bishop of West Texas.

Our families were very supportive throughout the process of our writing this book, and we are grateful for their love and encouragement. We thank Bishop Payne's wife, Barbara, and his two children, Elizabethe and Walter; and Hamilton Beazley's brother, Herbert Beazley.

We would also like to thank many unnamed members of the Diocese of Texas, both laity and clergy, who shared their personal stories of transformation with us, encouraged our work, and showed us the real power of the missionary Church living in miraculous expectation.

PROLOGUE

Yet if You say so, I will let down the nets.

—Simon Peter to Jesus Christ

A READING FROM the fifth chapter of Luke, verses 1–10:

Once while Jesus was standing beside the lake of Gennesaret, and the crowd was pressing in on Him to hear the Word of God, He saw two boats there at the shore of the lake; the fishermen had gone out of them and were washing their nets. He got into one of the boats, the one belonging to Simon, and asked him to put out a little way from the shore. Then He sat down and taught the crowds from the boat. When He had finished speaking, He said to Simon, "Put out into the deep water and let down your nets for a catch." Simon answered, "Master, we have worked all night long but have caught nothing. Yet if You say so, I will let down the nets." When they had done this, they caught so many fish that their nets were beginning to break. So they signaled their partners in the other boat to come and help them. And they came and filled both boats, so that they began to sink. But when Simon Peter saw it, he fell down at Jesus' knees, saying, "Go away from me, Lord, for I am a sinful man!" For he and all who were with him were amazed at the catch of fish that they had taken; and so also were James and John, sons of Zebedee, who were partners with Simon. Then Jesus said to Simon, "Do not be afraid; from now on you will be catching people."

This story of Jesus and the miraculous catch is a metaphor for the mainline denominations in the New Apostolic Age. Please keep it in mind as you read this book. We will return to it in the Epilogue.

PART ONE

THE NEW APOSTOLIC AGE

DENOMINATIONAL CRISIS AND OPPORTUNITY

I

SPIRITUAL HUNGER
IN AMERICA

---

*"It is written, 'One does not live by bread alone, but by every
word that comes from the mouth of God.'"*

—Jesus Christ (Matthew 4:4)

IN THE FINAL, PROSPEROUS YEARS of the twentieth century, no hunger
seemed deeper within the American soul than an unsatisfied longing for
spirituality. The new century and the new millennium have brought no
end to this spiritual yearning. Surveys consistently indicate that a large
majority of American adults remain dissatisfied despite the material
rewards they have accumulated, the physical pleasures they have experienced, and the leisure time they have taken (Barna, 1995, p. 22). Americans are reeling emotionally from daily life in a society traumatized by too
much violence, too many divided families, and too little job security. The
pain and isolation caused by reliance on material things and on human
resources alone has grown unbearable. People are searching for something
more meaningful and more enduring. As a result, tens of millions of
unchurched Americans are open to a set of spiritual truths that will free
them from the burdens of materialism and the shackles of worldliness. Increased sales of religious and spiritual books, spirituality touted as a solution to corporate problems, and advertising references to spirituality
characterize this new century as various segments of society seek to capitalize on the nation's spiritual hunger.

Even science has entered the spiritual arena by confirming the relationship between faith and health and offering scientific support for the medical value of a spiritual orientation. For example, at a Houston conference sponsored by Harvard Medical School on spirituality and healing in medicine, physicians heard how "belief in a higher power and prayer can give comfort from suffering, speed healing and improve health" (Jones, 1998, p. 8E). Consider these research findings, reported at the same conference:

- Open-heart surgery patients are twelve times more likely to survive if they have religious faith and social support.

- Mortality rates are 25 percent lower for men and 35 percent lower for women who attend religious services once a week or more.

- People who attend church or synagogue once a week are more likely to live longer.

- One-third of the medical schools in the United States now offer courses on medicine and spirituality. As reported by Jones (1998, p. 8E), Larry Dossey, a former Dallas internist and author of *Healing Words: The Power of Prayer and the Practice of Medicine,* says that the medicine-and-spirituality movement is "just exploding."

Some religious experts have suggested that America is on the verge of another great awakening—a prolonged period of religious interest that has occurred every so often in history. Michael Novak (1998, p. 11), writing in the *New York Times,* predicts that "the 21st century will be the most religious in 500 years," and he quotes George Gallup as having observed that "the focus of the 20th century has been on outer space, but the focus of the 21st century may well be on inner space" as spirituality receives increased attention in the new millennium.

And yet the incipient great awakening of the twenty-first century is already proving to be substantially different from previous awakenings. Why? Because this awakening is being driven, not by Christian religious denominations, but by spiritual individualism that honors spiritual values, discipline, and ethics while often rejecting the traditional religions from which they are derived. Tragically, the mainline denominations have not effectively responded to America's spiritual hunger, nor are they positioning themselves to do so. As Kew and White (1997, p. 20) have observed, "People are persistently asking spiritual questions for which the churches seem to have either mislaid or forgotten the answers." Thus spirituality in the new century is not necessarily grounded in established religion and may even be hostile to it.

As might be expected, the growth in unmet spiritual needs has paralleled declining membership in the mainline denominations over the past three decades. This decline is reflected in absolute membership and, more dramatically, in the number of members as a percentage of the American population. For example, the United Methodists are losing approximately forty thousand members per year and have shrunk from 11.1 million to 8.5 million over the last thirty years (Vara, 1999, p. 1E). Various denominations in the 1980s undertook initiatives to reverse these declines. In 1984, the United Methodist Church approved the objective of doubling its membership by 1992, the United Church of Christ made evangelism a priority from 1989 to 1993 (Hadaway and Roozen, 1995, p. 10), and the Episcopal Church declared the 1990s the "decade of evangelism." With the exception of recent modest gains by the Episcopalians, the decline in mainline denominational membership continues. By contrast, the Mormons have grown an average of 43 percent per decade for each decade of the past century (Stark, 1996, p. 7). Today, 50 percent of all churchgoing Americans are not members of mainline churches (Trueheart, 1996, p. 1).

Recent polls about belief in God are also disturbing. According to Broadway (1997, p. B7), writing in the *Washington Post,* the Gallup Poll recently found that 96 percent of Americans still believed in God (by comparison with 95 percent in 1947), but the Barna Poll found that one-third of the Americans who said they believed in God did not believe in the biblical God but in a "higher consciousness" or an Eastern god or even "many gods." Between 4 and 5 percent of Americans believe that they themselves are God.

American society has "edited out the sense of the 'spiritual' or 'holy' which pervades the lives of people in more traditional societies at every level and which was once an essential component of our human experience of the world" (Armstrong, 1993, p. 4). In so doing, Americans have divorced themselves from their spiritual nature. Ancient pagans, like contemporary Christians, believed that human beings were derived from the same divine substance as God. Until the Enlightenment, a few hundred years ago, it had always been assumed that human beings were innately spiritual, and divine involvement in human affairs was taken for granted. Although the origins of religion remain hidden, the idea of God is a constant presence in those human civilizations of which any records remain. Through the millennia, the world's organized religious traditions have embodied humankind's primary effort to give form and practice to its sense of the spiritual. Through the myths, stories, and religious doctrines that developed around their worship of gods, human beings have attempted to find an explanation for the mystery of their lives and the wonder of the universe. They have sought to experience what Rudolf Otto has called the numinous, the *mysterium tremendum*. The reverence for new life that we experience in the presence of a newborn infant is fundamentally religious, a manifestation of the religious dimension of our existence. The birth of a new family through marriage brings a similar experience of joy and reverence. Both provide a glimpse of the love and presence of God, to which we react at the deepest level.

Spiritual hunger can be understood as the deep yearning of the human soul for contact with God—the yearning for awareness of an ongoing relationship with the Transcendent, more profound than anything available in the material world. From this relationship with God flows a satisfying relationship with oneself and with others in the world. This desire for spiritual contact is a reflection of the call of the Creator to the created. It is a call that must be answered for life to be meaningful. The absence of spirituality can be described as a hole in the center of one's being that not even fame, power, wealth, beauty, or intelligence—the greatest prizes of the material world—can fill. This yearning for completeness, for the joining of human life and experience to the power and love of the immanent and transcendent God, exists in all human beings. It may be denied or rejected, but it is nevertheless defining, initiating in each human being a search for the divine or for some material substitute that might provide meaning and purpose.

Every human being worships at some altar. It may be at the altar of God, or it may be at the altar of fame, wealth, power, pleasure, or a hundred other forms of idolatry. Human life always has a reference point, something that is central and determining. Every human being has such a reference point—a faith relationship with something, whether this relationship is stated or not. A faith relationship entails trust in and loyalty to centers of value that are of ultimate concern to human beings and to the images of power with which they align themselves, centers of value and images of power on which people act in order to survive in an uncertain world. (This definition of a faith relationship is adapted from one developed by Fowler, 1991, p. 23.) Whether these centers of value and images of power are spiritual or purely materialistic, faith in them as the ultimate concern of life drives, directs, and motivates human behavior. The spiritual hunger in America is a reflection of faith relationships centered on material concerns rather than on spiritual truths. Christ's admonition that one cannot live by bread alone speaks directly to this point.

The hunger that drives this search for spirituality in America has several sources. One source of this famine of the soul is the absence of a meaningful relationship with the eternal God. Another source of spiritual hunger is the deeply felt need among the unchurched for hope and healing. As human weakness is exposed in the trials and tribulations of life, the resources of our humanity are overwhelmed and, intuitively, we turn for assistance to some greater power. One has only to read the newspaper or watch the news to find persistent evidence of the demonic in society. To rise above the self-defeating elements of existence and reject the false idols of the material world will require spiritual help. The psalmist writes, in Psalm 30:2, "O Lord my God, I cried to you for help, and you have healed me." Such spiritual healing, like physical healing, is a form of glorious personal transformation.

A third source of spiritual hunger is found in those who have felt, however briefly, the divine presence and want to experience more of it. Such men and women begin searching for someone or some institution to guide them along a spiritual path of which they as yet know very little. They are open to spiritual development and eager for it, but they do not often hear the call of God in the words and actions of the mainline Church. Instead, they search elsewhere and become prey to others who do reach out to their urgent hunger with promises of spiritual food.

In the first century, the Church proclaimed the answers to spiritual questions and sought to feed the spiritual hunger of the people. The story of the Christian Church is a story of self-transcendence and glorious transformation. Transcendence of the self leads to humility and to a sense of the interconnectedness of all things and of the sacredness of human life. With self-transcendence, we are relieved of some of the burdens of materiality, and we commune with the divine aspect of ourselves, which is beyond the pain and sorrow of mortality. By touching the eternal, we are empowered to find the joy that eludes us in our "lives of quiet desperation," to use Thoreau's famous phrase. Churches can foster such transcendence through their focus on God, love, and the need to serve others. Moreover, churches can provide a medium that makes it possible for such transcendence to occur. In the words of Christ, "I have said these things to you so that my joy may be in you, and that your joy may be complete" (John 15:11).

Imprisoned souls cry out for release from materiality and false gods. A spiritual rescue in which someone is saved from depravity and restored to wholeness and strength is the province of the Church and the work of God. Psalm 81:7 is a reminder of God's ever-present concern: "In distress you called, and I rescued you." The divine rescue finds its parallel in the eagerness of loving parents who restore their wayward child to a state of freedom so that the consequences of some ill-advised action will not be permanently damaging.

Less dramatic but no less important than a spiritual rescue are transformations that result from the acceptance of life's challenges. Such acceptance recognizes that suffering and struggle are part of psychological and spiritual growth and that divine assistance and comfort are available to strengthen and encourage the faithful. Christ's Resurrection after His acceptance of death on the cross illustrates the blessing that results from a commitment to the attainment of something larger and more significant than oneself. This lesson of struggle and sacrifice is a primary lesson of Christianity, and its validity is confirmed daily in Christian life.

Christianity is not a way to escape the trials and tribulations of mortal life but rather a way to overcome them, to handle them effectively and meaningfully and so find purpose in the pain they bring. Christ Himself was not denied freedom from suffering. He embraced it for the purposes it served. The way of the cross—of acceptance, love, and transformation—that Christ exemplified is the pathway to fulfillment and to the realization of our potential as God's creatures. It is one of the great promises of the Christian faith that is always kept in the lives of the faithful. Christianity leads us, through the example of Christ, to accept our own crosses, those burdens given specifically to us through which we grow in faith and service. As Christians, we are not called to ignore or deny the pain and suffering of the world but rather to find, in overcoming them, a transformation of our souls. With faith and the Holy Spirit, we need not cower before the uncertainties and difficulties of human life; rather, we can be reconciled to them. In such reconciliation, we encounter the presence of God and experience transcendence. And we are remade.

The early Christian Church was filled with stories of God's transforming power. Pagans became disciples, not because of what they read in the Bible (which did not exist in the earliest days), but because of what they experienced in the Christian community. And what they experienced was the awesome power of the love of God, expressed through the community of believers and felt directly in the depths of their souls. Pagans heard stories from Christians about miraculous changes in their lives, and they came to experience those changes themselves. People were converted because they saw and felt the power of God, were loved, and were healed. It is the experience of the Holy Spirit that changes people, and it is this experience that the unchurched seek. The Christian faith will satisfy spiritual needs in marvelous ways. To feed the spiritually hungry in the midst of so great a famine in America, however, will require the mainline Church to return to its roots, to the early Church, to the Great Commandment and the Great Commission of our Lord, Jesus Christ. It will mean a return to the experiential, to knowing the power and love of the living God in everyday life.

The role of the Church, therefore, is not to create a demand for religious experiences within people but rather to address and effectively satisfy the demand that already exists. This point is crucial in understanding the importance of evangelism in Christian life. Evangelistic activities are carried out in answer to a plea, even though the plea may be disguised or unstated. Evangelism is not intrusive; it is responsive. To reject evangelism is to reject the plea and ignore the hope of alienated individuals who are looking, through a relationship with God, for some meaning and purpose in their lives.

Spiritual development is a process. It unfolds through an organized program that provides instruction and that supports disciplined effort. Spiritual development occurs within an individual, but not in the absence of others. It is the product of interaction with other human beings and with God, who often uses human beings to carry out the divine work. Spiritual development is not an event but rather a way of life that leads to a deeper and more powerful relationship to God. Even sudden conversions are merely antecedents to spiritual work. There is no graduation from the Christian faith, just an ever-deepening experience of the eternal and its manifestation in the world. Spiritual development takes time, effort, and patience. It is both a commitment and a dedication.

The Church is particularly well qualified to direct spiritual development, understanding as it does the process that is involved and the structure that is necessary. As a community of spiritual wisdom, the Church holds thousands of years of knowledge about the myriad ways that God is present in our lives. As a depository of these spiritual experiences, the Church can support the unique journey that characterizes each individual's spiritual development.

What is equally important, the Church can set aside the too-easy, feel-good techniques of so-called spiritual development that are offered by some groups but that deny or minimize the existence of sin and imperfection and that reject or minimize the need for rigorous self-examination as a necessary element of spiritual growth. Spirituality is not about doing what one wants but rather about doing what God wants. Although spiritual development is not painless, it is deeply rewarding and enormously satisfying precisely because it represents a repudiation of false gods and impotent altars—a process of rededication and realignment that is not without suffering. Yet the pain of abandoning false gods is nothing in comparison to the joy of embracing the real God. Spiritual development marks a reunification of the estranged soul with its Creator, a realignment of the individual will with the divine will, and a rejoining of the beloved child with its divine Parent. Such experiences speak to the very essence of the soul, to the core of being.

The Church also provides an outlet for spirituality through the opportunities for service that it offers. Spirituality is faith carried into the world. It provides a way of dealing more joyfully and effectively with the trials and triumphs of life. Spiritual growth is not a retreat from the world but rather a bold venture into it. Churches need to reclaim everyday life and especially the workplace as a relevant setting for applying the Christian faith. The actions of Christ in the world were about the world and about the Kingdom of God in the world as well as about the life to come. Healing the sick, casting out demons, raising the dead, and feeding the multitudes were ways of solving fundamental problems of the world as well as of the spirit. The material world provides the field of practice in which a Christian applies and strengthens his or her spirituality and faith and so learns to face the daily challenges of life with joy and confidence.

Two broad responses have resulted from the failure of the mainline denominations to reach the unchurched and to fill the void that the absence of spirituality creates in the human soul. Each of these responses represents one extreme on a spectrum born of disillusionment and frustration; both are efforts to revise the inherited structure and meaning of the Christian Church. Religious fundamentalism, as one extreme, offers a concrete, absolute structure of belief that some find appealing, but that is ultimately restricting. Fundamentalist cults and sects unaffiliated with mainline denominations have grown up and flourished, providing rigid answers to the call for spiritual help. The other extreme has sought to discredit the theological language of the Church, even rejecting the Resurrection and denying the active role of God in human affairs. Heresies like these, long ago repudiated but recently publicized, distract the faithful from the real work of the Church.

Instead of these two empty responses to the spiritual crisis in America, a new one is needed, one that expresses the Christian faith in language that is secular enough to be understood by the unchurched but theological enough to be transformational. These goals are identical with those of Christianity in the first century, when the Church sought to spread the Good News and make disciples of the world. The primary focus of the early Church was the glorious transformation of lives. The stories of transformation that characterized the apostles and those whose lives were touched by Jesus Christ were expected to be replicated in the lives of believers. The Bible is a story of transformations. The apostles were gloriously changed by their relationship with Jesus. So were those people who experienced or witnessed His miracles—the feedings, the healings, the conversions. Jesus left this legacy of transformational power to His disciples, who were called on to continue this work. The early Church was a community where miracles of human transformation were courted and expected as a natural aspect of Christian life. In the ensuing centuries, however, the Church sometimes lost this life-changing focus; and today, at the beginning of this new century, we find ourselves in another such time. As a result, the Church is once again in need of becoming a missionary church in a largely unchurched world. Acceptance of this responsibility can be a force for liberation and empowerment, transforming the Church, its disciples, and those among the unchurched who are drawn to the promise of a glorious transformation of their lives.

Just as in the first century, the Church in the third millennium has a wondrous opportunity before it: to once again proclaim the Word of God to the world. If the Christian community can recover its sense of being God's agent for transformation, and if it can recover its passion for making disciples, it can reach out to the spiritually hungry and offer them the rich banquet of the Christian life. The spiritual hunger in America, like any other kind of hunger, will be satisfied one way or another, or the hungry will die. Spiritually hungry people can feast at the table of a mainline denomination, or they can make do with the spiritual equivalent of junk food, offered by whoever holds out the first morsel.

In the new century, the innate spirituality of the human being will find expression in some form of religion. The question for the mainline denominations is whether that religion will be in the mainline or take some other form. The answer lies not so much with the spiritually hungry as it does with us, the members of the mainline Church. We are the ones with the bounty to offer. We must choose between hoarding it and sharing it with others. This is no small choice, either for us or for them. Because upon that choice hinges the future of the mainline denominations in the new century and the lives of the people who need our help.

2

THE GREAT COMMISSION

*Go therefore and make disciples of all nations, baptizing them
in the name of the Father and of the Son and of the Holy
Spirit, and teaching them to obey everything that I have
commanded you.*

—Jesus Christ to His disciples (Matthew 18:16–20)

ON A MOUNTAINSIDE, the resurrected Jesus Christ appeared before His
disciples. When they saw Him, they worshiped Him. Jesus said to them,
"All authority in heaven and on earth has been given to Me. Go therefore
and make disciples of all nations, baptizing them in the name of the Father and of the Son and of the Holy Spirit, and teaching them to obey
everything I have commanded you. And remember, I am with you always,
to the end of the age." This instruction of the risen Christ to His disciples,
as recorded in Matthew, has been called the Great Commission of the
Christian Church. The central ideas of the Great Commission are not exclusive to the Matthean Gospel. They also appear, with different wording, in the Gospels of Mark, Luke, and John, and always in the context
of the disciples' experience of Jesus' Resurrection.

The Great Commission

The purpose of this chapter is to familiarize the reader with the Great Commission because this command of Jesus Christ is central to the life and
work of the Christian Church and to the new apostolic denominations of
the twenty-first century. The Great Commission provides the basis for

Christian evangelism, which seems to be seriously misunderstood by many in the mainline Church. The word *evangel* is a transliteration of a Greek word that means "good tidings" or "good news." In the New Testament, the word is used to refer both to the good news that Jesus proclaimed concerning the Kingdom of God and the good news that Jesus embodied with His life.

Five questions, adapted from Arias and Johnson (1992, p. 13), offer a fruitful way to understand the nature of evangelism, how it ought to be conducted, and what it means for congregations and the faithful who embrace it:

1. What is the process of evangelism, and how is it to be carried out?

2. What is the message of evangelism? In other words, what is the content of the Christian message that is being carried to the unchurched?

3. What is the reason for evangelism—that is, why do we carry it out?

4. At whom should our evangelistic efforts be aimed?

5. Who is responsible for evangelism?

Each of the four Gospels of Matthew, Mark, Luke, and John answers these questions in a somewhat different way. Together, the Gospels provide a comprehensive understanding of the nature of Christian mission. The Great Commission appears in the Gospels in the following ways:

> And Jesus came and said to them [the eleven disciples], "All authority in heaven and on earth has been given to Me. Go therefore and make disciples of all nations, baptizing them in the name of the Father and of the Son and of the Holy Spirit, and teaching them to obey everything I have commanded you. And remember, I am with you always, to the end of the age" [Matthew 28:18–20].

> And He said to them, "Go into all the world and proclaim the good news to the whole creation" [Mark 16:15].

> Then He opened their minds to understand the scriptures, and He said to them, "Thus it is written, that the Messiah is to suffer and to rise from the dead on the third day and that repentance and forgiveness of sins is to be proclaimed in His name to all nations, beginning from Jerusalem. You are witnesses of these things. And see I am sending upon you what My Father promised; so stay here in the city until you have been clothed with power from on high" [Luke 24:45–49].

Jesus said to them again, "Peace be with you. As the Father has sent Me, so I send you." When He had said this, He breathed on them and said to them, "Receive the Holy Spirit. If you forgive the sins of any, they are forgiven them; if you retain the sins of any, they are retained" [John 20:21–23].

The Process of Evangelism

In the Great Commission of Matthew, Jesus describes the process of evangelism as making disciples of all nations through baptism and teaching. The word *disciple* is derived from a Greek word meaning "learner" or "pupil." If discipleship is the heart of evangelism, then learning is the heart of discipleship. The goal of evangelism is not the development of nominal Christians but of devoted Christians who become disciples who make other disciples and whose lives are enriched by their relationship with God.

Discipleship is more than doctrinal instruction or religious training. It is word and deed combined; it is proclamation and demonstration. The Lord's commandment to His disciples was to teach all nations to obey everything that He had commanded them. Like the original disciples, contemporary disciples are called on to understand the doctrinal principles of the faith (orthodoxy) and the way to apply them meaningfully in daily life (orthopraxis). Jesus' life was the perfect example of this integration of word (teaching) and deed (action). Matthew recounts, "Then Jesus went about all the cities and villages, teaching in their synagogues, and proclaiming the good news of the kingdom, and curing every disease and every sickness" (Matthew 9:35).

Every Christian is called on to demonstrate his or her faith. We teach more effectively by example than by exhortation. In contemporary parlance, we have to "walk the talk." Matthew writes, "You will know them [the false prophets or true disciples] by their fruits" (Matthew 7:16). You will know them, in other words, not by what they say, but by what they do. Christ said, "Only the one who does the will of My Father in Heaven . . . who hears these words of mine and acts on them . . . will be like a wise man who built his house on rock. . . . And everyone who . . . does not act on them will be like a foolish man" (Matthew 7:21, 24, 26).

In the Marcan version of the Great Commission, the instrument of mission and evangelism is proclamation; in the Lucan version, it is proclamation and witness. This call to proclaim the Good News and to witness to it resonates with contemporary individuals. Human beings want to proclaim what is important to them, what has made a difference in their lives, and to share it with others who might benefit. A church that is alive with the spiritual power of Jesus Christ is a church that has witnessed the transforming power of the Holy Spirit and wants to share that power with others. For such a church, evangelism is inherent in the faith.

Message of Evangelism

In Matthew's version of the Great Commission, Jesus' commandment is to make disciples of all nations, "teaching them to obey everything that I have commanded you." In Mark's version, Christ's command is even simpler: "Go into all the world and proclaim the good news to the whole creation." New disciples are to be created by committed disciples, who continue to teach through word and deed what Jesus has taught and done. The content of mission—the message of evangelism—is therefore the Good News of Jesus Christ.

Reason for Evangelism

The motivation for evangelism, as described in Matthew, is the experience of the living Lord, the risen Christ. The power of the Resurrection focused and revitalized a scattered and demoralized group of disciples and turned them into a phalanx of believers who spread the Gospel to the farthermost reaches of the Roman Empire. The Resurrection converted cowardly people who had fled for their lives into courageous people who were willing to surrender their lives. It transformed a group of Jewish disciples into a core of devoted followers. In all the Gospel versions of the Great Commission, the risen Christ is the motivation to spread the Good News to all the nations. The power of the living Christ to continue His transformational work on earth, even after death, was news of such import that it could not be contained. The fervor of evangelism rose from this singular event in human history and from love of Christ, who had loved the sinners and had died for them.

In our time, evangelism is a gift that we offer out of gratitude and joy for what we have been given. It is through evangelism that the Holy Spirit moves in us and through us to connect us to other human beings with whom we share God's gift of life. We cannot, as good disciples, avoid our obligation to spread the Good News to the spiritually hungry. Evangelism is an activity that we carry out at Christ's command, for ourselves as well as for other people. Our own spiritual experience deepens through our sharing of our faith. If we do not engage in evangelistic activities, then we miss one of the great opportunities of the Christian faith: to be used by the Holy Spirit in the Lord's work.

Whom to Evangelize

The Matthean Gospel is clear about the objective of evangelism: to make disciples of all nations. There are not to be any exceptions in God's Kingdom. The Jews, Gentiles, Samaritans, men, women, children, prostitutes, tax collectors, and Roman centurions were all appropriate subjects for evangelistic efforts. The Marcan Gospel is likewise clear: "Go into all the world and proclaim the good news to all the world." The Kingdom of God is inclusive, not exclusive, built on love of neighbor and of God, and open to the whole of creation.

This aspect of the Great Commission is especially important in a society and a century of increasing diversity. Our missionary work is to embrace all those who are spiritually hungry—all of the unchurched, the lost, and the hurting—not merely those who seem like ourselves. We are united in creation by our divine Parent, who sees us as brothers and sisters, not as different races, genders, or job descriptions. We are the Body of Christ, each of us different, each of us crucial, each of us part of one another.

Responsibility for Evangelism

In the account of Matthew, the disciples are the ones to whom the Great Commission is addressed, but the call is much wider. The Great Commission is given to all who have heard the Good News. In the contemporary Church, responsibility for evangelism lies not just with the clergy but also with the laity, even primarily with the laity. Evangelical folk wisdom expresses it this way: "Shepherds do not make new sheep; sheep make new sheep" (Hunter, 1996, p. 157).

Nevertheless, it is the responsibility of the Church to prepare its people for evangelism by teaching them what evangelism means and how it is to be carried out. Even in this role, however, the laity play a critical part.

The Great Commandment

The Great Commission's instruction to obey everything that Christ has commanded springs from the Great Commandment, which the Great Commission therefore incorporates. According to Matthew (22:36–40), a Pharisee asked Christ this question: "'Teacher, which commandment in the law is the greatest?' [Christ] said to him, 'You shall love the Lord your God with all your heart, and with all your soul, and with all your mind. This is the greatest and first commandment. And a second is like it: You shall love your neighbor as yourself. On these two commandments hang all the law and the prophets.'" On these two commandments also hang the meaning and purpose of evangelism.

The love of God and of our neighbor impels us to engage in evangelism. Evangelism is God's work but our responsibility. It is a measure of our commitment to Jesus Christ and to God's commandments. Everything the early Church "was called to be and do in its worship, witness, fellowship, and service was infused and informed by evangelism" (Dunnam, 1992, p. 2). In the Christian faith, the love of God and of our neighbor pleads for experiential expression. How deeply we believe in the power of the Christian faith and of the triune God to transform lives will determine how committed we are to evangelism. In other words, if our own faith convinces us that Christ is the hope of salvation in this world and the next, then we cannot help spreading that news. The Great Commandment and the Great Commission provide a litmus test for individual faith and for the collective faith of a congregation, judicatory, or denomination.

Evangelism is not a program of the Church; rather, it is the essential work of the Church. It is not an option for Christians but an obligation, a fundamental commission of their Christ. Mission infuses all that the Church does. No person living richly and fully in his or her faith can ignore the call to make disciples of others. Evangelism, properly understood, is a powerful and rewarding activity of the faithful, a means of spiritual growth, and an invitation to an ongoing, intimate relationship with the God of abundant and everlasting life.

3

THE NEW APOSTOLIC AGE

Rejoice with me, for I have found my sheep that was lost.

—Luke 15:6

THE WORD *APOSTLE* comes from the Greek *apostolos*, which means "one who is sent out." An apostle is commissioned to accomplish a task and carries the authority of the person who sent him or her. In the Gospel tradition, the closest followers of Jesus were called apostles by virtue of their having been commissioned to preach and to heal, as Christ had done.

First Apostolic Age

The *First Apostolic Age* refers to the period in which the apostles spread the Good News of Jesus Christ throughout the Roman Empire and, ultimately, beyond, and in which evangelism was of paramount importance to the Church. The apostles and the disciples they baptized spread the word even "to the ends of the earth." Had evangelism not been central to the work of the Church in the First Apostolic Age, there would have been no Church.

In fact, all that the Church became (and splintered into) rose out of the act and process of evangelism. The Church did not develop its creed and literature and then, one day, with everything neatly packaged and ready, begin to evangelize. Rather, in response to the Great Commandment and the Great Commission, members of the early Church began to "make disciples." Through that process, they developed a creed and a literature that served their work. The New Testament did not predate evangelism; rather, evangelism predated the New Testament. The New Testament was a result of evangelism. It was a tool for the Church's evangelistic efforts, a permanent record of the Good News that the Church was seeking to spread. Therefore, the Church grew out of the effort to carry the message of Jesus Christ. What drove the formation of the early Church and fueled the growth of that Church was the power of God's Word. It is a critical mistake to reverse the order and think that evangelism is a child of the Church. The Church is the child of evangelism.

During the First Apostolic Age, members of the early Church fought against determined enemies and overcame daunting obstacles to survive and then to create, in a hostile environment, the Body of Christ that grew and prospered. Evangelism was the mission of the Church, and each member was an evangelist called on to witness to God's love in Christ. As Mead has pointed out (1991, p. 12), "The community [of the early Church] was to 'go into the world,' to 'be in the world but not of it.' It could not be true to its nature and play it safe. Its marching orders were to engage the world, not withdraw from it. . . . The congregation came to see that its front door was the frontier into mission. They were impelled to take the life they shared within the congregation and, in its power, cross over the boundary into the hostile world outside. They called it 'witnessing,' the Greek word for which is 'martyr.'"

Hunter (1992, p. 35) has identified four objectives that Christianity needed to achieve in the First Apostolic Age:

1. Teach people about Jesus Christ (because the population had no knowledge of the Gospel)
2. Convert people's attitude toward Christianity from hostile to favorable
3. Convince people of the truth (or at least the plausibility) of Christianity
4. Invite people to adopt the Christian faith and join the messianic community

Once these objectives had been met throughout the Roman Empire, the First Apostolic Age came to an end, and the Age of Christendom began. (Notice that these objectives are the same as those of the contemporary Christian Church when it is seeking to reach the unchurched.)

In American society, the apostolic paradigm existed from the time of the American Revolution, when multiple denominations developed, until about 1830 (Hadaway and Roozen, 1995, p. 110). During that time, the primary goal of the Protestant establishment was to Christianize the nation; everyone was an evangelical. According to Hadaway and Roozen (p. 111), "Beginning in the 1920s, but even more strongly after the end of World War II, churches in the ecumenical branch of evangelical Protestantism, what we now call the mainline, began to act less like distinct denominations on parallel missions and more like a single established church, with a highly developed collective sense of responsibility for 'its' culture." As had happened in Europe, evangelism faded as the primary focus of the Church.

In place of mission (and community), the Church in America turned its attention to pressing social issues, such as the Vietnam war, civil rights, and feminism. When the Church deemphasized the pastoral needs of its people and rejected evangelism as its central reason for being, it deprived its members (and potential members) of the sustaining power of the Christian faith and experience: spiritual transformation, the expectation of miracles, the experience of a loving community, and a deepening relationship with the triune God. In so doing, the Church moved from support for personal and congregational growth, which a missionary focus brings, to the stagnation engendered by a singular concern with issues. It moved, as a Church, from missionary expansion to the maintenance of its membership—to the assumption that those who should be Christian already were Christian or would somehow be attracted to the Church on their own.

Age of Christendom

Mead (1991, pp. 9–22) has described the difference between what he calls the apostolic paradigm, which characterized the early Church, and the Christendom (or postapostolic) paradigm, which characterized the Church after the conversion of the Roman Emperor Constantine in 313 A.D. By the end of the fourth century, Christianity had become the official religion of the empire. During the Age of Christendom, the Church had been successful in creating a Christian civilization in which it "became the source and center of Western Civilization, influencing every area of Western humanity's life, thought, and activity" (Hunter, 1992, p. 23). The period of the High Middle Ages was the apex of the Church's influence, when the creation of a Church-dominated world was complete. It was, after all, the pope who, with the Line of Demarcation, divided all the lands of the earth between the nations of Spain and Portugal. The Church even collected taxes throughout the realm, and the officials of Church and of government were often the same people.

In the Age of Christendom, everyone was assumed to be a Christian, and the difference between a good citizen and a good Christian was indistinguishable. Because everyone was a Christian in medieval Europe, the term *evangelism* was meaningless; there were, by definition, no unchurched people to whom the message of the Gospel might be addressed. There were children, of course, but they were growing up in a Christian environment, were sent to church, and were therefore Christian. The attention of the Church turned from evangelism to internal issues.

Maintenance Versus Mission

Another way to contrast the First Apostolic Age and the Age of Christendom is in terms of Church models based on focus. The First Apostolic Age was characterized by a model that emphasized community and mission. The Age of Christendom was characterized by a model that emphasized community without mission—that is, maintenance of the status quo. Today's maintenance-centered Church ministers primarily to the faithful— to those, that is, who are already Christian, were raised Christian, and are expected to die Christian. It is not particularly attentive to the unchurched except philosophically, paying only lip service to the idea of evangelism. In the maintenance church, both clergy and laity lose sight of their obligation to make disciples. The inevitable result is a significant decline in membership as new sects arise to satisfy the unaddressed and unmet spiritual needs of the unchurched.

In the First Apostolic Age, the early Christians had a clear picture of who and what they were. They had a vision, imparted to them by Christ, that informed their lives and vivified their days. For all the squabbles and sects that rose and died, the early Christians articulated, to those they knew, their vision of life transformed. These Christians lived their faith, risked their lives for their faith, and found their lives in that faith. That situation and that time are much to be envied in contrast to the confusion and meekness of our own days and our own witness. The religious tolerance and theological openness so valued by the mainline Church have driven its members to a conspiracy of silence about their religious beliefs and about the effects of those beliefs on their lives. As a result, the maintenance church is silent, largely irrelevant to the unchurched, and disconnected from them. For fear of imposing answers, the mainline has left unanswered the ultimate questions that Americans are asking. This problem is not confined to the Church's dealings with the unchurched. The maintenance church deals no better with its own members, for whom it provides little spiritual direction. As Hadaway and Roozen observe (1995, p. 77), "Ironically, their openness to other religious understandings gives mainline 'seekers' permission to explore their spirituality elsewhere, on their own—without any assistance, guidance, or support from their church or from the rich tradition of Christian spirituality and mysticism. As a result, interest in spiritual formation has led spiritually oriented mainstreamers away from the Church, most frequently into individualized expressions of religious experience but also into evangelicalism."

In the missionary-centered church, by contrast, as in its first-century counterpart, evangelism informs all activities. What the missionary church experiences that the maintenance church does not is the powerful effect of evangelism on the life of the believer. Evangelism is not merely a means of spreading the Good News. It is also a means of living the Good News, of incorporating it into daily life. Evangelism is a form of teaching that leads to learning. It is an essential exercise of the Christian soul, an exercise that strengthens, enriches, and transforms.

Post-Christian Age

The Age of Christendom has slowly been dissolving since the High Middle Ages. According to Hunter (1992, pp. 26–30), the decline of Christendom and the secularization of the West (that is, "the removal of whole areas of life, thought, and activity from the control or influence of the Church") were hastened by six major cultural events spanning several centuries: the Renaissance, the Protestant Reformation, the rise of nationalism, the rise of science, the Enlightenment, and urbanization. More recently, the movement in the West toward democracy and individual freedom has led to a succession of events in which individuals and societies have struggled to free themselves from ecclesiastical domination. Even the American sexual revolution of the 1960s was an effort to be free of constraints that were largely placed on human beings by the Church.

With the dissolution of Christendom as the de facto state religion in America, powerful vestiges of influence from the Age of Christendom have waned. American society has been increasingly without reference to God in the decisions it makes. Christian sexual morality is largely disregarded by society as a whole. Violence that makes mockery of the value of human life is glamorized on television and in motion pictures. Divorce grows increasingly common, and the laws of the nation are regularly made without regard to applicable Christian principles. The religious core that has guided the country's destiny since its founding has given way to a secular philosophy of right and wrong. Prayers have been removed from the schools, and morality and ethics are often recast as secular philosophies devoid of explicit religious references. Therefore, from a practical standpoint, it is possible to talk about the late twentieth century and the first years of the new century as the Post-Christian Age. In this age, however, are the makings of the New Apostolic Age.

New Apostolic Age

The New Apostolic Age is potentially as exciting and fruitful as the First Apostolic Age. It carries great risk as well as great opportunity for the mainline Church. The great opportunity is for the Church to recapture the transformational power of first-century Christianity through adoption of a missionary model. The great risk is that the mainline denominations may not do so. If the mainline continues to rely on a maintenance model, it will continue to decline in membership. In the Post-Christian Age, the maintenance church has no long-term future; it is headed for extinction. It is possible, on the basis of current trends, to plot an extinction curve for each of the mainline Protestant denominations, identifying the year in which each will become a dead religion. If nothing changes, the situation is that simple, and it really is that dire. But it is not hopeless. As St. Matthew reminds us, "For everyone who asks receives, and everyone who searches finds, and for everyone who knocks, the door will be opened" (Matthew 7:8). We stand in the doorway.

4

DENOMINATIONAL CRISIS, DENOMINATIONAL OPPORTUNITY

There is one body and one Spirit, just as there is one hope to which God has called you.

—Ephesians 4:4

THAT THE MAINLINE Protestant denominations are in crisis at the beginning of the new century is a fact that is widely recognized at virtually every level of the Church. Denominational statistics tell an irrefutable story of declining membership and increasing rejection by the unchurched. What the statistics do not tell, but newspaper articles do, is an equally irrefutable story of dissension, conflict, and threats of schism that have wracked the Church, driven many members from its embrace, and repelled others who might have sought its shelter. This sad story of decline, in its many manifestations, does not have to be recounted here.

Rather than focusing on symptoms, such as membership decline, the purpose of this chapter is to focus on the root cause that has given rise to these symptoms and to suggest a new hope based on the inherent value of denominations to the faithful. Metaphors are powerful ways of understanding complex situations. One of the most useful metaphors for the current situation of the mainline denominations is illness. This metaphor can help us to understand the cause of the Church's decline in membership and influence and to develop possible treatments for restoring its vitality.

Denominational Crisis

As every physician knows, it is important to treat life-threatening symptoms of illness, but it is more critical to get to the underlying disease that is generating the symptoms so that the illness itself can be cured; otherwise, there can be no permanent restoration to wellness. The metaphor of illness is especially appropriate because it helps us understand that what we are seeking is a healing in the Body of Christ. It may also let us develop greater compassion with respect to those with whom we find ourselves in disagreement and those whom we would ask to change.

The principal cause of the symptoms affecting the mainline denominations—the basic disease afflicting the Church—is that *the mainline denominations have lost their common vision of being a missionary church dedicated to community, discipleship, and personal transformation.* This loss of a common vision creates multiple symptoms. As in any other serious illness, denial is present. Denial about the seriousness of the disease afflicting the Church pervades every level of the mainline denominations. Church members acknowledge that something is wrong, but the guiding belief seems to be that the problems of the Church are caused by external rather than internal factors and that, somehow, things will work out. In fact, however, the central problem is an internal one.

Without a unifying vision of their mission, denominations dissolve into conflict and become self-serving institutions. They turn the primary focus of their energy and efforts to contentious issues. For years, such issues have dominated the agendas of the mainline denominations and captured national headlines. Thus, rather than vibrant waters of interchange refreshed by evangelism, the denominations have become dead seas. Their congregations, for the most part, are ingrown, isolationistic, and competitive. They function independently within their judicatories, each congregation concentrating on what is important to the clergyperson in charge, to the detriment of common missionary vision and alignment of purpose and direction. Their insularity militates against diversity, ministry to the poor, and outreach to the unchurched. Without a unifying judicatory or denominational vision to anchor the development of objectives, strategies, and tactics, goals may vary, and they may even conflict from congregation to congregation. Moreover, networking among congregations is virtually nonexistent.

Lack of interest in the plight of the unchurched accompanies the loss of a missionary vision. In contemporary society, the Church has made itself largely irrelevant to the unchurched, who therefore regard the Church with apathy and search elsewhere for spiritual sustenance. The wealthy but aging members of the mainline denominations often find, sadly, that they cannot attract their own children and grandchildren to the faith.

This litany of symptoms could be expanded, but the point is this: If the denominations are to survive, denominations in the New Apostolic Age will have to be different from those in the Age of Christendom, and denominations in the twenty-first century will have to be substantially different from those in the twentieth century. The question is not whether denominations will exist by the end of the twenty-first century but rather what forms they will take, and whether denominations at the close of the twenty-first century will be mainline denominations or new and emergent ones that were unknown in the year 2000.

Denominational Opportunity

Is there a case to be made for the mainline denominations? Should we care about them, or should we let them die? Three general responses seem possible.

A first response is to let the denominations continue declining in membership, ultimately to the point of their extinction. This alternative is based on the assumption that the era of denominations is over, and that denominations should be permitted to die their slow death, gradually to be replaced by an emergent network more in tune with the postmodern world. This position has its adherents.

A second response is functionally identical to the first, and it seems to be the majority response. This one suggests that we should care very deeply about the state of the mainline denominations, but that there is, unfortunately, little or nothing we can do to renew them. Therefore, we should keep doing what we have always done while hoping that the outcome will somehow be different.

The third response is that we should care very deeply about the state of the mainline denominations because of what they have to offer, but that we should also recognize that they cannot continue in their present form and still be effective in the New Apostolic Age. Therefore, our task is to manage the transition of the denominations from their twentieth-century form to their twenty-first-century form.

This book espouses the third response—and, indeed, there may be growing sentiment within the Church that just this kind of transformation must take place. Although naysayers flock around the DENOMINATIONS ARE DEAD banner, those who have thoughtfully considered the potential of the mainline Church seem encouraged to take on the task of dramatic Church-wide renewal. The painful fighting that has wounded the Church for decades seems less palatable now to all concerned. Here are some reasons for devoting ourselves to the transformation of the mainline denominations:

○ The mainline denominations represent, in a variety of ways, the "one holy catholic and apostolic Church" of the Nicene Creed in which we as Christians anchor our belief. As members of the mainline Church, we are the direct heirs of the apostles, in a line of succession unbroken from the days when St. Peter and St. Paul carried the Good News to the Roman Empire. As congregations of the mainline Church, we enjoy this bountiful inheritance; as individual congregations divorced from the mainline churches, we do not.

○ The mainline denominations are a rich treasure of wisdom, experience, and financial resources, all of it developed through centuries of committed study and effort. The mainline denominations house the knowledge of generations of men and women whose lives, intellects, and fortunes have been devoted to the Church. These collective assets of the Church are brought to the life of each church member in each congregation of each denomination.

○ The denomination is the repository of the faith traditions, the procedures, the laws, and the obligations that have ensured the functioning of the Church for centuries and that have maintained the integrity of the faith. Christians believe that God's revelations were not given once and for all but continue to be given. As the world changes dramatically through advances in technology, medicine, and science, new issues come to the fore and must be addressed. The teachings of the Church continue, grounded in God's Word but forever new as the world is made new. The teachings of the Church that formally address the issues of the day come from the Church as a whole—that is, from the denominations. The history of the denomination gives it a long-term perspective that congregations and even judicatories often lack, protecting against ill-advised change while, ideally, encouraging well-designed innovation. Congregations are more subject to trends, fads, and local biases, lacking the panorama of two millennia and the broad experience of the "one holy catholic and apostolic Church." It is the denomination that provides an essential forum for discussion and for personal discernment, ensuring that the tenets of the faith will be guided by doctrine rather than driven by personalities. Denominations provide structured opportunities to continue the conversation on the meaning and practice of Christianity in an ever-changing world, allowing different voices to be heard on difficult issues of the faith, in a context of tolerance and prayerful inquiry.

○ There are thousands of denominational institutions devoted to various causes and good works. Their existence has had a profound effect on the human condition for decades, even centuries. These institutions depend on the denominations for financial support and coordination. From missions abroad to summer camps at home, from seminaries to universities, from shelters for homeless people to retreat centers, the denominations and their judicatories support thousands of well-designed and well-coordinated efforts to relieve suffering, bring hope, and inspire faith. At their best, these institutions of good works can be maintained only on a denominational basis, by seeking funds and support from hundreds of congregations throughout the country. Because of their size and experience, the denominations are able to provide these services more efficiently and at lower cost than could be managed by independent congregations, alliances of independent congregations, or well-publicized private charities. In this way, the return on every dollar contributed is maximized. Through these institutions, Christians unite as one body in reaching out to the poor, the sick, and the unfortunate.

○ Congregations, judicatories, and denominations acting in concert can carry out the Great Commission and the Great Commandment more effectively than isolated congregations could. Each congregation and judicatory has a unique set of experiences and resources that can be brought to bear on the Church's mission. When an individual congregation's resources are combined with those of other congregations and denominations, the result is a potent mutual effort.

○ Denominations and their judicatories provide expanded career opportunities for clergy while protecting them from abuse by dysfunctional congregations. Denominations and their judicatories provide due process in disputes, to ensure justice and act as a brake on unruly passions.

○ Denominations provide a variety of administrative services to clergy and congregations that would otherwise be unavailable to them. Examples are low-interest loans to congregations and health and pension plans for clergy.

○ Denominations provide a unifying and reassuring national structure, identity, and community. Our own faith is reinforced by the faith of others. We worship with all the other members of our faith, whether physically or spiritually, when we gather for the worship service. Denominations also give us a "home" church wherever we travel or move, and they provide a safe harbor of beliefs to which we can refer over and over in our own spiritual pilgrimages.

○ For two thousand years, the Church has been the repository of a program of spiritual development that is available to all who seek it. This legacy of the promise of spiritual growth, personal transformation, and expectation of miracles ought to be centered in the mainline denominations. The fact that individuals seeking spiritual answers do not see the mainline churches as the established spiritual authority is merely a reflection of the Church's focus on maintenance. To maintain its integrity, the Church must be fundamentally missionary and profoundly spiritual and thus offer itself as the primary resource for those seeking spiritual growth.

○ Denominations, more so than congregations individually, have an opportunity to reach the poor, the diverse, and the underserved in many ways. The potential is there, which is another reason to retain but transform the denominations.

○ The letters of St. Paul to the scattered Christian churches of the first century make it clear that the interconnectedness and interdependence of Christian congregations is an essential part of the faith. The Body of Christ is no mere phrase. It represents the unity that we find in Christ, the solvent that eradicates our differences and makes us brothers and sisters. The "blessed company of all faithful people" to which every Christian belongs is one that extends beyond the boundaries of a single congregation or even a single judicatory. If a congregation were to withdraw from its denomination and the national community of believers that it represents, the congregation would enter a state of isolationism inconsistent with the teachings of Christ. The drive toward interdependence, toward "one community," toward close cooperation with others, is inherent in the faith. Therefore, if the denominations did not exist, they would have to be created. From a practical standpoint, it is not reasonable to destroy an existing structure that will have to be replaced, if that structure can be transformed into one that meets the needs of those it is striving to serve.

○ The mainline denominations, as now constituted, provide barely a glimpse of what they could be. We have fallen so far short of fulfilling the potential of the denominations that we have lost sight of what that potential is. One of the strongest reasons for maintaining the mainline denominations lies not in what they are but in what they could be. It is their potential that is so promising and so exciting. The denominations have the basic elements in place to create, at the dawn of the new century, a new Church of enormous power and relevance. Much will have to be done, of course, to achieve that goal, but the potential is there. We cannot afford to throw away the opportunity or give up on trying to achieve it.

Pathways to Healing

A critical illness in a human life is often a turning point. It offers the potential for bringing an individual face-to-face with the crucial life issues that he or she ignored in days of better health. Suddenly the unexpected heart attack or diagnosis of cancer realigns priorities, makes life more precious, and brings about a new approach to living. Such a crisis inevitably offers great spiritual opportunities that the individual may or may not embrace. It also generally requires a significant change in lifestyle if the individual is to recover and maintain health.

But the initial response to very bad news—loss of a job, diagnosis of a serious illness, death of a loved one—is very often denial. In order to benefit from treatment, work through a crisis, or recover from grief, however, the individual must first accept that the underlying problem exists. For decades, the mainline denominations have been in denial about the severity of their problems. Furthermore, to an organization, the fear of death is not necessarily a compelling argument for change. Indeed, many organizations have died despite years of warnings about decaying health and impending death. Rather like a human being, an organization seems to need a persuasive reason to live in order for it to change, and this principle applies to the mainline denominations as well. Scare tactics aimed at reversing their demise have not been persuasive for the past thirty years; in and of themselves, such tactics are unlikely to be persuasive now.

The Healing Vision

Over the past three decades, the mainline Protestant denominations have functionally abandoned the Great Commission in America. They have lost their common vision as a missionary church. The central Christian idea of a community of disciples making disciples has been relegated to occasional programs or obscure committees. Is it any wonder that the mainline Protestant denominations are in decline? Splintered by issues rather than united by a vision, the denominations have lost their way. It has remained for a few congregations, here and there, to find their way back to the Great Commission and the Great Commandment. The denominations have not yet done so.

The experience in the Diocese of Texas has been that a unifying vision can propel a judicatory and its congregations along a new and invigorating path. The experience in Texas also suggests that a unifying vision has the potential to do the same for whole denominations. The inculturation of a unifying vision into denominations, their judicatories, and their congregations is the first task of anyone who seeks to renew the mainline denominations. Ironically, it is also the creation of such a unifying vision that would be required in the new century in order to create a new denomination or a new form of network to replace the denominations.

A unifying vision provides more effective motivation than do continual references to declining health or past failures. It is preferable to focus on the positive—on what yet can be—instead of on the negative. Sometimes we are not really aware of how sick we have been until our recovery begins; only in hindsight do we see how close the call was, or how much potential was lost. After five years of the missionary model in the Diocese of Texas, it is only now becoming possible for us to see how far we have come, how rich the future is, and how much we were missing.

Wounds on the Body of Christ

One advantage of a missionary focus is that it deemphasizes the divisive issues and emphasizes the unifying issues in a congregation, a judicatory, or a denomination. A common vision will relieve the symptom of discord and strife that threatens to destroy the mainline denominations and has alienated so many of the unchurched. The missionary church keeps its members living the Christian message of love by drawing them into missionary lives based on the Great Commission and the Great Commandment. Church members avoid making currently controversial issues into litmus tests of the faith when they practice tolerance and acceptance in their work with the unchurched. For example, issues that revolve around homosexuality, feminism, and women in leadership roles are important, but they also have the potential to paralyze a judicatory or a denomination, negating both the expectation of the miraculous and the glorious transformation of its members. The missionary church concentrates on core values that can be universally accepted by the faithful. It realizes that justice can be legitimately claimed by people with differing points of view. Therefore, members of the missionary church, accepting that some controversial issues cannot be easily resolved, direct their energy toward what can be helpful and effective, believing that the Holy Spirit will ultimately lead the faithful into all truth.

The tendency to devote time and energy to divisive issues is often great in the mainline denominations: it is far easier (and also felt to be "holier") to fight than to build. But judicatory leaders, lay leaders, and the clergy must be resolute in refusing to support this preoccupation. As a judicatory shifts to a missionary stance, some church members and some clergy will bait the judicatory leader, trying to draw him or her into the conflict they are trying to create or sustain. In the Diocese of Texas, the bishop remains true to the diocesan vision, reminding his clergy and parishioners that the church's primary goal is to make disciples and to address the needs of the underserved, the poor, and the disenfranchised. The personal position of the bishop on controversial issues is a matter of record and is publicly known. What is equally clear is his resolve to keep from debating these issues as tests of the faith in the winner-take-all atmosphere of a vote in the Diocesan Council.

These divisive issues that set Episcopalian against Episcopalian, Presbyterian against Presbyterian, or Methodist against Methodist are not definitive issues of the Church unless the faithful surrender the Church's mission to the 5 percent on each extreme of an issue. Instead, these controversial issues are distractions from the principal work of the Church— making disciples—as pursued in obedience to the Great Commandment and the Great Commission. As long as the spiritually hungry in America go unfed, a missionary church cannot afford the indulgence of focusing on issues that are unlikely to be resolved in this decade. For the most part, people do not go to church to get involved with issues. They go to church to get involved more fully with God. As Christians, we have an obligation to reach out to all those who are suffering and offer them the healing power of Jesus Christ by bringing them into the Christian fold.

On the divisive issues that threaten the Church, Bishop Payne has this to say:

> The vision of our diocese is clear: we are one Church of miraculous expectation and glorious transformation. We are living the core Christian value of love, and we are carrying the Good News of Jesus Christ to those around us in terms they can understand. We are experiencing the miraculous in our lives and we are being transformed. We cannot—and will not—be distracted by lesser issues unrelated to the Great Commission. I hold very strong opinions on these issues, but I know that we are called as a diocese and a Church to a larger vision. I am committed to that missionary vision and, with God's help, will do all within my power to make it manifest in this diocese and in all its missionary outposts.
>
> We cannot rebuild the Episcopal Church in this country and fight about issues. What we can do is focus the Church on evangelism and still consider the issues that divide us through forums specifically established and even facilitated for that purpose. These forums will allow all voices to be heard and all opinions to be considered, but in the context of Christian love and compassion. We must choose a middle ground between fighting in loud voices and completely shutting down those voices. We cannot build the Church in hate. We can build it in love and through mission. We can be unified in purpose yet diverse in our beliefs as we struggle to know God's will for us. The Diocese of Texas is committed to community and to mission. It has chosen to

build in the spirit of St. John's admonition, "Beloved, let us love one another" (I John 4:7).

These divisive issues must be considered thoughtfully and prayerfully, and without the public diatribes that injure other disciples of the one church of the diocese, the Body of Christ. As long as these issues are causing hurt to other members of the body, all members should be concerned. Extreme positions, which some individuals may perceive as purely ideological, actually reflect experiences of pain for others and cause pain to still others. And yet, as disciples of Christ, we are called on to love one another, bear with one another, and console one another. In dealing with potentially destructive issues, it is imperative that we take this human and holy dimension into consideration instead of antiseptically considering the ideological or theological or intellectual or rational or political aspects of the issue.

Those who take extreme stands on these issues are still loved by the great majority of the members of their dioceses, who do not want to lose them or see them hurt. The goal is for all to find a way of going forward together in Christ and working toward solutions to these largely intractable problems. As part of our discipleship, we are called on to act in a certain way toward one another—to respect and love one another. This relationship is governed by the Great Commandment and nurtured by mission and is far more important than the issues themselves. St. Matthew writes (Matthew 5:23), "So when you are offering your gift at the altar, if you remember that your brother or sister has something against you, leave your gift there before the altar and go; first be reconciled to your brother or sister, and then come and offer your gift."

These great issues are certainly a threat to the Church, but they are also an opportunity that can be explored as such. By reaching down into the depths of who and what the Church is as the Body of Christ, we may find new ways of dealing with these matters on the basis of the unique perspective of the Christian faith. This perspective on handling conflict is something that the newcomer and the seeker may not have seen in the secular world. They are familiar with conflict but not necessarily with resolving it in an atmosphere of love and respect. The Church is not an arena in which the winner takes all. It is a community in which the humble are raised up and the righteous are recognized by their efforts to know the will of God and to bring peace. The Church has available to it all the resources necessary for healing and reconciliation.

The clergy and the bishop, in their pastoral roles, can draw on the great resources of the Church—meeting with the aggrieved parties, praying with them, having them pray for one another, laying hands on them in prayer, praying for healing, hearing the confessions of the parties in conflict, and celebrating Holy Eucharist with them. One should never underestimate the power of prayer to bring healing in such a situation, for we never pray alone. Christ always prays with us: "Peace be with you."

When the conflict is seen in this way, as a wound on the Body of Christ, healing becomes a process and not an event. The answer lies not in a vote but in a reconciliation. Opposing parties find a way to deal with irreconcilable issues and still be reconciled. The vision of the Diocese of Texas gives mission a higher priority than fighting over issues. It also reinforces the concept of the diocese as one church, a community of disciples living together in expectation of the miraculous. This remarkable power of the vision—to relegate divisive issues to secondary status—reflects the values of the Christian Church of the first century. The early Church faced and ultimately resolved issues that could have destroyed it without the presence of a missionary vision. The same vision that served the early Church and that has served the Diocese of Texas so well can also serve the mainline Church in the new century. As in the apostolic Church of the first centuries, unresolved issues in the contemporary Church will be settled, in time, on the basis of mission.

Schaller (1996, pp. 33–34) reports on the Texas Southern Baptists meeting in convention at a time when serious disputes between fundamentalists and conservatives had erupted into a fight for control over denominational agencies and seminaries. At the same time, the convention had to deal with several divisive statewide issues, among them Baylor University's decision to dissolve its relationship with the denomination and the sudden removal of Southwestern Baptist Theological Seminary's popular president. One predictable outcome of the convention might have been a bitter fight over these issues, had the convention not been challenged to plant fourteen hundred new congregations over the next four years. Instead of taking sides, the convention participants took up this challenge, and the battle never erupted.

Reimagining the Denominations

Another pathway to healing, one that proceeds naturally from the vision, is the willingness to examine the changing expectations of disciples and unchurched alike and to consider how their expectations might be translated into a new denominational form. What do church members and the unchurched want from congregations? from judicatories? from denominations? What is the best way to meet these needs? At each level of a denomination, there are questions to be asked:

What is the value added by this level?

What can the congregations do for members that members cannot do alone?

What can the judicatories do that the congregations cannot do alone?

What can the denominations do that neither the judicatories nor the congregations can do alone?

What can the three levels do together that none can do alone?

Reimagining the denominations means replacing competition with collaboration and reaching for a consensus, being sustained by similarities rather than divided by differences. All the tools necessary for transformation are already available to the Church, but we must let go of the past in order to hold to the future.

In Chinese, the identical character is used to mean both "crisis" and "opportunity," a fact reflecting the Chinese belief that each phenomenon embodies the other. The mainline denominations face both a crisis and an opportunity. To ignore the crisis is to forgo the opportunity. To rise to the challenge of the crisis is to take advantage of the opportunity. The New Apostolic Age is an era of unparalleled opportunity for the mainline Church precisely because it is an era of crisis unmatched since the first century.

Denominations in the New Apostolic Age

What might the mainline denominations look like in the New Apostolic Age if they embrace the missionary model and seize the opportunity available to them?

○ The missionary vision of the Great Commission and the Great Commandment will guide the mainline Church, calling its members to become disciples making disciples. Evangelism, spiritual growth, personal transformation, community, and the expectation of the miraculous will characterize the lives of the faithful and the life of the Church.

○ The rigid hierarchy that once characterized the Church will give way to a more collaborative, relationship-based structure in which denominations, judicatories, and congregations serve as resources for one another, integrating their efforts, perspectives, and talents into a more powerful and effective whole.

○ Authority that was once granted to the top of the hierarchical pyramid will be dispersed throughout the denomination so that decision making is more participatory, collaborative, and closer to those most knowledgeable about and most affected by decisions. The preferred leadership model will be servant-leadership, Robert Greenleaf's concept of leading through service to others.

○ Denominations and their congregations will be more responsive, more spiritual, and more relevant to daily life. They will look and feel less like institutions and more like the Body of Christ.

○ People will be more deeply involved in their church, and their church will be more deeply involved in their lives. The separation of church life from work life and of both from family life will lessen as spiritual formation leads church members to carry their faith into their daily lives and into all that they do.

○ Church members will be more knowledgeable about the Christian faith, will expect more from it, and will give more to it. Evangelism will lead members to greater commitment to prayer, Bible study, and service.

○ Worship services in multiple forms, to meet different needs, will be richer, more meaningful, and more relevant. The quality of sermons will rise to meet higher expectations. Music will be better chosen to unify and inspire the worshipers. The congregation will participate with greater enthusiasm. A sense of the presence of the Holy Spirit will pervade the worship services.

○ Divisiveness over issues, a condition that characterized the denominations in the last decades of the twentieth century, will be replaced by greater forbearance, more earnest listening to opposing sides, and an authentic sense of community that is uniting and strengthening. A model of Christian compassion, prayer, and patience, grounded in love of God and others and based on the values of the Christian faith, will guide discussion and action on difficult issues, providing a powerful example of the Christian faith to the unchurched and the nation. The importance of issues for their own sake will lessen.

○ Laypeople will be used more extensively. They will play a greater role in the activities of the Church through evangelistic activities, strategic evaluation in planning, lay ministries, small groups, and the pursuit of pastoral duties, and their greater involvement will enrich the Church.

○ Church members will be more concerned with, interested in, and able to identify with the unchurched and their spiritual needs. They will be more compassionate, understanding, and welcoming of them, intentionally reaching out to these "lost sheep" whose inchoate spiritual yearning is an invitation to the Church to enter their lives.

○ Racism will lessen as disciples purposefully seek to know and understand those of different races, cultures, and socioeconomic backgrounds, intentionally reaching out to all sorts of people in all kinds of conditions.

○ The mainline denominations will grow in size and authority and will reemerge as potent forces in the shaping of American culture and values, not as institutions but as communities of the faithful whose individual members carry their spirituality and Christian principles as a transforming influence into society as a whole.

Are these extravagant hopes for the mainline denominations in the new century? We think not. They are expectations that, to varying degrees, have found tangible expression in the Diocese of Texas as a direct result of the missionary model's implementation, and they are being realized at greater depth and with greater frequency as the diocese lives its vision. Like the fruits of mission experienced in the early Church, they grow naturally out of the vision and the model. They can be and are meant to be as much a part of the Christian faith in the third millennium as they were in the first.

PART TWO

THE NEW APOSTOLIC DENOMINATION

FROM MAINTENANCE TO MISSION

5

THE NEW APOSTOLIC
DENOMINATION

---

*So if anyone is in Christ, there is a new creation: everything old
has passed away; see, everything has become new!*

—II Corinthians 5:17

CHAPTER FOUR DESCRIBED what the mainline denominations might look like in the New Apostolic Age. This chapter describes the essential elements necessary to create those denominations in the new century. Its purpose is to provide a conceptual model that will be fleshed out in subsequent chapters. Although the model is based on the experience of the Episcopal Diocese of Texas, its basic elements are just as applicable to any other judicatory or denomination of the mainline Church. From the standpoint of the model, the denominations are scaled-up judicatories that can use the same concepts, principles, and strategies employed to implement the model in the Diocese of Texas.

Purpose of Vision

"Where there is no vision, the people perish" (Proverbs 29:18, King James Version) is a simple but eloquent reminder of how important it is for every community to remain continuously aware of the core values that shape its identity and that define its mission. Without ongoing reflection on and thoughtful recommitment to its vision, a community will die. Jesus had a vision that sustained the early Church. So did His disciples. Probably no group has ever accomplished anything great without a defining vision. The founders of the American republic had a vision of freedom and equality. Henry Ford and his company had a vision of producing an automobile so affordable that every American could buy one. Bill Gates and his team had a vision of a new electronic world linked by easy-to-use personal computers. A vision provides focus and power in the same way that a laser generates a more penetrating beam of light than an ordinary light bulb because it aligns and focuses the light waves.

A vision sets the guiding values and determines the goals that allow diverse people and groups to align their labor in a common effort with a singular focus. A vision steers, inspires, and motivates. It also clarifies, aligns, and facilitates. Every congregation, judicatory, and denomination has a vision. It may be an overarching vision shared by many, a collection of visions shared by few, or a fuzzy vision shared by none. It may be a nascent vision or an obsolete vision or a failed vision.

The missionary vision of the Diocese of Texas states clearly what the diocese is about. In so doing, it fulfills several important functions of a vision that are applicable to all mainline denominations:

○ It sets goals for the judicatory and the missionary outposts and therefore provides direction.

○ It guides all decision making by establishing a standard to which to adhere.

○ It unites the congregations in the judicatory by aligning and integrating divergent interests in the pursuit of a single, overriding purpose.

○ It focuses the judicatory outward on the unchurched rather than inward on itself.

○ It brings out the best in people by offering them a context and a purpose for their offerings of time, talent, and treasure.

The Missionary Vision

The Bible is fundamentally visionary. It catalogs vision after vision in its pages: Sarah and Abraham's vision of the Promised Land; Moses' vision of deliverance; Joshua's vision of conquest; the Old Testament visions of a great kingship, of deliverance, and then, in exile, of a return to the Promised Land; John the Baptist's vision of the kingdom about to come, and Christ's vision of the Kingdom of God at hand. God has given us all a vision that sustains us at every stage of our lives. When we are children, it is a vision of expanded abilities—talking, walking, reading. When we are adolescents, it is a vision of growing independence—driving a car, earning money, making decisions. When we are adults, it is a vision of marriage, of family, of making a meaningful contribution to the world. There are also visions of the spirit: finding purpose in life, experiencing love, being touched by God. Visions of satisfaction and joy and "the peace that passeth all understanding" flood the adult consciousness as life presents its challenges and opportunities. All such visions are powerful motivators that can lead to growth and change.

The Church, too, has a vision. It is a vision of transformation, miracles, and eternity, of growth, triumph, and love. The vision of the Diocese of Texas reflects this vision of the Church. It was cast in response to the growing legion of unchurched in America, in reaction to a world of disbelief and unbelief that mimics the Roman world of the first millennium. The Diocese of Texas returned to first-century Christianity for its model of the missionary church, but it cast its model in terms of the new century. This model—rooted in the historic evangelism of the Christian faith but designed for the contemporary world—is not a tweaking of the system but rather an overhaul so major as to represent a reformulation. The new model restructures the relationships of judicatories to congregations, congregations to other congregations, congregations to disciples, and disciples and congregations to the unchurched. Grounded in the realities of the new apostolic age, the vision is a forceful answer to the bold and prophetic call for a missionary church in the new millennium.

Taking its name from its primary purpose, the missionary model replaces a maintenance mentality with evangelistic focus, reuniting the community and missionary polarities of the first-century Church. In this model, mission in accordance with the Great Commandment and the Great Commission becomes the heart of the Church's work. This vision of the missionary church is cast in the purpose statement of the Diocese of Texas, which is as follows:

> The Diocese of Texas has a vision of being One Church, under the leadership of Jesus Christ as a "Community of Miraculous Expectation." It is a missionary diocese, whose bishop is the Chief Missionary, localized in missionary outposts and missionary institutions, utilizing the historic catholic structures of classic Anglicanism, and whose purpose under the Great Commandment to love is focused on the unchurched with a goal of growing to 200,000 by the year 2005. This is growth beyond mere numbers toward discipleship and seeks to include all sorts and conditions of people, bringing joy to those who are reaching out and to those who are reached.

Another denomination or judicatory may choose different wording for its own vision, yet these central unifying elements are likely to remain consistent across denominations, reflecting the promise of the early Church. Here, as described in the vision, are the governing principles of the missionary model:

- Each judicatory is perceived as one church (that is, one huge congregation) rather than as a collection of congregations.
- Each congregation and institution within the judicatory is viewed as a missionary outpost of the church as a whole (that is, of the judicatory and then of the denomination).
- Congregational members perceive themselves as disciples making disciples by bringing the Good News of the Christian faith to those around them. The focus of the Church is thus external and evangelistic—that is, it is on the unchurched (biblically referred to as "the lost").
- The judicatory (which includes each of its missionary outposts) perceives itself as a community of miraculous expectation.
- The community's core value is love based on the Great Commandment.
- In denominations with episcopal polity, the bishop is the chief missionary and symbol of the unity of the one church of the judicatory. In denominations with congregational polity, the chief officer of the judicatory is the chief missionary and symbol of the one church. The Church's offer to both the faithful and the unchurched is the glorious transformation of lives.
- The result of participation in the church community and of a commitment to something greater than oneself—a commitment to God—is a feeling of profound joy.
- Through many lay-based ministries, the missionary outposts of the one church meet the spiritual and emotional needs of both the churched and the unchurched among people from multiple cultures and various ethnic backgrounds and of all ages. Just as the Gospel message of new and abundant life was extended to all in the first century, so does the scope of the vision embrace all creation.

Another way to analyze the vision is in terms of its core attributes:

- *Core objective:* the glorious transformation of lives, which was the result of Jesus' teaching, preaching, and healing. In changing the lives of individuals, Christ changed the society in which they lived.

○ *Core value:* to love. The Great Commandment is to love God with all one's heart. The second is to love one's neighbor as oneself and is linked to the first. Evangelism is grounded in love.

○ *Core focus:* the lost, the needy, the suffering—what today would be called the "unchurched." The parables of the lost sheep of the House of Israel (Luke 15:3–7), of the silver coin lost by the woman (Luke 15:8–10), and of the prodigal son lost to his father (Luke 15:11–32) make clear Jesus' concern with those who are lost and hurting. The missionary church is focused on these lost sheep, on the unchurched. After Zacchaeus' encounter with Jesus, which led to Zacchaeus' glorious transformation, Jesus said, "For the Son of Man came to seek out and to save the lost" (Luke 19:10).

○ *Core means:* discipleship and the baptismal covenant.

○ *Core result:* joy. "Well done, good and faithful servant. Enter into the joy of your master," reads the biblical passage. Glorious transformation produces the fruits of the spirit described in Galatians 5:22: love, joy, peace, patience, kindness, generosity, faithfulness, gentleness, and self-control.

Table 5.1 compares the explicit vision of the missionary model to the implicit vision characteristic of the maintenance church. The elements are still the same, and the vision functions in the same way, regardless of whether the vision is at the denominational or the judicatory level.

Envisioning the New Apostolic Denomination

The explicit vision of the missionary model is in sharp contrast to the implicit vision of the maintenance model. The contrasting visions of the two models—maintaining the status quo of the Church versus making disciples—infuse all aspects of denominational life. The choices a denominational, judicatory, or congregational leader (lay or clergy) makes will depend on the model to which he or she adheres. All judicatory leaders, clergy, and laity inherit the maintenance model. It is the predominant model in the Protestant mainline in America, and therefore it is difficult to break through. Nevertheless, internal reform is possible when a new vision energizes a judicatory or a denomination, and when adherents of the vision seize the opportunity to drive significant change.

The passages that follow summarize the major characteristics that distinguish the vision of the new apostolic denomination (that is, the missionary church) from the vision of the denomination in the post-Christian era (that is, the maintenance church). Subsequent chapters explore the application of these concepts in detail.

**Table 5.1 Elements of the Vision: Comparison
of Maintenance and Missionary Models.**

Element	Maintenance Model	Missionary Model
Inevitable results	Membership decline	Membership growth
Goals	Ministering to church members; maintaining and improving the church as an institution	Development of effective structures in the congregations and judicatories to build community and further mission; making disciples; living in miraculous expectation; glorious transformation of lives
External focus	Weak or none	Making disciples of the unchurched; spiritual development of seekers
Internal focus	Church members; issues of the time that are sometimes divisive; the congregation as an association of individuals; focus implicit or vague	Discipleship, community, spiritual development; judicatory understood as a community of miraculous expectation; focus explicit
Basic denominational unit	Congregation	Denomination and judicatory as one church composed of all its congregations
Denominational functions	Geared to maintaining the status quo, with minor tweaking	Geared to making disciples as a missionary church; serves as a resource for judicatories and congregations; advances the unifying vision of the denomination and its congregations
Judicatory functions	Monitors congregations	Unifies and integrates the congregations while capitalizing on individual congregational differences; serves as a resource for congregations; supports the missionary vision; implements the missionary model

Table 5.1 Elements of the Vision: Comparison of Maintenance and Missionary Models, Cont'd.

Element	Maintenance Model	Missionary Model
Congregational identity	Each church as separate from other churches in the judicatory, isolated and sometimes in competition with them	Each church as a missionary outpost of the one church of the judicatory and the denomination, networked to other congregations, cooperative with them, and synergistic
Role of the miraculous	Miraculous sometimes experienced but not expected	Miraculous expected and experienced
Expectation of personal transformation	Occasional at best	Glorious transformation expected and experienced
Membership	Largely restricted, although not by design	Comprehensive and inclusive

Goals: Making Disciples and Transforming Lives

In the missionary model, the primary goal is to make disciples in accordance with the Great Commandment and the Great Commission. From discipleship and the practices and commitments it brings flow all kinds of other blessings, which include the transformation of lives.

By contrast, the goal of the maintenance model is to maintain the Church as it is. A few refinements may be made here and there, but the primary objective is to keep the congregation, judicatory, or denomination unchanged and operating smoothly. Innovation is neither sought nor embraced. Management is by exception—that is, whatever goes wrong gets the leader's attention so that it can be rectified and the status quo can be reinstated. The congregation is focused on its own members, not as a community of disciples making disciples but as a collection of individuals whose concern is largely with their own group. Dramatic growth in membership is not expected, although some growth may be considered a desirable goal, at least in theory.

External Focus: The Unchurched

In the missionary church, the goal of evangelism creates a strong external focus on the unchurched. This orientation is a radical departure from that of the maintenance model. It creates an outward-looking community of the faithful intent on making disciples, and, in the case of the Diocese of Texas, it returns the diocese to its biblical roots and to the *Book of Common Prayer*. The Episcopal catechism defines the mission of the Church as the restoration of "all people to unity with God and each other in Christ."

The external focus of the maintenance church, by contrast, is weak or virtually nonexistent; the maintenance church's preoccupation is largely with its own members. Church membership is viewed as a concluding goal rather than as an initiating step that will lead to dedicated discipleship. There is little or no perceived need for making new disciples, and this lack of external focus leads to insularity, which further distances the church community from the unchurched.

Internal Focus: Discipleship, Community, and Spiritual Development

The internal focus of the missionary church is a reflection of its external focus on evangelism. Because it takes a disciple to make a disciple, evangelism encourages congregational discipleship, which builds community and leads to individual spiritual development. Together, the three interrelated elements of discipleship, community, and spiritual development form the core internal focus of the missionary church. All activities and programs of the congregation reflect this internal focus.

By the end of the twentieth century, approximately 40 percent of all Americans had joined some kind of small group to experience the sense of community that it affords, the support that it offers, and the opportunity for spiritual development that it frequently provides (Wuthnow, 1994). About three million such groups meet regularly in America to fulfill a variety of needs. Nearly two-thirds of them have some connection with churches or synagogues, and more than half of them (54 percent) are Sunday school classes or Bible study groups. The rest are self-help groups or special-interest groups, such as book clubs, discussion groups, political organizations, or sports teams.

The growth of small groups is rooted in the breakdown of society's traditional support structures (neighborhoods, families, churches, and employers) that once provided a sense of community for Americans (Wuthnow, 1994). Small groups meet the need for community. A sense of community, whether it is found at home, at church, or through a small group, pulls people out of their self-centeredness, loneliness, and alienation and puts them in touch with the spiritual (Wuthnow, 1994). It is a powerful attraction for those who are isolated, unchurched, and seeking spiritual answers. A sense of community has always been part of the Church, but it becomes a rallying cry when it is made explicit and emphasized. Such a promise not only attracts seekers but also awakens church members to the realization that they have failed to expect enough of their faith. St. Paul's benediction in this area in instructive: "Glory to God whose power working in us can do infinitely more than we can ask or imagine" (Ephesians 3:20).

First-century Christianity was exciting and contagious because in community it transformed the lives of the disciples and the lives of those whom the disciples touched. It was a world and a time of expectation—of miraculous expectation. Word of mouth spread the news of the power of the risen Christ, of the sick healed and the dead raised to life. Expectation fueled the hope of transformation and of a more abundant life. By such hope, and through the power of the Holy Spirit, pagans were converted to Christianity. Expectation is a legacy of the Church, passed from generation to generation through two thousand years to the present time. In the missionary church of the new millennium, miraculous expectation characterizes the attitude of the Church community.

Christ's life began with a miracle and ended with a miracle, and in every sense of the word it was a miracle. It should not be surprising, therefore, that miracles are a natural part of the Christian life, even in the twenty-first century. Christians pray to invoke miracles, and they pray to thank God for miracles. When they follow the will of God, they have a right to expect miracles in their lives. A community of miraculous expectation is a community alive with the power and potential of the living God. It is an exciting place to be, one that acknowledges the presence and purpose of God in human life and that gives thanks for God's gifts bestowed on the faithful. Expectation is a powerful, energizing, hope-filled emotion. It lifts us out of the narrowness of our world and into a richer, more satisfying universe filled with God's love and compassion. Expectation is the right of every Christian—expectation of miracles, of blessings, of strength, of power, and of personal growth. A congregation that is not expectant is not living the fullness of the Gospel. A congregation in strong expectation of God's response to its prayers and its life is a vibrant, transcendent community for which the manifestation of the Good News is proven and palpable.

Christian doctrine confirms the reality of miracles in the lives of the faithful because it confirms the continued activity of the Holy Spirit in the affairs of humans. Although the Christian faith encourages miraculous expectation, it does not promise the fulfillment of every entreaty made to God, nor does it promise specific miracles in response to specific requests. "God's will be done" is properly part of every Christian's prayer, demonstrating explicit acceptance of divine authority over human life and the recognition that divine perspective is superior to the limited knowledge that any human being can bring to bear on a given situation. Therefore, Christians are not to be resentful if their prayers are unanswered; instead, they are to be accepting of divine omniscience. Expectation in the Christian sense, then, is not identical to expectation in the ordinary sense of anticipating that something very specific will happen. Christians can expect miracles in their lives, but they do not know how, in what ways, or over what period of time these miracles may occur.

This emphasis on community and on the miraculous in the Diocese of Texas has helped its members identify the miracles that have already occurred in the diocese and to anticipate more, boldly and eagerly. It has also led them naturally toward a greater commitment to evangelism. The concept of a community of miraculous expectation contains three promises to the spiritually hungry: a sense of community with God and other people, the expectation of miracles, and personal transformation.

For a generation of young adults who view institutions with suspicion, the word *church* carries a negative connotation rather than a positive one because it is often considered synonymous with the term *institution*. The word *community*, by contrast, is not a pejorative term to the young; in fact, it is quite the opposite. The phrase "a community of miraculous expectation" is more meaningful to youth than the word *church* and carries a lot less baggage. It is also more effective as a description of what a missionary church is to its members.

A community of miraculous expectation is a community of Christians whose members experience a sense of the miraculous, of the transforming power and presence of the Holy Spirit in their lives. Such a community embraces the power of prayer and recognizes divine involvement, encounters the holy in daily life, and is confident of experiencing miracles and God's ever-faithful care. In this kind of community, miracles occur and are recognized, lives are changed, and the joy of transformation is spread from disciple to disciple and from disciples to the spiritually hungry and unchurched. Other phrases that might be used synonymously are "a community of miracles" and "a community of the miraculous." The words themselves are not important as long as some phrase is developed and used to convey the specific idea of miraculous expectation.

By comparison with the dynamic focus of the missionary church, the internal focus of the maintenance church is much more static. Concerned primarily with the status quo and with the church's existing members, the maintenance church manifests less enthusiasm for Christian education, youth ministry, outreach, and lay ministries, all of which enrich the lives of church members, and all of which grow naturally from evangelism. The maintenance church also becomes preoccupied with largely irreconcilable differences among its members, many of which are divisive, provocative of anger, and disruptive of community.

Glorious Transformation

Glorious transformation is another outcome of the missionary model. To some, the phrase sounds fundamentalist and perhaps even somewhat corny, yet it grows on people because it vividly captures an essential element of the Christian faith. Other judicatories, of course, can coin their own terms for the same phenomenon. The phrase refers to the changes wrought within an individual by the Holy Spirit that lead to a greater alignment of the individual's will with God's will and to an experience of the "fruit of the Spirit." As described in Galatians 5:22–23, this fruit includes love, joy, peace, patience, kindness, generosity, faithfulness, gentleness, and self-control. In a world beset by trials and tribulations, the promise of personal transformation, which will enable one to surmount and even embrace such difficulties, is much to be desired. Glorious transformation puts the individual in touch with eternal spiritual values that satisfy rather than with temporal and materialistic values that disappoint. Spiritual growth and centering and a release from the traps of false idols are all aspects of the glorious transformation that a life in Christ provides. "And the peace of God, which surpasses all understanding, will guard your hearts and minds"(Philippians 4:7).

Christ's encounter with the hated tax collector Zacchaeus, as described in Luke 1:10, provides a vivid biblical illustration of glorious transformation. Zacchaeus wanted to see Jesus as He passed through Jericho. Because of his small stature, the tax collector climbed a sycamore to get a better view. When Jesus came to the tree, the story goes, "He looked up and said to him, 'Zacchaeus, hurry and come down for today I must stay at your house.'" Upon being called, Zacchaeus immediately came down "and received Him gladly." In that instant of responding to Christ's call, Zacchaeus was gloriously transformed. Zacchaeus said to Jesus, "Behold, Lord, half of my possessions I will give to the poor, and if I have defrauded anyone of anything, I will give back four times as much." This internal transformation—a miracle of change wrought by the power and presence of Jesus Christ—was as complete in Zacchaeus as it was instantaneous. Zacchaeus the greedy tax collector became Zacchaeus the generous benefactor, giving away half of all his possessions and agreeing to repay fourfold those whom he had defrauded. Zacchaeus' encounter with the living God was gloriously transformational, and it serves as an illustration of the Christian promise for those living in miraculous expectation within the community of faith.

The Diocese of Texas is replete with stories of transformations and miracles that have been revealed as a result of the vision. These stories—of people being healed of diseases, comforted in their pain, finding love, beginning new ministries to the poor or underserved or lost, discovering companionship, acting on faith and being blessed, building a community, expanding a church, finding meaning and purpose in their lives—are reported over and over and have become a source of hope and joy for others. The vision gives people permission to speak of the miracles in their lives, of the changes that have been wrought by their church and the Holy Spirit. Because they can talk about these manifestations of the presence of the living God, they can carry the message of transformation to those in need of hope and power, renewing the faithful and inspiring the unchurched. When personal transformation and miraculous expectation become topics of conversation, the nature of the church changes. Disciples of the faith witness to God's love and compassion, to divine involvement, and to exquisite change. They expect more of their faith, and so they receive more from it. In such an apostolic environment, people speak openly of answered prayers, spiritual growth, and new lives. Their experiences and their language reflect those of the early Church, when the electrifying story of the risen Christ converted an empire.

The Denomination and the Judicatory as One Church

One of the characteristics of a spiritual person is his or her sense of the wholeness of the world, of the interconnectedness of all things and all people. Spiritual individuals focus on the commonalties of human experience rather than on the differences. As God's creations made in the divine image, we are all holy. The phrase "brothers and sisters in Christ" reflects the relationship that we share by virtue of our divine Parent. As members of the Body of Christ, we have different roles to perform and functions to fulfill, but we are all necessary.

The judicatory as one church is an exciting vision that can dramatically shift the perspectives of church members and congregations. At the judicatory level, it means simply that the diocese, synod, conference, convention, region, or association is perceived as being one huge congregation.

This concept allows church members to envision closer cooperation with members of other missionary outposts in their judicatories. It also enables them to see themselves as part of a much larger body and as more influential in the work they do.

For example, in the Diocese of Texas there are some eighty thousand Episcopalians spread over 156 congregations. Many of these congregations are very small and can feel quite isolated. By seeing themselves as members of one church, however, as belonging to one body with more than eighty thousand members, they become part of a much larger effort that they can call their own. This perceptual change, from many churches to one church, is not mere wordplay. It represents a fundamental shift in how disciples view themselves in relation to the church, their individual congregations, and one another. From this new worldview flows a different set of attitudes and behaviors. The new perspective frees the congregations from debilitating and distracting parochial concerns and allows them to refocus their attention on the larger issues of the Christian life and faith.

The concept of the judicatory as one church emphasizes our relationship with one another in Christ and our relationship to the Church. It builds community by reminding us of the oneness of our divine condition rather than of the separateness of our human condition. Because each congregation is only one part of a larger whole, it has a responsibility to each of the other parts as well as to itself and to the whole. When the judicatory is envisioned as one church, individual congregations can work together to provide complementary and supportive services to each other. Programs that work well in one congregation can be replicated in another, and programs that are best offered by a special congregation can be opened to members of other congregations who want to participate in those programs' activities (for an example, see the discussion of cluster conferences in Chapter Ten).

Rapid advances in technology make it possible to translate the mental construct of the judicatory as one church into workable reality. By exploiting the Internet, e-mail, fax machines, videotape, teleconferencing, and CDs, congregations and members of congregations have the ability to access massive amounts of information while dealing with each other one to one. Technology allows congregations to share vast resources that would have been unavailable to them even a decade ago. The power of technology to reshape the Church and the experience of Church is so important that it is discussed in a chapter of its own (see Chapter Fifteen).

The denomination as one church reflects the same principle as the judicatory as one church but brings its potentiality to the denomination as a whole. The one-church concept offers a sense of community, encourages networking of judicatories, and recasts the denominational office as a re-source for the judicatories.

JUDICATORY FUNCTIONS. In the missionary model, the judicatory func-tion is integrative and geared toward making disciples rather than nar-rowly focused on the monitoring of congregational activities, as in the maintenance model. The judicatory serves as a resource for its congrega-tions, providing the services individual congregations need, handling those matters relevant to all the congregations, coordinating various activities among the congregations, creating synergy among congregational proj-ects, providing networking opportunities for congregations, and sup-porting the judicatory vision, all in the interest of making disciples and building community.

DENOMINATIONAL FUNCTIONS. The denominational function in the new apostolic denomination parallels that of the judicatory, but on a larger scale. Whereas the maintenance denomination is primarily con-cerned with maintaining the status quo or making minor improvements, the missionary denomination is geared toward making disciples. All its functions are oriented in that direction. In contrast to the maintenance de-nomination, the missionary denomination serves as a resource for its ju-dicatories and congregations and advances the missionary vision. Some of the denomination's functions seem to remain essentially the same. These include its functions of serving as a clearinghouse for denomina-tional missionaries sent abroad; providing a forum for the denomination to wrestle with important issues; speaking for the denomination as a whole; coordinating the work of the judicatories; sponsoring outreach; dealing with ecumenical, interfaith, and other global issues and concerns; and handling relationships with other denominations of its own tradition around the world. Even these functions, however, are fundamentally re-cast when they are performed in the service of a unifying vision of mission.

The Congregation as Missionary Outpost

The image of a missionary outpost hardly seems to fit the congregations of the mainline faiths in the United States, with their historic buildings, inspiring music, and traditions of worship, and yet mainline congrega-tions are indeed missionary outposts in the increasingly secular world of America. Every neighborhood and every congregation is somewhere on the frontier of the unchurched. The lines that divide the churched from the unchurched cut through the high school across the street, the apartment house around the block, and the office buildings downtown. Church members move through a world of unchurched souls who are seeking spiritual food but who do not know where to find it or even how to ask directions to it.

The perception of each congregation as a missionary outpost has several advantages. It reinforces the concept of the judicatory as one church and of evangelism as its central function. As missionary outposts, all congregations, regardless of their size, are equal in their need to fulfill their missionary purpose. As with first-century Christianity, evangelism is still properly centered in the congregation, the front-line unit of the Church. The term *missionary outpost,* applied to a congregation, transmits far more energy and meaning than the term *individual church.* It has a dynamic rather than static quality, and it challenges the larger congregations, which can easily become complacent about growth, to continue to see their mission in evangelistic terms.

As a missionary outpost, each congregation looks to the judicatory for overall direction and coordination of its evangelistic activities. Each congregation also relies on other outposts for resources, and on the judicatory as a clearinghouse to provide missing or complementary resources. Conferences organized throughout the judicatory around topics of concern to the congregations permit the missionary outposts to share their experiences and resources with one another and to share their members, whom they may send to other congregations for activities unavailable in their own. Different missionary outposts can cater to different segments of the unchurched and, in combination with one another, can enable the judicatory as one church to minister to people of all ages, all races, and all ethnic, cultural, and socioeconomic backgrounds.

Comprehensive and Inclusive Membership

This element of the vision is related to the comprehensiveness of membership and is based on Christ's command to "make disciples of all nations." The Diocese of Texas is eager to become multicultural, multiracial, and multiethnic. This kind of comprehensiveness constitutes the Anglican Communion worldwide, but it does not describe the Episcopal Church in the United States. Episcopalians have not effectively evangelized across cultural, racial, or ethnic lines. As a matter of fact, they have not even evangelized very well across socioeconomic lines. This socioeconomic failure promotes racism, something that the Church abhors publicly but promotes structurally through the maintenance model. Episcopal membership is predominantly in the middle and upper classes. This condition promotes elitism, something that, again, the Church abhors publicly but promotes structurally through the maintenance model. Mission strategy has not been aimed at making disciples from among the poor. This strategy has not been intentional, but it results nevertheless from a structure that uses missionary dollars to plant new churches in the more affluent areas. As the old aphorism puts it, "If you keep doing what you've always done, you'll keep getting what you've always got."

In his address to the 149th Diocesan Council, Bishop Payne spoke to this issue in these words:

> If we believe, as we do, that ours is a more comprehensive way [than religious fundamentalism], a more compassionate and loving Gospel-centered life, we stand condemned when we surrender the mission field, saying we can't grow in certain areas or with certain types of people. That is blasphemy. The truth is too often that we choose not to try. Consequently, I remind you again of the potential we have when we view ourselves as one church, a community of miraculous expectation, reaching out to the unchurched, to all sorts and conditions of people.

The increasing diversity of the American population may be the most significant demographic fact of the new century. A missionary church, in contrast to a maintenance church, is open to all people and seeks to evangelize all people. Not every missionary outpost will necessarily appeal to all ethnic, social, age, and economic groups, but every judicatory as a whole can do so through its various and varied outposts. When the judicatory is perceived as one church, it can create or sustain different congregations to meet different needs and preferences. In this classic win-win situation, everyone can find a congregation that is meaningful.

For example, St. Alban's Episcopal Church, in Houston, was an established, predominantly Anglo-American congregation in the midst of a neighborhood with changing demographics. It adapted to the growing number of Hispanic people in the parish by incorporating them into the church, its ministries, and its services. As Vicar Heber Papini recalls, "Our church had to choose between the menace of closing the doors or opening them wider to welcome the new neighbors, fulfilling in the best sense our Lord's Great Commission to His disciples." St. Alban's is a vibrant manifestation of the diocesan vision. To become the truly multicultural community of faith that the congregation is today, says the vicar, "we had to learn what it means to be one church and also how to have miraculous expectation."

Under the new missionary model, the Diocese of Texas began its first Asian ministry. It is also working diligently to increase the number of disciples among African American and Hispanic people. The diocese was highly instrumental in providing facilities for Santa Maria Virgen Episcopal Church, the first church building constructed from scratch for a Spanish-speaking congregation in the Episcopal Church of the United States. Situated on six acres, the new building seats 450 people for worship and contains offices and a parish hall. It was built with the first $600,000 collected under the bishop's new Partners in Mission program, which was created to fund new congregations. Santa Maria Virgen is an example of the diocesan commitment to bringing all ethnic and socioeconomic groups into full partnership in the life of the diocese.

The diocesan vision is clear about its intentional inclusiveness, reaching out, in Bishop Payne's words, to "all the expressions of human life," whether white, African American, Asian, Hispanic, American Indian, or of any other race or ethnicity. The 1998 Diocesan Council of the Diocese of Texas included music from all the major ethnic groups in the diocese and offered worship in Spanish during one main service. By introducing Anglo-Americans to the Spanish service and thereby showing them what it is like for Hispanic people to worship in English, the bishop again focused on the intentional multiculturalism of the church's mission. Bishop Payne has lived out this mission by learning Spanish so that he can say the liturgy and deliver his sermons in Spanish when he visits a Spanish-speaking congregation. The third-largest missionary outpost in the Diocese of Texas is now Hispanic, with an average Sunday attendance of more than one thousand disciples.

The Vision in Action

In the late summer of 1996, Patrick Gahan gave his first sermon as rector of St. Stephen's Episcopal Church in Beaumont. A total of 121 people attended all three worship services in a sanctuary built for 450. The rector observed that the worshipers "were rambling around in that huge nave like elderly parents wandering around in a house that had been built for a lively brood of children, long since gone." In the mainline denominations, the sight of only a few people scattered among many empty pews in a beautiful church is not unusual. If the dilemma is common, however, Father Gahan's reaction was not. He decided that the appropriate response was to implement the missionary vision of the Diocese of Texas, which the bishop had articulated. The congregation agreed, primarily because of the urgency of the situation. "We put everything we did under the microscope," said the rector, "to see whether it was a promising missionary enterprise or simply a stale furniture-rearranging endeavor."

Three years later, the state of the church was very different. During that period, the census more than doubled (from 121 to 325), the size of the choirs quadrupled, vacation Bible school attendance tripled, mean membership age dropped by ten years, and a temporary building had to be built to house the overflowing children's programs. After-school care, "mother's day out," handbell, and drama programs were all added, and a teenage ministry that is hailed as one of the best in the city was created. The church staff increased from four to twenty-four, and the annual budget grew from $221,000 in 1996 to $550,000 in 2000.

What happened? According to the rector, "The growth we've had in a city where the population is relatively stable is the consequence of the power of the missionary vision of the Diocese of Texas. That biblical vision has meant salvation for St. Stephen's. Once we took our eyes off ourselves and centered them on the needs of those not yet within our doors, we prospered." As one aspect of being a missionary outpost, St. Stephen's instituted a system of welcome that emphasizes the importance of seekers and unchurched people to the life of the congregation. In the week after a new person's visit, he or she receives a phone call from the rector by Monday or Tuesday evening, a letter from the rector explaining something about the parish and inviting the visitor to the church's Newcomer's Café, a program for all new people who are interested in the congregation for whatever reason and with whatever religious background (or even no religious background), a handwritten note from the Angels on Assignment ministry team, a current issue of *Ecclesia* (the church's weekly newsletter), a loaf of homemade bread that is delivered by the bread ministry, and a call from one of the staff members as a follow-up. The rector reports, "We have yet to have someone say, 'I wish you hadn't called.' Our assumption is that those who are returning to church after a ten- or twenty-year hiatus or coming for the first time do not want to remain anonymous. If they wanted to be anonymous, they would have stayed home on Sunday, had their coffee, eaten their bagels, and read the Sunday paper."

The Newcomer's Café, an idea that St. Stephen's adapted from Trinity Episcopal Church, in The Woodlands, consists of five sessions designed for anyone interested in the church. It runs every Sunday morning from 9:00 to 9:45. The first Sunday session is titled "The Big Story." In that seminar, the basics of the Biblical salvation story are presented. The second seminar is titled "The Episcopal Story," and it describes how the Episcopal Church has tried to live the "big story." The third session is titled "The St. Stephen's Story," and it describes how the congregation at St. Stephen's has tried to live the "big story." The fourth session is titled "What Is Your Story?" and it deals with what has brought the visitors to St. Stephen's, how they might see a new chapter in their lives opening at St. Stephen's, and what opportunities they will have at St. Stephen's to enter into its many ministries. A fifth session introduces those who have chosen to become new members. A liturgical rite of new membership is celebrated, a reception is held in their honor, and their pictures are posted on the Newcomer's Café bulletin board.

The transformation at St. Stephen's is remarkable. It reflects the qualities of the diocesan vision, however, and so it should not be considered unusual—remarkable, yes, but not surprising for a congregation in an apostolic judicatory in the new century. St. Stephen's grew and prospered as a community of faith because its members gave themselves to discipleship, evangelism, and the glorious transformation of lives. It lived into the vision, becoming a community of miraculous expectation that looked outward to the lost sheep and concentrated on how to bring them into the fold. Like the first-century Church, it offers welcoming arms, the rich story of the risen Christ, the presence and power of the Holy Spirit, and the promise of grace: "We know that all things work together for good for those who love God, who are called according to his purpose" (Romans 8:28). That has been the case at St. Stephen's, a congregation devoted to mission and thus living the Great Commandment and the Great Commission.

6

IMPLEMENTING THE VISION

If God be for us, who can be against us?

—Romans 8:31

JUDICATORIES AND DENOMINATIONS are dynamic and complex systems involving the most glorious of God's creations: human beings. As such, they are unique and unpredictable, filled with opportunity and occasionally littered with disappointments. The principles enumerated in these chapters, and the stories that unfold, are part of the Diocese of Texas's journey through its vision. The process of implementing a missionary model is organic rather than mechanistic. It is not possible to develop a "cookbook" of "recipes" that will describe, in an unequivocal way, the requisite steps to transform a maintenance-driven denomination into a missionary one. The work of transformation is ultimately the work of the Holy Spirit; there must be space for divine leading to accommodate the special needs and talents of each person called to the Lord's work.

The adoption of a missionary vision spurs objections from some people, just as it elicits praise from others. Continuing discussions among church members about the purpose, design, and implementation of the vision are a significant opportunity for disciples to assess their own faith, their role in the Church, and their commitment to Christ. Self-analysis in this area is healthy for an individual, a congregation, and a denomination. The clergy and laity of each congregation will interpret and implement the vision in a way that is meaningful to the people of their respective congregations and to the unchurched people they are trying to reach.

The missionary model can be adapted for use by any mainline Christian denomination and initiated at any level of the denomination. The model may be easier to apply in those denominations with more centralized judicatories: the Roman Catholic Church, the Greek Orthodox Church, the Episcopal Church, United Methodist Church, and the Evangelical Lutheran Church of America. It may be more difficult to apply in denominations with less centralized congregational polity because the denominational structure provides for less direct and less extensive involvement of the judicatory and the denomination in the operation of the congregations. Nevertheless, the model will work in these denominations as well.

This book does not claim to have all the answers to designing or implementing a missionary model. The Diocese of Texas is a work in progress, an ongoing experiment that challenges a powerful status quo that has a long and honored tradition. Some of the discoveries made in the diocese were not made quickly or easily, and other important discoveries have yet to be made. As a result, the model described in this book is still evolving and, in that sense, is not yet nearly complete. Undoubtedly, many who use the model will make new discoveries about it and can share them with the Diocese of Texas and with other judicatories and denominations making their way along this exciting new road.

The maintenance model of the Christian Church was centuries in the making; it will not be abandoned easily. An apt metaphor for changing a denomination, judicatory, or congregation from a maintenance model to a missionary model is the metaphor of changing the direction of an ocean liner that is under way. Such a change in direction cannot be made quickly—there is too much forward momentum—but change will come when a new direction is plotted and when pressure is consistently applied to the wheel.

The process of implementing a vision begins when it is created and ends when it is lived by those who have adopted it as their own, but that envisioning never ends, and so the process is never complete. A great vision grows richer and more pertinent over time as those who live it expand the depth of its meaning and the breadth of its application to their lives. The vision of the Diocese of Texas can serve as an example of how a vision is constructed and implemented and how powerful it can be in the life of a denomination. In the Diocese of Texas, the vision was created at the judicatory level, with the help of the congregations, and it spread downward and outward to the missionary outposts. But the vision does not have to begin at the judicatory level. It can begin at the congregational level and spread outward to other congregations and then upward to the judicatory, or it can begin at the denominational level. For denominations with congregational polity, the Texas experience provides guidelines for building cooperation and coordination among the congregations, by using the existing structure of the judicatory. Although the process is not exactly the same as with episcopal denominations, it is analogous, and it strengthens the mutual efforts of the congregations as they unite in a shared vision.

Surveying the Judicatory

The initial planning process of vision development should include a survey of members of the judicatory to determine what they desire for themselves and their church. In the Diocese of Texas, this survey was called *Shaping the Future,* and it was distributed through congregations to the church membership. The survey yielded important data for developing the vision. For example, one set of questions asked how fully members lived their faith and how readily they would share it with others if called on to do so. The results were encouraging. The responses contained overwhelming affirmation that church members relied on their spiritual roots in their day-to-day living. More than three-fourths of the respondents were ready to share their Christian life with others; they just needed to know how. This discovery was crucial to development of the vision because it confirmed the people's willingness to participate in evangelistic activities. The stumbling block was not lack of willingness but rather lack of knowledge about the process. The answers to these questions suggested a receptivity to evangelism and mission that might otherwise have been missed. Other survey questions, designed to identify the needs and priorities of diocesan members, revealed that the top priorities were ministries of youth, Christian education, and evangelism.

The survey also generated demographic data from the congregations that could be used for evangelistic purposes. It revealed, for example, that a congregation adjacent to, and essentially part of, the campus of the University of Texas at Austin had almost no student attendance despite a university enrollment of more than forty-eight thousand students. The discovery of this deficiency directed the attention of the congregation to a campus ministry for the university.

The process of developing the survey proved to be almost as important as the data. The survey was, in many ways, the first manifestation of the diocesan vision of one church. It drew the members of the diocese together by focusing on common goals and by assessing common strengths. Congregational members appreciated being surveyed about their views and their hopes, and some commented that it was the first time the diocese had asked them anything significant in years. The survey-development process provided an important opportunity for the bishops to work with the clergy and for the clergy to work with lay leaders in rethinking the identity of the church and the nature of its mission. Answers to such questions as "What is the purpose of the church?" and "What would God have us become?" helped shape a new vision for the diocese.

It is an accepted principle of organizational behavior that those who participate in making a decision are more likely to support its implementation than those who do not participate. The self-examination that was required to respond to the survey instrument increased the involvement of parishioners in the analysis of the diocese and its future and so strengthened their ownership of its emerging vision.

A Gathering of the Diocese

A vision can be introduced to—but not imposed on—a congregation, a judicatory, or a denomination. The vision must be chosen by the people themselves. It must be adopted as their own and made a part of their lives. How a vision is introduced to church members, so that it ultimately becomes their own vision, is extremely important. The mechanism developed to launch the diocesan vision of one church and to introduce the missionary model to the Diocese of Texas was an event that was called "A Gathering of the Diocese: New Horizons, New Perspectives, New Disciples." In essence, the Gathering was to be a diocesan conversation about the future of the church, about the role of the diocesan ministry staff, and about adoption of a new vision. Every member of the Diocese of Texas was invited. The Gathering was unprecedented. Instead of coming together to settle issues, the newly chosen Bishop of Texas declared, the people of the diocese would "gather to celebrate our life together."

The enthusiasm among those who witnessed and participated in the Gathering was palpable. The Gathering is considered in some detail in this chapter because of its critical role in the launch of the vision. Symbolically, it signaled a major shift in diocesan thinking and purpose. Practically, it introduced the vision to the diocese and inspired those present to believe in it. Furthermore, it was a form of renewal that had a major impact on the diocese. The Gathering was not a small undertaking. It required a year and a half of preparation and involved some fifteen hundred church members from all over the diocese, who came together in a forty-thousand-square-foot tent on the campus of Episcopal High School in Houston. Every congregation sent someone to the Gathering.

As unaccustomed as they were to tent "revivals," the assembled Episcopalians responded enthusiastically to their bishop's call to sing God's praises, to worship, to share, to pray, to dream, and to envision. For two days, this amazing diocesan conversation continued, infused with laughter and insights, new hopes, and the promise of grander horizons. By its conclusion, a virtual miracle had occurred. The presence of the Holy Spirit had touched the lives of those assembled, reuniting them in the fellowship of Christ and inspiring them with new dreams and possibilities. From the Gathering, they went back to their congregations and to the world with a renewed commitment to their faith and to their diocese. At last they had something to unite them and something to strive for: a set of goals that were meaningful to them. According to the Right Reverend Leopoldo Alard, Bishop Suffragan of Texas, "What caused the vision to incarnate in the people of the diocese was the Gathering. It was there that the vision took flesh and dwelt among us."

Design of the Gathering

The Gathering was modeled on a structure described in the Leadership Network's *Church in the Twenty-First Century* series. It had the following major components:

- Two plenary sessions, which explored such subjects as the forces driving change in the Church, the conflicting worldviews of different generations, and the nature of the Church in the twenty-first century
- Thirty-two workshops conducted by leaders from all around the diocese, who showcased their expertise in such traditional and contemporary areas as Christian education, music, worship, outreach, stewardship, bioethics, singles ministries, practical ways to reach and incorporate newcomers, medical missions at home and abroad, moral questions raised by dramatic advances in science, and ministries to youth in crisis
- Theatrical presentations that portrayed biblical themes in contemporary settings
- Traditional, contemporary, gospel, and rock music provided by a piano, an organ, singing groups, and choirs
- Group singing

- Morning and afternoon worship services
- Open-space technology, a process of organizing small-group discussions on any topic of interest, which was developed in 1985 by Harrison Owen (see Owen, 1990) and was facilitated at the Gathering by the Reverend Dr. David Galloway, rector of Christ Church, Tyler
- A closing address by Bishop Payne, in which he articulated the new diocesan vision

During the open-space technology session, everyone at the Gathering was invited to come up to the microphone, announce a personal topic of interest, and offer to form a group to discuss that topic. After the initiating person announced the topic, he or she was given a meeting time and a room number, which were posted on the wall along with the topic. All who wanted to join the initiator in addressing that particular topic met in the assigned room at the appointed time. A scribe chosen by the group kept a record of what was discussed. The process rules were simple: whoever showed up was supposed to be there, whatever happened was supposed to happen, "when it's over, it's over," and any participant except the convener was free to leave at any time to find something more meaningful (the "law of two feet").

Eighty-three individuals brought up such topics as contemplative prayer, hospices, racism, rural schools, the use of computers in evangelism, liturgy for baby busters, homeless people in affluent suburbia, and reinstatement of the 1928 prayer book with 1979 rubrics. Bishop Suffragan Alard recounts that when one person announced an interest in a small-group discussion on friends and families of gays and lesbians and "nobody booed," it signaled the turning point in a diocese that had been deeply divided over the issue of sexual orientation. An invigorating, freeing atmosphere of openness, tolerance, and acceptance infused the Gathering. Written summaries of the discussions were transcribed, printed, and bound in time for delivery to the participants at breakfast the morning after the open-space technology session. When those in attendance received their bound reports, "it started," says Bishop Alard. In that event and at that time, the Gathering became a grassroots meeting of the diocese as one church.

Themes of the Gathering

The themes of the Gathering were presented in five thematic words, each beginning with the letter *I*.

INSPIRATION. Inspiration, a gift of the Holy Spirit, was invoked on behalf of those in attendance. The first fruit of the Gathering was inspiration by the power of faith, the fellowship of believers, the potentiality of transformation, and the hope of miraculous expectation. The size of the crowd, the diversity of the participants, the innovative agenda, and the talented presenters all contributed to the inspiration that became a hallmark of this two-day event.

IMAGINATION. Imagination is the God-given ability to see what has not yet come to pass—to perceive the impossible as possible and thus to accept a vision as a realizable dream. Imagination was essential in order for members of the diocese to see the Church as they wanted it to be, and it was crucial to their belief that such a Church could be. Imagination shapes a dream and makes it real, and so imagination powers the diocesan vision, showing disciples how profound a difference the Church can make in their own lives and in the lives of others.

INFORMATION. The theme of information was chosen as a reminder of the Information Age, of the technology that birthed it, and of the need for continuous learning that characterizes it. Continuing education is a hallmark of contemporary life, including life in the Church. Education is expansive because it broadens the range of viable options, and it is necessary because the world is changing so rapidly and so dramatically.

The revolution in electronics has transformed communications and the nature of education. It has invested each missionary outpost and many homes with the telecommunications and computing power that few companies enjoyed even a decade ago. Using the Internet, we can reach our clergy, our church offices, and our prayer groups in seconds. We can study the stories of the Bible, the words of Jesus, the doctrines of the Church, and the nature of evangelism from our own homes. We can participate in virtual conversations with other churchgoers. We can check the church calendar, the sick list, the prayer list, the birthday list, or almost anything else the denomination, judicatory, or missionary outposts want to make available electronically. We are in an age in which the distance between us has been virtually eliminated so that we have new opportunities to connect with one another.

INCORPORATION. The theme of incorporation was chosen to capture the need to incorporate the elements of the diocesan vision into daily life and into the life of the congregations. The Gathering was a tangible manifestation of the diocese as one church. It was an opportunity for disciples throughout the diocese to talk, network, share, pray together, and revel in their commonalties instead of focusing on their differences. In community and fellowship, diocesan members could experience the vision for themselves—a sense of miraculous expectation for what God had in store for them.

INAUGURATION. The theme of inauguration was a reminder that no vision is meaningful until it has been implemented. Someone must blow the trumpet at a time when enough people in the community are willing to hear and respond to the call. The Gathering, as the Episcopal version of an old-fashioned tent revival to which everyone in the diocese had been invited, represented that time. The trumpet was sounded to inaugurate a new vision and a new era for the Diocese of Texas, and the people responded.

Symbolism of the Gathering

The Gathering was designed so that its elements were highly symbolic of the vision to which it called the people. Some of the elements may have been included unconsciously, but they nevertheless sent a powerful message to members of the diocese. The Gathering included the following important symbolic elements.

GUEST LIST. The invitation list was intentionally inclusive. All members of the diocese were invited to gather together for the purpose of celebrating their life together. Congregations were urged to send at least 10 percent of their members.

LOGO. As shown in Figure 6.1, the logo created for the Gathering consisted of a circle of fish, with each fish drawn in the form of the ancient

Figure 6.1. Logo of the Gathering.

Christian symbol, head facing inward. The logo conveyed a sense of the unity of the diocese: a gathering of Christians in a perfect circle that symbolized eternity and unity. The way in which each fish was drawn and placed created the illusion of a sunburst at the center of the circle around which the fish were gathered. This symbol of the faithful, gathered in perfect union around the light of God, was powerful and persuasive.

MEETING PLACE. The tent as a gathering place for those who attended was filled with meaning and symbolism. The tent is a metaphor for the "pilgrim church" in which one is always a pilgrim, never arriving at the final destination but continually growing in faith. In the Exodus experience, God was present in the tent. Tents in a religious setting are often associated with revivals, and so the tent was a reminder of the need for revival in the Church and of the power and purpose of evangelism. Because its use at this event was unprecedented, the tent symbolized a radical abandonment of the old ways of doing things, an invitation to innovation, and something entirely new for the Diocese of Texas. A tent is also associated with movement and change, and so its use suggested that the diocese was on the move and that big changes lay in store. More specifically, the tent symbolized a readiness to move where God called.

LOCATION. The Gathering was held on the grounds of Episcopal High School, a setting that was highly symbolic for two reasons: first, as a diocesan school, it symbolized the whole diocese; and, second, Episcopal High came into being in 1982 only because the Diocese of Texas had functioned as one church to create it. (That achievement itself, a remarkable expression of miraculous expectation, had required the purchase of thirty-five acres of prime land.)

OPEN-SPACE TECHNOLOGY. Open-space technology provided convincing evidence that everyone in the diocese had a right to be heard, that all voices were welcome, and that all opinions would be respected. It symbolized a new bishop as well as a diocese confident enough that it could allow divergent opinions to be expressed without allowing them to become distractions from the primary objective of making disciples.

NETWORKING. By emphasizing networks and providing time for networking, the Gathering symbolized a new way of operating, one based on cooperation among the congregations, a flattened hierarchy in the diocese, and 360-degree communication (up and down, down and up, and horizontally across all levels of the diocese).

HIGH STANDARDS. In its design, process, content, and execution, the Gathering met very high standards. From the logo to the speakers to the music to the food, the superior quality of all the elements symbolized the setting—and meeting—of high expectations. It was a challenge to dare, to dream, and to achieve.

Results of the Gathering

It would be hard to overemphasize the positive effect of the Gathering on the members of the Diocese of Texas or the role it played in the people's acceptance of the new vision. As a dramatic, unprecedented event, it generated excitement and talk in the diocese. It also heralded a new time, one filled with fresh possibilities, the expectation of miracles, and the promise of glorious transformation. There were a number of other results as well:

- Spiritually and emotionally, it united those who were present and created a sense of community. It gave every person who was present a preview of what the diocese as one church could be like.

- In an atmosphere of acceptance, tolerance, and understanding, it allowed members of the diocese to share with each other, and with clergy, those issues that were most important to them. No one was punished or judged; everyone was heard. As one parishioner said, "It was like a fresh air blowing through the diocese."

- It permitted direct, two-way communication between diocesan and congregational leaders and among all participants, building trust and permitting a free exchange of ideas. It also enabled people to make connections with other disciples in the diocese and to begin the process of networking.

- It opened the minds and hearts of participants to the possibility of focusing outward toward the unchurched instead of inward on themselves.

- More than thirty workshops on potential church programs seeded many new initiatives in the missionary outposts.

- It was in the moment of the Gathering that the vision came alive for the people of the Diocese of Texas, and so the Gathering allowed the participants to buy in to the vision. More than that, however, it helped them create the vision by taking it back to their congregations and turning its promises into reality.

Perhaps the most remarkable aspect of the Gathering was what it proved to a doubting diocese: that people in the community of faith who had different interests could focus on an overarching vision of the miraculous and the transformational, a vision that could guide their endeavors and lessen their divisiveness. For example, one of those who reluctantly attended the Gathering was an individual who had been a prominent delegate to the diocesan councils until a series of divisive councils, focused on issues of gender and sexual orientation, made him "too sick at heart" to continue attending the councils. This earnest Episcopalian described the Gathering as "the first time I saw a vision that all the diocese could embrace. It was a holy vision based in Scripture that did not draw lines in the sand to divide us. We didn't have to say that another Episcopalian was evil or wrong but could stand together for something more important than the issues that had separated us. It got me and others thinking about the Church in a new way—something we had never done before as a diocese. The gathering was a turning point for me. I decided that I would leave my law practice of twenty-three years and asked Bishop Payne to find something for me to do. The vision made a place for my ministry and created a team of which I could be a part."

The favorable results of the Gathering led the Bishop of Texas to arrange a video teleconference that would introduce the vision to more members of the diocese. Downlinks were established in each of the ten regions of the diocese so that they could receive a special three-hour broadcast. The teleconference focused on the vision and on providing information about the Gathering to those diocesan members who had not been able to attend. The teleconference exemplified the innovative use of communication technology to shrink the diocese and re-create it as one church.

Challenging Assumptions

Because the maintenance model has firmly gripped the Church, many assumptions that are taken for granted must be questioned and changed. The new apostolic model requires a thorough analysis of judicatory and congregational operations. In analyzing what is working and what needs to be done differently, it is helpful to pose a number of questions to each judicatory and congregation and to each congregational or judicatory function. Such questions involve the clergy and laity in discussions that build community, identify obsolete assumptions, and orient them toward evangelism and mission. Here are some of the questions, always in relation to the vision, that should be asked:

- Who are we?
- What is our unique work?

- How can we involve the laity?
- How can we involve the clergy?
- How can we involve the professional staff?
- How can we best assess the needs of the communities in which we have our congregations and our judicatory institutions?
- How can we involve the people we will serve in the processes of program assessment and design?
- What is working, and why?
- What is not working, and why not?
- How can we live the vision?
- How can the judicatory better serve its congregations?
- How can the denomination better serve its judicatories and congregations?
- What opportunities for education and training (for example, lay training in evangelism, or staff training in team building, or clergy training in the missionary model) should be offered in order to facilitate the shift from maintenance to mission?

For all the changes wrought by the missionary model, the model itself will seem very familiar to most Christians because it captures the heart of the Gospel: sharing the Good News with others. Properly planned and implemented, the missionary vision will have a powerful effect on the members of a denomination, its judicatories, and its congregations. It will renew their faith, inspire them to new and deeper expressions of ministry, and bring them to a more profound awareness of the power and presence of the living God in their lives; that, at least, has been our experience in the Diocese of Texas.

7

CHANGING ORGANIZATIONAL STRUCTURE AND CULTURE

For just as the body is one and has many members and all the members of the body, though many, are one body, so it is with Christ.

—I Corinthians 12:12

THIS CHAPTER DESCRIBES the changes in organizational structure and culture that took place as a result of our implementing the missionary model in the Diocese of Texas. Although our experience is based on what occurred in the Episcopal Diocese of Texas, these changes also apply to other mainline denominations and their judicatories. Some allowances will have to be made, of course, to accommodate differences among denominations and judicatories, but the essential principles remain unchanged.

Organizational Realignment

The organizational structures of most of the judicatories in the mainline denominations are based on a hierarchical model of management that is typical of the maintenance church. In a maintenance denomination with episcopal polity, the organizational chart is pyramidal, with the bishop at the top and everyone else below, at descending levels of power and responsibility. In this autocratic model, decisions are made from the top down. There is little interaction between functions. The bishop instructs the clergy and congregations in the mode of "father knows best"; their input may or may not be valued. Loyalty to the bishop is expected.

In the missionary model, by contrast, the organizational structure of the judicatory is aligned with its missionary purpose to create a less hierarchical, more network-focused, technologically centered, and service-oriented institution. These changes parallel those that are taking place in other large organizations seeking to enhance their effectiveness in the turbulent, change-driven operating environment of the new century. In the Diocese of Texas, for example, the traditional pyramidal hierarchy has been replaced with a ministry-team model that includes significant lay involvement. This reorganization has eliminated the rigid boundaries that used to separate such diocesan departments as Christian education, communication, and finance so that these departments can now work together in areas of overlapping interest. In the new design, the laity have become partners in the parishes, and the diocese itself was re-created as a resource for congregations. The various lay advisory boards to the diocesan staff now work for the staff members, rather than vice versa, and so serve as resources to the congregations.

This kind of restructuring is necessary in response to a changing environment that is no longer hospitable to top-down, pyramidal organizations. The same basic forces that have battered secular organizations have also had a serious impact on the Church: rapid technological change, greater "consumer" diversity, demands for improved service quality and greater competence, increased competition, information explosion and overload, dramatic demographic changes, and, in terms of church membership, shrinking "market share." The hierarchical management model of the maintenance church cannot meet the needs of the mainline denominations in a period of turbulent change. In fact, it is a threat to their continued survival.

As opposed to the maintenance church, the missionary church is based on the leader as servant. When Robert Greenleaf developed the concept of servant-leadership, he identified several defining characteristics of this different way of understanding leadership. Greenleaf wrote that a servant-leader is a person who wants first and foremost to serve. From that desire to serve, he or she chooses to lead. Those who report to the servant-leader, according to Greenleaf, are empowered, grow in self-confidence, achieve greater autonomy, and are more likely to become servant-leaders themselves. Jesus Christ is the exemplar of the servant-leader.

The spoke-and-wheel management model is the one used to reorganize the diocese (see Figure 7.1). Significant characteristics distinguish this management model from the hierarchical pyramid:

Figure 7.1. Spoke-and-Wheel Management Model.

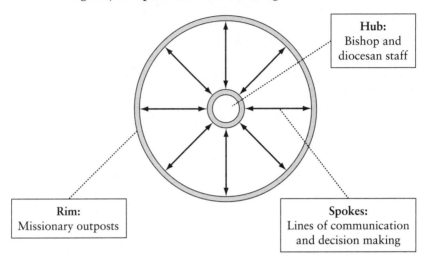

Hub: Bishop and diocesan staff

Rim: Missionary outposts

Spokes: Lines of communication and decision making

○ Symmetry and balance in communication and decision making replace the unbalanced, top-down hierarchy of the pyramid. Because two-way communication among all parts of the wheel is necessary to maintain the system in balance, communication flows both inward and outward. In adhering to this management model, a judicatory leader seeks the counsel of the missionary outposts when making decisions, listens to their needs, and responds to those needs.

○ Decision making is also spread across the wheel and is balanced. Decision-making authority is delegated to the congregations on the basis of perspective, knowledge, and experience related to the particular decision. In other words, those who are most qualified to make decisions are the ones who make them. The hub is composed of the bishop (at its center, not at the top) and members of the diocesan staff. The function of the hub is to serve the missionary outposts on the outer rim in their efforts to make disciples of the unchurched.

○ Although this feature is not shown in Figure 7.1, the diocesan staff is cross-linked within the hub through a team structure that ensures integration, coordination, and strength. Staff members also have cross-functional capabilities.

○ The spokes represent lines of communication and the provision of services among the hub (the bishop and his staff), the deans of the regional convocations, and the clergy and laity of the missionary outposts.

○ The outer rim of the wheel is the line of missionary outposts that are cross-linked through direct communication with one another and that have a direct interface with the unchurched.

○ Because real church growth occurs on the rim, where disciples in the missionary outposts touch the unchurched, the wheel's energy and focus are always directed outward, as if the wheel were in motion, creating centrifugal force.

The Bishop of Texas restructured the diocese by using elements that were largely in place. Therefore, his reorganization is not characterized as much by new elements (the planning groups and Episcopal Health Charities are notable exceptions) as by a reordering of relationships among existing elements. Other judicatory units can reorganize according to the same principle of re-creating relationships in order to achieve new judicatory goals.

Teams

The bishop employs a team-based management style throughout the diocese. Within the hub of the spoke-and-wheel model, he uses weekly meetings of the ministry staff to keep team members informed, to coordinate and integrate their activities, to work through problems and anticipate problems, and to modify plans, programs, and projects as feedback comes in. One result of this team-based approach is that each member of the ministry staff can effectively address the vision of the diocese and can respond on a current basis to issues raised by the missionary outposts. Because there is considerable cross-functionality in the team, and because the work of the team is integrated, any single member can generally make decisions for the group as a whole. This approach generates increased responsiveness, innovation, and synergy. Furthermore, project task forces can be created quickly and easily to provide support for individual staff members assuming responsibility for new projects; for example, staff members responsible for communications, resource development, and Christian education might be assembled on a task force to help the director of youth ministry on a specific project.

This team approach creates a strong sense of community among staff members. It allows them to develop trust for one another and to lead from their value systems. It also teaches them a constructive way to work with others, which they can model in their interactions with committees, missionary outposts, and judicatory institutions. In some instances, team-building programs or exercises may be necessary to teach staff members how to work more effectively together in the new environment.

When the judicatory is large and diverse, as in the Diocese of Texas, the judicatory staff must be proactive in visiting the missionary outposts. Staff members go to offer encouragement, to nurture the vision, and, where necessary, to teach about new initiatives. They also seek data and counsel from those who are engaged most directly in the evangelistic effort. Each congregation is thus taught to see itself as complementary to every other; the success of one becomes the success of all.

Accountability

The principle of accountability, with regular performance evaluations, is accepted in industry as essential to good management, but this concept is somewhat alien to the Church. Clergy must conform to certain moral and ethical standards, of course, but not necessarily to performance standards related to the quality of the work they are doing in a congregation. And yet it is reasonable for a judicatory leader to ask the clergy, for example, "Why aren't you offering more discovery classes?" or "Why aren't you doing more baptisms?" or "Why are there no outreach programs?" Indeed, without a judicatory or congregational articulation of what is expected, it is difficult for clergy to determine how well they are doing or to be held accountable for the quality of their work. Therefore, performance measurements that reflect the vision should be instituted, and various aspects of the clergy's performance in the missionary outposts should be regularly reviewed, so that the clergy can be assessed on how well they are ministering to the needs of their congregations.

In the missionary model, the judicatory leader establishes performance standards for the clergy, and these standards reflect the vision. This kind of assessment is easier, of course, in denominations with episcopal polity. With respect to statistics, for example, a judicatory leader might be interested in the average annual Sunday attendance, the number of pledging units, the number of baptisms, and the number of adult confirmations and receptions that the congregation has recorded over the past decade. In nonstatistical areas, a judicatory leader might be interested in the congregation's ministries, in the extent of lay involvement, in the congregation's plans for the future, and in other ways in which the congregation nurtures and lives the vision. Because these key indicators have the bishop's attention, they will also have the clergy's attention, and the clergy will know that "doing well" includes these aspects of congregational life.

Judicatory leaders who expect their clergy to perform well and to work hard should expect the same of themselves; accountability for performance is a two-way street. Through formal surveys, informal surveys, and conversations across the judicatory unit, a judicatory leader and staff members can measure their own performance and hold themselves accountable for the work they do. Performance standards for the judicatory leader might include the ability to maintain trust; consistency in implementing the vision; fairness in dealing with both clergy and laity; willingness to learn, adapt, and be corrected; openness and accessibility; ability to delegate and empower; willingness to recruit people who have leadership and entrepreneurial skills; and ability to model a servant-leadership form of leading. Regular publication, in the judicatory newspaper, of a judicatory leader's monthly calendar and of a journal discussing his or her activities can be an effective means of reinforcing performance.

The work of the missionary church is more demanding than the work of the maintenance church. It requires more effort, and it entails more risk for judicatory leaders, clergy, and laity. To some extent, it means stepping out into the unknown. In this respect, it is stressful, but no more so than dealing with the self-absorbed, internal struggles of the maintenance church, and it is stress in the service of productivity and achievement. The psychoanalyst Wilfred Bion was convinced that real psychological growth occurs only through tension, and that the absence of tension indicates the absence of learning and of growth.

Regional Planning Groups

In the missionary church, congregations are given more decision-making responsibility in the areas where they are most affected, most knowledgeable, and most qualified to make decisions. A shift to more participatory decision making at both congregational and judicatory levels acknowledges the diversity of a judicatory and the competence of its congregational leadership. It also recognizes that the judicatory is one church, and that each congregation has a stake in what it does and so should have some input into the decision-making process. When decisions are moved lower in the organization to more people, creativity generally increases, commitment strengthens, responsiveness rises, and decision quality improves.

Site selection for new churches in the Diocese of Texas is a good example of a decision set that has been delegated to local areas. Resident laity are more familiar than diocesan staff with local history and real-estate trends and values and are more intimately concerned with the decisions that are made. The first effort of the Bishop of Texas to involve the missionary outposts in decisions that were once reserved by the bishop concerned the start-up of a new congregation in Austin. Bishop Payne created the Austin Regional Planning Group to deal with this issue. It was led by native Austinite Billy Gammon of All Saints' Episcopal Church and was made up of visionary lay leaders from several Austin parishes. The group studied its assigned problem by collecting and analyzing relevant data and then made its recommendations. In the process, it brought local knowledge and insight to bear and, later, could field questions that arose in the Austin congregations about the start-up. The result of the committee's work was far-reaching. It handled the issue of the new congregations well, and yet the more lasting effect was something else: the group changed the way the Austin congregations viewed one another and the diocese. The congregations were led to a more cohesive stance that reflected their acceptance of the diocese as one church. A prime example of their cooperative spirit was their strong support for the start-up of the new congregation (discussed in more detail in Chapter Ten).

Thanks to the vision, the work of the Austin Regional Planning Group, and the Austin parishioners, the Austin congregations continue to work well together. They are joined in their mutual support of El Buen Samaritano, an outreach ministry to low-income persons and particularly to pregnant woman and others who are not receiving public social services. Together they are supporting the possible relocation of two existing Austin churches, and they share a master plan for the future development of new churches. Kevin Martin, Canon for Congregational Development, summarized the Austin experience when he wrote, "Austin Episcopalians are getting a firsthand experience of what it means to live into the vision of being 'one church.' They are learning that the Diocese of Texas is not a place, nor is it only the Episcopate. They are the diocese, and the diocese does not exist apart from them" (Martin, 1988, p. 4). The Houston Planning Group and the Southeast Regional Planning Group perform similar functions in their respective geographical areas.

Mission Funding Decisions

The Diocese of Texas depends on financial support from its congregations to carry out a variety of ministries. Historically, the diocesan Department of Finance has developed the annual missionary budget for the diocese. On the basis of an established formula, the budget is apportioned into a "missionary commitment asking" for every congregation. After prayerful consideration, each congregation pledges the asking amount or some other amount. The Executive Board takes the total amount pledged and recommends to the Diocesan Council a diocesan missionary budget indicating how the funds will be spent.

In 1995, Bishop Payne appointed a special committee to review the system of mission funding and to make recommendations for improving it. After two years of prayer, study, research, and brainstorming, this committee recommended a radically different approach. It suggested that the diocese abandon the old policy of asking the congregations to support the budget while allowing the diocese to decide how to spend the funds that were pledged. Instead, the committee recommended that the diocese allow each congregation to determine not only the specific ministries it wanted to support financially but also how much financial support it wanted to provide. This change in procedures would move the funding decision from the diocesan level to the congregational level, involving the congregations, their clergy, and the laity more directly in diocesan funding decisions.

This method was approved by the Diocesan Council, and the Mission Funding Committee in 1999 prepared the inaugural edition of its *Episcopal Diocese of Texas Mission Opportunities Catalog,* forty-six pages long, using the slogan "One Church in Mission." In addition to the catalog, the committee furnished each congregation with a thick notebook that contained more details on each ministry. Representatives of each of the ministries went to the congregations to explain the funding opportunity and to answer questions. The audience for the presentation was determined by local choice: the whole congregation, the governing body (vestry), or a special committee. The catalog lists all the ministries seeking funds from the diocese, and it divides the mission opportunities into five categories—mission congregations, college ministry, outreach programs, diocesan support ministries, and the bishop's contingency fund for mission and programs—but it adds two new categories: cooperative projects (that is, specific projects jointly proposed and developed by three or more congregations) and dream budgets (that is, the hopes of existing ministries for which extra financial support is being sought). The catalog describes the cooperative projects in this way: "Mission work that may seem impossible for one missionary outpost to do alone can be possible through combined efforts. God calls us to work together, support each other, and combine our resources to accomplish extraordinary tasks. When congregations cross the invisible walls that divide them, they find brothers and sisters in Christ striving to serve the same Lord. Suddenly being 'One Church In Mission' becomes a reality" (Episcopal Diocese of Texas, 1999, p. 38). The catalog describes the dream budgets in this way (p. 40):

> Opportunities to dream excite the hearts and imaginations of God's faithful people. Dreams have been the seeds planted by God that have

resulted in the most fruitful ministries. 150 years ago, the Diocese of Texas was just a dream in the minds of a few.

Faith, belief in the possibilities, hard work and the financial commitment of the greater Christian community brought the Episcopal Church to Texas. The seeds were planted, the ministries born.

Never before have the ministries represented in this catalog been able to imagine the possibilities for new or expanded work and to seek financial support for these dreams on a diocesan-wide basis. Now they can. Take a few moments to read and consider these dreams. Your financial support can make them a reality. Do they stir your imagination for the extension of God's kingdom?

Seeds planted, ministries born . . . imagine the possibilities!

The new system of mission funding was not without risks, and several fears and objections developed in addition to the general fear of change:

- Fear that diocesan needs that were not considered "attractive" (for example, clergy travel) would not be met
- Fear that ministries that were not considered glamorous would not be funded
- Fear that those who could not make dynamic or dramatic presentations in the catalog or through their representatives would not be funded
- Objections from ministries that had always been funded but that would now have to "compete" for funds
- Objections that it was the bishop's job, not the job of the congregations, to make these determinations
- Objections that it meant more work for the congregations, which would now have to study the catalog to decide which ministries to support

After the first year, however, it became clear that these fears were not to be realized, and that the objections had been overcome. The remarkable change in philosophy and method of funding, a change embodied in the catalog of offerings, had both practical and symbolic importance for the diocese and entailed a number of results:

- Contributions to mission funding increased by 15 percent. This was the single largest percentage increase in mission funding in the history of the diocese, and it was even more impressive for having followed years of declining contributions.

○ Despite the fears, funds were still available for the "unattractive" projects—even larger sums, in fact, than in the past.

○ Because the congregations were given a voice in how their money was spent, they took ownership of that spending and of the funding program as a whole, becoming involved in what the ministries were about and becoming more committed to them.

○ Individual congregations developed, often for the first time, a full understanding of all the ministries of the diocese. The congregations came to see that the diocese was conducting wonderful and important ministries, and they came to understand what constituted the ministries of the Church.

○ The congregations realized that they were in these projects together (as one church in mission), that each congregation was part of all the ministries, and that they needed to support these ministries of the diocese. This realization raised awareness of the diocese as one church. Perhaps for the first time, the laity realized that they were part of a group of ministries that was larger than themselves and their congregations.

○ The view of the diocese as an interfering "big brother" changed. As one rector put it, "The new method transformed the way the lay leadership thought about the diocese."

○ The process of fund allocation and determination created bonds among church members and generated a new spirit of excitement about and involvement with the ministries of the diocese.

○ The shift in funding decisions, from the diocese to the congregations, empowered and inspired the congregations and led them to take a greater interest in diocesan ministries, make a greater commitment to them, and imagine for themselves new ways to work with other congregations in the one church of the diocese.

This revolutionary delegation of decisions about mission funding was in fact a courageous step. By delegating authority to the congregations, the bishop allowed them to support the ministries they chose, with the idea of growing those ministries together. He believed that the essential needs of the diocese would be met, but he also understood that some ministries might fall by the wayside. The new approach and its very satisfying results are in line with the diocesan vision of one church in action, supporting more than seventy ministries.

Many people in the pews have said that the revolution in how mission funds are raised and allocated is the greatest story of the diocese. They see at last what it means to be involved in the work of the church as a whole, and they get excited about their favorite ministries. For example, one congregation gave $10,000 more than it was asked to give, even though it was not a large church: its members got so excited about the process and the ministries that they were unable to compromise on what to fund and what not to fund, and so they simply funded everything they wanted to fund! Another congregation studied the catalog for three months because its people were so excited to be part of the process. As one parishioner said, "The bishop empowered a group of people to make a radical change in the diocese." Another individual added, "The lesson is that if you want the congregations to support something, go to them and ask them what it is they want to support." There is an interesting postscript: one of the individuals who complained loudly about the new system, because the bishop was giving up his authority to decide on mission spending, is now serving happily and ably as a volunteer mission coordinator.

One of the cooperative projects that best illustrates the power of the diocesan vision of one church in mission is the Heart of East Texas Episcopal Cooperative, developed by four sponsoring churches. The coordinator of the cooperative is Sherry Peterson, whose congregation, All Saints' in Crockett, was one of the first missions to have its funding eliminated under the bishop's new program, which called for missions to become self-supporting. Despite the elimination of diocesan funding, the mission remained open on its own, but its members began to turn to other congregations for help. Ms. Peterson, a musician, began to arrange visits among members of several small missions in East Texas, in order to provide better music for special occasions. Once the churches began working together on music, they started to get excited about some other things they might do. Each of the congregations put in some money and decided to offer a joint vacation Bible school. At this point, Ms. Peterson began talking with Mary MacGregor, senior mission coordinator for the Diocese of Texas, who suggested that they make application for mission funding as a cooperative. The description for the Heart of East Texas Episcopal Cooperative, as it appeared in the mission-funding catalog, reads as follows:

> The Episcopal Church was established in East Texas 150 years ago in St. Augustine. Since that time, Missionary Outposts of the Diocese of Texas have been established throughout the region. These various Outposts have always been friendly toward one another, but very rarely have we worked together for an extended period of time. The Bishop's vision of 'One church in Mission,' coupled with the new mission funding initiative, has opened new vistas for the Outposts in the Heart of East Texas. Our plan is to draw these Outposts together into a cooperative that will provide:

○ Vacation Bible Schools

○ Hispanic and Native American Ministries

○ Youth Ministry Networks

○ Music, Drama and Liturgical Dance Workshops

○ Stewardship Workshops

○ Summer Camps for the Underprivileged

○ Children-Led Worship Services

○ Seeker Services

Our intention is to develop these programs (no more than three the first year funding is available) in such a way as to bring those who have yet to respond to the Gospel within the reach of our Lord's saving embrace, thus being responsive to the Great Commission in the Heart of East Texas. Miraculous Expectations, indeed, but all things are possible through Christ who strengthens us.

The Cooperative requested $29,900. It was fully funded [Episcopal Diocese of Texas, 1999, p. 39].

Sherry Peterson talks about the benefits that have developed as a result of the project. "I think it has been good for the people of East Texas," she says. "Formerly, we were content to stay behind the doors of our church. Now we reach out to others." Reaching out to others means reaching out to sister congregations as well as to the unchurched. "It means something to go to another church on your own vacation time to make something happen for someone else," Peterson says. "The result has been unbelievable camaraderie and a special sweetness to the worship services that comes from so many people networking with each other." The cooperative has been good for the clergy as well, proving to them that multiple congregations can work effectively together. Finally, it has been a blessing to the members of these small churches, who have found an outlet for their unique talents and capacities. "These eagles," as Sherry Peterson calls them, "can join with people from other churches to soar. In their cooperative work, they find a dimension added to their lives that they otherwise would have missed."

Changes in Organizational Culture

The culture of an organization reflects the basic values, beliefs, and attitudes that guide the organization and the people in it. Cultural norms describe acceptable and unacceptable behavior, cultural values infuse organizational decisions and actions, and cultural symbols provide meaning for

those individuals whose lives intersect the life of the organization. Organizational culture is thus a reflection of as well as a driver of organizational behavior. Because the culture of an organization will facilitate or
hinder organizational change, and because organizational culture is itself
a target of such change, it is one of the keys to organizational transformation. Whenever organizational transformation is to occur, there must
be a transformation in organizational culture, and the Diocese of Texas
is no exception to this principle.

As more and more diocesan members embrace and act on the vision,
the culture of the Diocese of Texas changes and itself becomes an instrument of change. The new missionary vision and the culture it inspires are
altering how church members view their congregations, their diocese, and
their Christian responsibilities. What is more profound, the new missionary vision and culture are changing how church members relate to God,
to themselves, and to their fellow human beings. These changes in the
norms of behavior and in the values of the faithful are leading to a deeper
and more intimate relationship with Christ and to a more powerful and
expansive discipleship. The diocesan culture, as it affects the individual
members of the congregations, has changed and is changing in five significant directions, discussed in the passages that follow.

Spiritual Rather Than Institutional Orientation

In the maintenance model, church members are so concerned with maintaining the institution of the church that they lose sight of the larger spiritual purpose that it serves. As the means through which the community
of the faithful come together, the institution of the church is important,
but it is not to be emphasized at the expense of the results it is designed
to achieve. Seekers and the spiritually hungry are attracted, not to the institution of the church, but to what it has to offer. The Church is a vehicle
for spiritual transformation, whose forms and doctrines have changed
over the centuries in response to changing times and conditions but whose
central promise of transformation and salvation has remained the same.
The Church serves a holy purpose but is not to be worshiped itself. In the
missionary church, the institutional dimension of Christian life is secondary to the dimensions of service and mission. Since the first century,
Christianity has offered hope, miracles, and personal transformation. A
missionary church speaks soul to soul with those who are hurting and
fearful. "Ask, and it will be given you; search and you will find; knock
and the door will be opened for you," Christ promises (Matthew 7:7;
Luke 11:9). "For everyone who asks receives, and everyone who searches
finds, and for everyone who knocks, the door will be opened."

Focus on Others Rather Than on Self

Although evangelism is inwardly rewarding, it is outwardly focused. It leads to compassion for others and away from self-centeredness and self-indulgence. The beatitudes, the Sermon on the Mount, the parable of the talents, and the commandment to love one's neighbor all address the need to be outwardly focused in the Christian life. And yet, paradoxically, such a focus provides internal rewards: in helping others, one is helped; in giving, one receives. Evangelism provides a compass for this outward orientation and a means for its manifestation.

Congregational Collaboration Rather Than Isolation and Competition

A judicatory vision of one church allows each missionary outpost to see itself as an integral part of the whole. When the judicatory operates as if it were one church, congregations are led to collaborate, and each makes a unique contribution that is valued by the whole. The tendency for individual congregations to compete with one another, or to suffer in isolation, is therefore reduced. As in the Diocese of Texas, start-up congregations are supported (rather than opposed) by existing congregations. Denominational structure becomes an asset rather than a liability in attracting new disciples to the work of the Church.

Sharing Rather Than Hoarding

"The measure you give will be the measure you get" (Matthew 7:2). Evangelism and congregational development encourage us to share our spiritual treasure with others so that all can be enriched. Evangelism and congregational development teach us not to hoard what has been given to us but rather to share it so that it can be multiplied. The maintenance church is grounded in selfishness because it does not reach out to share its spiritual treasure with the unchurched. The Church, by hoarding what God has commanded that it give away, loses its vital connection to God's will in this area, and so it withers. A missionary church, by contrast, is eager to share its good news with the suffering people outside its walls. Like the good Samaritan, the missionary church stops to offer aid to those along life's highway who are hurting, unconcerned about whether they are "like us" but concerned only with whether they are in need. This attitude of sharing outside the Church can easily spread to sharing time, talent, and treasure within the Church.

Love Rather Than Hate

Evangelism leads to love and away from hate. A judicatory that envisions itself as one church living in miraculous expectation of glorious transformation, and that carries that vision outward to the unchurched through its missionary outposts, is a community living in love. Such a community does not focus on issues that divide but rather on the call of our Lord to make disciples of all nations. Self-righteousness, intolerance, and condemnation are replaced by compassion, discernment, and acceptance. In the spirit of the Great Commandment to love, people are allowed to change and grow. In following the mission of the early Church—to spread the Good News of God's love—the denomination, its congregations, and its members become both messenger and the message, a hope for the unchurched and a joy to each other. This emphasis produces the much needed diversity to which a missionary church aspires, and it simultaneously attacks racism in a tremendously positive way as the faithful are energized to reach outward to different sorts and conditions of people.

Inspiring Trust

The presence or absence of trust is a defining characteristic of an organization's culture. In the maintenance model, especially in denominations with episcopal polity, trust tends to be weak because loyalty to the judicatory leader, or to the denomination, is the primary criterion by which performance is rewarded. This kind of loyalty is a feature of the maintenance church because maintaining the church as it is, or in slightly altered form, is the heart of its work.

In the missionary church, by contrast, the central thrust is not maintenance but evangelism: the making of disciples. The task of the missionary church is so fluid and complex that its members must be trusted to carry out their responsibilities and to work with others in ways that are innovative, imaginative, and appropriate. Trust is also crucial because of the number of people involved and because it takes the denomination, the judicatories, and the congregations all working together to succeed in their missionary effort. In the missionary church, "where the action is" is not the top of the organizational pyramid, as in the maintenance church, nor even the hub of the spoke-and-wheel model, where the judicatory leader is; the rim is where the action is because this is where the missionary outposts make disciples. The vision leads the church, and so loyalty to the bishop is actually loyalty to the vision, and this means making disciples, not defending issues. In the missionary model, energy is focused outward, toward the unchurched, not upward or inward, toward the bishop.

In mainline denominations, trust begins with the judicatory leader. It arises because the leader's character, management style, and goals inspire trust among the members of his or her staff and the people of the judicatory. In the Diocese of Texas, the bishop consciously sought to develop trust in the diocesan office from the beginning of his episcopate. That trust has been an essential part of the success of the missionary model in the diocese. The previous culture had created an atmosphere in which the congregations mistrusted the diocese; the general consensus was that the diocese could not do much to help the congregations. As a result, when the bishop announced that he was going to be a resource for the congregations and lead the diocese into a new vision, the people did not put much credence in this announcement. The mistrust was not overt, but it was there; in Texas there had been little recent history of a diocese serving as a resource for its congregations, or of a diocese empowering its congregations. Therefore, the bishop sought by word and deed to establish the new culture, taking particular care to deliver what he had promised and not to promise what he was unwilling or unable to deliver. In the Diocese of Texas, trust grew out of the following factors:

○ The Bishop of Texas is and is known to be trustworthy. Publicly and privately, he can be relied on to do what he has said he will do; he does not say one thing but do another, nor does he make promises that he does not keep. He can also be relied on to listen to opposing points of view with respect, openness of mind, and a willingness to be convinced by the other party. Further, he can be trusted to reveal truthfully what his thoughts and feelings are about an issue that has been raised, or about an opinion that has been expressed; he does not take one position in public and another in private, nor does he favor an issue in talking with one group but oppose it in talking with another.

○ The bishop and the diocesan missionary staff believe in and live the missionary vision in its many manifestations. They are exemplars of what they preach, modeling the principles they teach in the work they do.

○ As a resource to congregations, the bishop and his staff serve the congregations rather than expecting the congregations to serve them. They play a productive and active role in helping the congregations fulfill the vision among their members.

○ The bishop delegates responsibility and decision-making authority to those individuals and entities who are most directly concerned, and who, by virtue of their familiarity with a situation, are most competent to make decisions about it. This delegation of authority to diocesan staff and congregations empowers clergy and laity, and it builds trust because it is itself built on trust.

○ The bishop trusts the members of his staff and the clergy and laity of the diocese to carry out the vision.

This sense of trust spreads throughout the judicatory. For example, in conducting its business, one vestry (governing board of a congregation) in the Diocese of Texas intentionally moved from a very formal, businesslike, maintenance model to a more trusting, faithful, leadership-empowerment model. Meetings were begun with prayer, Bible study, and sharing time. The success of this model led to its adoption for monthly ministry and team meetings. The team concept for all ministries was encouraged, and teams replaced committees. The change was more than semantic because the spirit of trust, which had been modeled by the diocese and then by the vestry, had infused the congregation. To prevent any one person from developing a sense of owning a particular ministry, one congregation encourages the rotation of leaders, with an emphasis on development of new leaders. Twice a year, "Leadership Saturdays" are held to teach leadership skills, increase communication among members, and further cast the vision into the hearts and minds of the members. Existing leaders are asked to bring two other representatives with them, as a way of helping to raise new leaders.

The missionary vision is expansive. It is meant to be incorporated into the life of every Christian and to manifest itself in ways that are unimagined except by God. People grow into the vision individually and collectively— stretching their horizons, developing spiritually, and maturing as Christians. Each person who lives the vision adds to the vision, multiplying its effects and creating unexpected wonders. The vision is not to be constrained; rather, it is to be unleashed. Those who follow it must be trusted to apply their unique gifts and talents in whatever ways they are called by the Holy Spirit to do as they go about making disciples, building community, and expecting the miraculous.

8

MANAGING CHANGE

For everything there is a season, and a time for every matter
under heaven.

—Ecclesiastes 3:1

THE PROFOUND CHANGE in organizational culture represented by a shift from the maintenance model to the missionary model does not come quickly or easily. Even in a time of distress, turbulence, and uncertainty, a time that demands innovative responses to dramatic new challenges, the Church moves slowly. The potential for resistance to change is great. The issue is not whether such resistance will arise but rather how to manage it effectively so that it does not block or erode the change effort. This chapter describes the resistance to the missionary model that surfaced in the Diocese of Texas and how that resistance was managed.

The reason an entire chapter of this book is devoted to overcoming resistance is twofold. First, resistance to change is a serious potential impediment to implementing the missionary model and must be acknowledged as such and dealt with effectively. Second, those who have been attracted to the power of the missionary model implemented in the Diocese of Texas have nevertheless raised the fear that it could never be done in their denominations (or judicatories, or congregations) because those entities are not as rich (or as diverse, or as rich in resources, or as united, and so on) as the Diocese of Texas. These objections have been so widely expressed that they must be confronted and put to rest.

A great deal of research has been conducted on organizational change, particularly change in organizational cultures. This research has resulted in the development of various models for overcoming, reducing, or otherwise managing resistance to change. Two of these models are particularly helpful to clergy and lay leaders in denominations, judicatories, and congregations seeking to change the culture of their organizations. Each of these models provides the change leader with insights and principles through which to lead a denomination, judicatory, or congregation out of the maintenance model and into a persuasive commitment to mission and discipleship. In fact, these two models describe the process through which the missionary vision was created and introduced in the Diocese of Texas and how, through use of the principles described by these models, resistance was effectively managed.

Force Field Analysis

The social psychologist Kurt Lewin (1952) developed a model that provides an excellent overview of the process involved in bringing about major change. Lewin called his approach *force field analysis* because he postulated that the culture of an organization at any given time is the dynamic result of two opposing force fields. One field is made up of driving forces working in favor of change, and the other field is the sum of the restraining forces working against change. Whether or not change occurs will depend on which of these two fields is the more powerful. When the fields are equally balanced, which is the case most of the time, the organization is said to be in a state of equilibrium. In that state, change does not occur; the status quo is maintained.

But suppose that the status quo is no longer an effective response to new developments affecting the organization. Suppose that the organization needs to change in order to prosper or even survive and yet remains wedded to the same way of doing things and unresponsive to the new imperatives. How does one change such an organization? Lewin used the metaphor of the status quo as something frozen that needs to be thawed so that it can be changed into something new. His model is used to disturb the equilibrium of the status quo, create a new desired state, and then institute permanent change. The model has three stages:

1. Unfreeze—disturb the status quo by making members of the organization aware that a change is needed in existing attitudes and behavior.

2. Change—move from the old state into the new one by changing attitudes and behavior.

3. Refreeze—make the new attitudes and behavior relatively permanent and resistant to change.

Lewin's first contribution was that he identified the status quo as an equilibrium state that was kept in balance by opposing force fields (hence the name of his model). Change depended on which field was stronger. An additional insight of Lewin's model concerns the necessity not just of increasing the strength of the driving forces but also of reducing the strength of the restraining forces. Because driving forces always produce restraining forces that counter them, and because driving forces are always in existence, the most productive change efforts include attempts to reduce or remove restraining forces. The restraining forces, however, are more difficult to deal with than the driving forces are because they often involve individual psychological defenses or group norms. Even so, savvy change agents work to reduce the number and strength of the factors opposing change at the same time that they increase the number and strength of the factors favoring change. From a practical standpoint, the former approach means combating fear of change in whatever form it takes and working to alter group norms. Assurances, reasonable alternatives, counseling, emotional support, and a powerful vision are examples of ways to reduce the force field that opposes change. The forces that create fields favoring and opposing change are many. They may be technological (for example, when new technology drives change or creates resistance to change), economic (when economic threats from competitors drive change, or when the economic threat of losing one's job restrains it), regulatory, environmental, competitive, intellectual, and emotional.

Stages of Change

Kotter (1996) has developed a model that maps out eight stages that a change agent must induce in order to bring about the process that Lewin described nearly fifty years ago. Kotter draws his model from his study of major change efforts that have failed in corporate America. Each stage in his process is designed to counteract one of the management errors that he identifies as having torpedoed an attempt at major change. These eight stages and the steps they require are equally valid for bringing about change in denominations, judicatories, and congregations.

Of course, one has to be cautious in adapting a model based on research in the corporate world, and yet the principles Kotter describes seem to be generalizable to any organization, including the Church. The change effort in the Diocese of Texas was undertaken without benefit of the Kotter model. Even so, the model fits the actions that were taken in the Diocese of Texas to create and implement its vision of the missionary church and to counter the resistance that the vision and its implementation created. Therefore, the Kotter model is a good description of what happened in the Diocese of Texas and is thus an effective change model that other judicatories and denominations can use.

Two principles, unmentioned by Kotter, are nevertheless important to the model when it is applied to the Church: first, pray for and expect the miraculous for the denomination, its judicatories, and its congregations and for each individual in the Church; and, second, give thanks in all things (in the fullness of gratitude for what we have been given, we are led to share it). Moreover, an implicit assumption, which needs to be made explicit, is that the individual chosen to lead the change effort in a denomination, a judicatory, or a congregation must be a change leader— that is, a person who possesses significant leadership qualities, including skills in change management. Training in such skills is available, but the change leader must have an intuitive grasp of the vision and how to accomplish it. Members of the mainline Church have a collective responsibility to identify visionary leaders and elect them to positions of authority from which they can lead their denominations toward evangelism and unity in the new century.

One caveat is in order: the experience of the Diocese of Texas is that the process is a good deal messier than Kotter's model of eight stages may suggest, for two reasons. First, any organizational change effort is really a collection of many smaller change efforts. These individual efforts, which constitute the whole, do not move through the stages in tandem; later efforts, obviously, are in earlier stages than initial efforts. Therefore, with the different individual efforts in their respective stages, it is not as easy to discern the stage of the overall change effort as the model may make it appear. Second, the stages are not as discrete and sequential as the model implies; the first four stages in particular have a greater degree of simultaneity because efforts made in those stages are likely to be taken in parallel. Despite this caveat, however, the model is useful in describing the various elements (if not the precise stages) involved in major cultural change.

The following passages describe each of the stages of the Kotter model. Each goal description includes the goal of the stage and the typical error that blocks its achievement. Kotter's goals have been reworded to fit the reality of the Church rather than that of a business enterprise, but the underlying principles have not been altered. The examples that illustrate the applications of the principles are taken from the Diocese of Texas.

Stage 1: Establishing a Sense of Urgency

GOAL: *Identify and discuss crises, potential crises, or major opportunities that can create enough urgency among people in the denomination, the judicatory, or the congregation to drive change.*

TYPICAL ERROR: *Allowing too much complacency*

The biggest mistake the change agent can make is to plunge ahead without first instilling a strong sense of urgency among lay leaders, clergy, and members of the judicatory and the congregations.

COMMENTARY. A sense of genuine urgency is what drives change by making people willing to reject the status quo, accept initiatives, leave their comfort zone, and make sacrifices. Urgency is built from all the forces for change (the "driving forces" in Lewin's model) that the change leader can identify and use. The leader's goal is to identify as many such forces as possible and portray them as vividly as possible. Lack of urgency defeats a change effort, no matter how well intentioned it may be.

APPLICATION. Bishop Payne created a sense of urgency in the Diocese of Texas in a variety of ways. He and his staff relentlessly reminded the diocese about its problems, potential problems, and potential opportunities, especially with respect to the following issues:

- The membership decline in the Episcopal Church, which paralleled declines in other mainline denominations over the past four decades
- The failure of the diocese to increase its membership sufficiently to avoid a decline in its membership in terms of a percentage of the total population within the diocesan boundaries
- Destructive polarization over issues, both in the Diocese of Texas and in the national church, especially in regard to gender and sexual orientation
- The graying of the church, with proportionately fewer and fewer young people
- The increasing secularization of society and the declining influence of the Church, even though parts of the diocese were in the so-called Bible Belt
- The large numbers of unchurched people who were not looking to the Church for answers to their spiritual questions
- The failure of the Church to adequately address the enormous spiritual hunger of the unchurched, even when they came to church looking for spiritual sustenance
- The diocese's failure to reach out to all sorts and conditions of people

At the same time that the bishop raised these problems, he emphasized the potential opportunities they represented—making disciples, creating community, reaching out to the unchurched and the young, being intentionally inclusive, and so forth. In particular, he emphasized the possibility of personal transformation, spiritual development, and expectation of the miraculous. Therefore, the driving forces for change were efforts not just to avoid impending negative consequences but also to achieve positive ones.

Bishop Payne and his staff also took the following steps:

- Set challenging targets that were achievable but too high to be reached without major change (for example, increasing the diocese's membership by more than 100 percent within a decade)
- Changed the performance measures of the diocese (average Sunday attendance, for example, and number of confirmations and baptisms) to reflect the missionary vision of making disciples
- Benchmarked diocesan and congregational performance to outstanding judicatories and congregations, thereby establishing criteria for both superior and inferior performance
- Conducted a general survey of the diocese, to gather information on what the members of the diocese thought should be its priorities

Stage 2: Creating a Guiding Coalition

GOAL: *Put together a group of individuals with enough influence, capability, and expertise to lead the change effort, inspire trust, and function well as a team.*

TYPICAL ERROR: *Failure to create a sufficiently powerful guiding coalition*

One way in which this error may be expressed is in the failure to put together a coalition and to recognize that unfreezing, changing, and refreezing the culture is too great a task for one individual to achieve, no matter how capable or charismatic he or she may be. Another way in which this error may be expressed is in the failure to put together a coalition that is capable and collaborative enough to guide the change. This error may also be expressed in both of these ways.

COMMENTARY. Kotter proposes the following criteria for selection of each member of the guiding coalition:

- A formal title that suggests strong positional power
- Broad expertise

- A solid reputation that carries high credibility in the organization
- Ability to operate in a team environment
- Ability to trust, which can be enhanced through team-building events
- Devotion to the common objective represented by the vision
- Commitment to excellence
- Capacity for leadership
- Skills in change management (people can be trained in these skills, to some extent)

In the corporate world, Kotter warns, a secondary objective is not to leave anyone out of the coalition who can easily sabotage the change effort. Nevertheless, individuals should be excluded if they have large egos and no grasp of their own weaknesses, or if they destroy trust among team members. Moreover, if people of this kind are powerful enough to block a cultural transformation, then their resignation or their retirement is the preferred recourse.

APPLICATION. Because resistance to change emerges at every point, the need to build a capable guiding coalition cannot be overemphasized. The Diocese of Texas is evidence of this principle of creating a highly qualified team. Indeed, one reason why resistance has been effectively managed is the commitment to excellence, the dedication to the vision, and the high level of expertise and competence of the diocesan staff and the lay and clergy leaders who joined the guiding coalition to introduce the missionary model to the Diocese of Texas.

While he was still the bishop coadjutor (that is, before becoming the diocesan bishop), Bishop Payne put together a small think tank to test some ideas he had about diocesan change. He knew from the beginning of his tenure as bishop that mission and evangelism would be the focus of his episcopate. He also knew that his primary goals would be to reach the unchurched and to create a state of wellness that would put an end to the infighting that had divided the church. One of the members of the think tank asked, rhetorically, "Do you understand the full ramifications of focusing on the unchurched?" After some consideration, the bishop replied, "I don't think we have any option if we're going to be faithful to our calling." One of the ideas that came out of the think tank was the mission event known as "A Gathering of the Diocese: New Horizons, New Perspectives, New Disciples," or simply as "the Gathering" (see Chapter Six).

The guiding coalition that the bishop put together was built around the members of his diocesan staff, some of whom already held their positions at the time of his election and some of whom had not yet been hired. In addition to his staff, however, he reached out to clergy, lay leaders, and other influential members of the diocese, seeking to gain both their commitment to the vision and their help in its achievement. In every case, the bishop sought the most capable leaders in the diocese, men and women whose skills, abilities, and expertise most closely matched the demands of the positions for which he was recruiting them. Over time, he assembled a remarkably talented and dedicated group of individuals who had made a commitment to serve the diocese and its new vision.

Stage 3: Developing a Vision and a Strategy

GOAL: *Create a vision to direct the change effort and develop strategies for achieving that vision.*

TYPICAL ERROR: *Underestimating the power of a vision*

A sense of urgency and a strong guiding team are essential to major change, but they are not enough. An inspiring vision of the future is also required, one that is clear and easily communicated. This vision must then be translated into logical strategies and comprehensive plans, which should include well-thought-out budgets.

COMMENTARY. The function of a vision is twofold: to clarify the direction of change in order to coordinate people's actions, reduce confusion and conflict, and simplify decision making; and to motivate people to change, even when change is painful or not in their short-term self-interest.

Kotter lists six characteristics of a vision that can achieve these objectives:

1. It offers a picture of what the organization will be like in the future.
2. It appeals to the long-term interests of all who have a stake in the organization.
3. It is realistic, setting attainable but challenging goals.
4. It is clear enough to guide decision making.
5. It is general enough to permit individual initiative.
6. It is easy to communicate and can be fully explained within five minutes.

A seventh criterion, not mentioned by Kotter, is required for church-related visions: they must be biblically based.

Coalition members play a critical role in the development and implementation of the strategy designed to achieve the vision. The development of this strategy includes force field analysis, that is, an analysis of the forces working for and against the proposed changes implicit in the vision. When coalition members attempt to identify the primary forces working against the proposed change (the "restraining forces" in Lewin's model) and how to reduce them, they examine systems, structures, traditions, procedures, and so forth, as well as personnel. This analysis attempts to anticipate who (or what) will resist the change, in addition to why, how, and to what degree. It also attempts to identify opposing strategies that opponents are likely to employ, as well as the means through which to develop or maintain relationships with them to ensure ongoing communication that can educate or persuade.

The coalition will also address the forces driving change. Its analysis should include individuals who are natural allies, as well as those who may be undecided but whose help will be required to move the change effort along. The analysis should also include the systems, structures, traditions, procedures, and so forth, that will facilitate change. The ultimate goal of the final strategy devised is to increase the number and strength of the forces working to bring about change while attempting to reduce the number and strength of the forces opposing change.

Preparing a budget for implementation of the missionary model is a another way to identify changes that will have to be made, as well as forces that will drive or oppose them. Some resources (financial and otherwise) will have to be reallocated in accordance with the new priorities. A comprehensive educational plan should be developed for clergy and laity in areas where instruction is needed to carry out the missionary vision. For example, clergy members will profit from studying the difference between the maintenance church and the missionary church and how their roles will change with adoption of the missionary model. The judicatory staff may benefit from team-building exercises to help its members in their more integrative roles. The laity will gain from a better understanding of the meaning of the Great Commandment and the Great Commission, the nature of evangelistic activity in the mainline Church, and their role as disciples making disciples. The process of developing both the plan and its supporting budget is an effective focusing exercise on what is entailed in implementation of the missionary model.

APPLICATION. All six of Kotter's criteria for an effective vision, as well as the seventh criterion, are fulfilled by the vision of the Diocese of Texas and by the diocesan vision statement:

> The Diocese of Texas has a vision of being One Church, under the leadership of Jesus Christ, as a community of "Miraculous Expectation." It is a missionary diocese, whose bishop is the Chief Missionary, localized in missionary outposts and missionary institutions, utilizing the historic catholic structures of classic Anglicanism, and whose purpose under the Great Commandment to love is focused on the unchurched with a goal of growing to two hundred thousand by the year 2005. This is growth beyond mere numbers toward discipleship and seeks to include all sorts and conditions of people, bringing joy to those who are reaching out and to those who are reached.

At the same time the vision was being developed, so was the Gathering that would be used to implement it. In the process of creating the vision, it became clear that much would have to change in the Diocese of Texas for the vision to be achieved. The bishop and his staff started work on an implementation strategy as they thought through what the new vision would mean in terms of how the diocese was structured and how it operated. They began to get a sense of the fundamental change that would pervade the diocese and its congregations if they were to live the vision.

Upon becoming diocesan bishop, Bishop Payne used a sermon in Tyler, Texas, to lay out the bare bones of the vision. The next day, in a business meeting of the Diocesan Council, he elaborated on it. The vision was well received by those who heard the sermon, and it was well received in the Diocesan Council's business meeting. Thus began a honeymoon, but there was a plan to use the honeymoon period to develop the future.

Stage 4: Communicating the Change Vision

GOAL: *Use every method possible to continually communicate the new vision and strategies, and have the guiding coalition model the behavior expected of clergy, staff, and laity.*

TYPICAL ERROR: *Seriously undercommunicating the vision by referring to it only infrequently or by using only a limited number of communication channels*

COMMENTARY. Church members are bombarded with communications from many, many different sources. Unless the vision is relentlessly repeated and modeled, it cannot take hold. Kotter offers seven principles for communicating the vision:

1. Keep the vision simple. Eliminate "in" words, jargon, wordiness, and words that are not easily understood.

2. Use metaphors, analogies, and examples. They convey complex ideas simply and efficiently, and they are often emotionally powerful.

3. Use many different forums to communicate the vision. In the Church, these may include speeches by laypeople and clergy, church papers, Web sites, sermons, Sunday school classes, visits from the bishop, church bulletins, memoranda, press releases, posters, informal conversations, formal reports, conferences, seminars, and so forth.

4. Lead by example. Change leaders (the bishop, diocesan staff, clergy, lay leaders) must model the vision in what they say and do. Seeing someone "walk the talk" is more convincing than hearing mere words. Failure to model change is one of the reasons why many change efforts fail.

5. Listen and be listened to. Listen to what clergy, lay leaders, and members of the congregation have to say about the vision. Take the time to explain the vision to them.

6. Expressly address apparent inconsistencies between the vision and the actions taken. If some action seems to contradict the vision, specifically confront the presumed contradiction, and explain the inconsistency.

7. Repeat, repeat, repeat. The vision cannot be communicated too often.

APPLICATION. Implementation of the missionary model in a denomination, judicatory, or congregation is impossible without the help of most of the clergy and lay leaders. In general, however, implementation requires some kind of short-term sacrifice. In the Church, short-term sacrifice often takes the form of behaving in a new way that is uncomfortable at first. People will not make such sacrifices unless they believe that the potential benefits of the change are attractive and that the change itself is possible. They must believe in the vision. It takes a lot of credible communication to capture the minds and hearts of the clergy and the laity and lead them to a new vision.

The Gathering (see Chapter Six) was the vehicle used to launch the vision in the Diocese of Texas, and its announcement was the point at which

resistance began. The bishop had wanted (and expected) a very large number of people to attend from all the congregations of the diocese. He and
his staff spent well over a year planning the Gathering and were excited
by its possibilities. When the invitations went out, however, the response
from the congregations was unenthusiastic. The attitude in the diocese
was that this event was just one more diocesan meeting.

Excuses were plentiful. Some people had become so turned off by continuous diocesan infighting related to issues that they refused to attend
another meeting where they expected conflict to erupt without any kind
of resolution. Others did not want to bear the cost of attendance because
a fee was charged to underwrite the event, and travel and lodging ex-
penses were required for many. Still others stayed away because of simple inertia. In order to get people to attend, the bishop resorted to
assigning suggested attendance quotas to each congregation. The bishop
and his staff personally pressured as many people as they could to attend.
In the case of the mission congregations, the bishop simply directed their
clergy to come (the clergy of missions are called vicars, and they report
directly to the bishop). They were appalled by the directive, but they
came. For all others, however, attendance was voluntary, and there was a
lot of foot dragging. Nevertheless, about fifteen hundred people (out of a
diocese of seventy-three thousand) did come.

The results of the Gathering, in terms of communicating the vision and
building support for it, cannot be overestimated. What the Gathering did
was to expand and solidify the first three stages of the change process. It
created a sense of urgency in the people who came, and therefore it built
a much larger guiding coalition. At the Gathering, plenary speakers addressed the dissolution of Christendom and the need to reorder the
Church, the differences among generations, and the necessity of understanding the different kinds of unchurched people if they were to be
brought into the Church. The bishop talked about the Great Commandment and the Great Commission, explained what evangelism is and how
it is conducted, and talked about how the spiritually hungry could be engaged. He emphasized that the diocese did not even understand its own
model of evangelism, and that too often the focus was on membership
rather than on spiritual development. The bishop also acknowledged the
stress associated with change, and especially with adopting the missionary model, but he pointed out that in the maintenance model there is also
stress, which takes the form of internal strife and the low morale it breeds.
The stress that comes from implementing the vision is biblical and to be
expected. It is the stress experienced with any prophetic call; it is the stress

of achievement. It is the stress that Jeremiah endured for his faithfulness to God, and that Moses experienced when he answered the divine call at the burning bush to lead his people to the Promised Land. This stress is also the kind faced by the apostles in the trials, tribulations, and burdens of their discipleship. Missionaries throughout every age have had to deal with stress. We are also missionaries; small wonder that we experience the same.

In order to make the Gathering still more comprehensive, a presentation on youth was included, and plenty of youth were present. All the urgent problems of the Church—secularization, spiritual hunger, the decline in national membership, the graying of the membership, divisiveness— were directly addressed. The gathering created a critical mass for communicating the change vision, and it was absolutely crucial to the success of the new vision. The whole transformation plan would have failed without the Gathering. Afterward, the people of the diocese knew that something was different. The bishop had said that they were not going to spend time fighting over issues, and when they did not spend time fighting over issues, that was a manifestation of serious change.

In the aftermath of the Gathering, every channel of communication available to the diocese was used to communicate the vision. Virtually every aspect of the diocesan newspaper, including its masthead ("A Community of Miraculous Expectation"), had some connection to the vision. Whenever any of the bishops spoke or delivered a sermon, they preached on the vision. When the Web site was added, it emphasized the vision. The themes chosen for diocesan meetings enhanced the vision. Diocesan communications on evangelism, congregational development, outreach, Christian education, and youth ministry were all related to the vision.

Stage 5: Empowering Broad-Based Action

GOAL: *Empower people to implement the vision by removing obstacles to its implementation.*

TYPICAL ERROR: *Permitting obstacles to block the new vision*

Obstacles that block the new vision, whether they are structural, cultural, political, or related to human resources, must be confronted and overcome or substantially eliminated.

COMMENTARY. Kotter lists ways to empower people for broad-based action in an organization seeking to change:

1. Restructure wherever necessary to remove structural barriers and make it possible for people to achieve the vision. In particular, remove structural silos and replace them with teams.

2. Provide the skills training that is necessary to implement the vision. Examples might include training in skills related to team building, communication, conflict resolution, and diversity.

3. Make sure that systems affecting performance evaluation, decisions about compensation and promotion, and recruitment and hiring are aligned with the vision.

4. Encourage risk taking and nontraditional ideas, activities, and actions.

5. Confront people in authority who undercut the change that is needed. When they are unwilling to change or incapable of changing, conduct an honest dialogue with them, and seek their assistance. Ask them what they can contribute to help achieve the vision. If enlisting their help is a lost cause and they need to be replaced, then their replacement will be easier after such a conversation. By contrast, if they are cooperative but just do not know what to do, then such a conversation can be helpful.

APPLICATION. The Diocese of Texas took each of these steps in order to remove or substantially reduce the obstacles that blocked achievement of its new vision. Some of these changes have already been described; others will be detailed in subsequent chapters. In general, however, the bishop took the following actions:

○ He restructured the diocese by integrating diocesan functions. He replaced functional silos with teams, empowered congregations to make or participate in many decisions from which they once had been excluded, and served as a resource for congregations. The spoke-and-wheel organizational form developed from this effort (see Chapter Seven). In the process, all judicatory staff, regardless of their functional areas, were involved in congregational development and planning.

○ In light of the vision, he reviewed every diocesan program with the diocesan staff. He discarded what was not working, regardless of how long it had been in place or how popular it was. The cardinal principle was to barbecue the sacred cows.

○ He used the vision to drive all decisions, actions, resource allocations, and activities in the judicatory, its missionary outposts, and its institutions. It is in service to the vision that clergy are called, churches are built, programs in Christian education are developed, fundraising is carried out, staff members are assembled, and themes are chosen for judicatory councils.

○ He encouraged experimentation, risk taking, nontraditional ideas, and innovative activities that furthered the vision. He rewarded successes and refused to punish innovations that failed, recognizing that failure is an inevitable part of creative responses, innovative approaches, inventive solutions, and change. Implementation of the missionary model requires decisions and actions that are often without precedent. In these conditions, it is impossible not to fail. When failure did occur, the bishop and his staff admitted it and took responsibility, acting as quickly as possible. They were open and honest about what had not worked. The cumulative success that experimentation and innovation engendered was far greater and more meaningful than the failure that sometimes accompanied it.

○ He realigned the systems for performance evaluation, promotion, compensation, and recruiting and hiring in order to reward achievements that reflected the missionary goals of the vision.

○ He provided clergy and laity with the training necessary to implement the vision. For example, in the case of the Diocese of Texas, the bishop spent the first two years of his episcopate visiting each of the ten convocations in the diocese and talked about the vision, evangelism in the Anglican tradition, and making disciples. His presentation, titled *The Bishop's Teaching Series,* is available on video in every missionary outpost. Because the members of mainline denominations generally have unclear or distorted perceptions of evangelism, implementation of the vision begins with teaching both what evangelism is and how it can be accomplished in the denomination's tradition.

○ He inaugurated or incorporated other training events, such as stewardship conferences; cluster conferences, in which laity and clergy from congregations of similar size discussed issues of mutual interest (see Chapter Ten); and conferences for new vestry and wardens (elected congregational leaders). In each case the objective was to provide training and support, and in each case there was resistance. Attendance lagged behind expectations, but each event was well received by those who did attend, and they spread the word. Training programs in communication, Christian education, and youth ministry were also instituted.

○ He called on the experience, expertise, and dedication of the laity. In the maintenance church, use of the laity is generally limited to staffing for church services and Sunday school. In the missionary church, the laity play these and many other roles, both inside and outside church buildings.

o He reminded people that it is easier to tear down and fight than to build and create. The bishop refused to be distracted by denominational issues that could divide, fracture, or demoralize the diocese and its congregations. He refused to be seduced into debating these issues for the purpose of voting on them in a "winner take all" context.

o As necessary, he dealt in an appropriate manner with people in authority who blocked achievement of the vision.

At the same time, the diocesan staff began the slow process of remolding the work of its departments—communications, Christian education, youth ministry, outreach—to fit the vision. Staff members promoted the vision whenever they interacted with the congregations, and they changed the way in which they dealt with them. This direct effort counteracted the long-standing idea that the diocese could not do anything to help: staff members went to the congregations to assist and empower them. For example, the purpose and design of the various conferences held on Christian education, youth ministry, and communications all were changed to reflect the missionary vision and what the diocese was about in the way of ministry. The old youth meetings, which had been modeled on a politics-based legislative process, were changed so that they now focused on leadership training and evangelism.

Through all these changes, there was resistance. Some of the resistance stemmed from the ingrained belief that nothing could be done about the decline of the Church, and that whatever was done would not make much difference. Moreover, not everyone wanted to be empowered, nor did everyone want to engage in evangelism. It took time to convince people otherwise, but the bishop, his staff, and other key change leaders persevered. Whenever they promised something, they delivered it, and they delivered it well.

Most of the clergy enthusiastically embraced the missionary vision. Others, as they saw the power of the vision made manifest, were brought along without the need for direct confrontation. Some clergy, however, despite education and training in the missionary model, will remain more comfortable with the old model. Such individuals generally retire or transfer, although they are given every opportunity and encouragement to adapt. Resistance to the new model requires great compassion and wisdom on the part of the judiciary and the congregations, as well as acknowledgment of these clergy's years of dedicated service to God and to the Church. These clergy have spent their lives in another model and are suddenly asked to change. At any rate, the few who cannot or will not change eventually leave for their own sake, as well as for the sake of their congregations. Because of the accountability required in the new model, it is stressful for clergy who remain maintenance-oriented to be in a missionary church. We can believe, however, that God has a plan for each of us, and that those who are uncomfortable with the new paradigm are meant to be somewhere else. New programs and extensive training have reenergized some clergy. Most have adapted eagerly, simply because of the unspoken but perceived understanding that a change was desperately needed. Because the transformation has been biblically centered, it has been all the more readily received and accepted.

Nevertheless, some fallout will inevitably occur with a paradigm shift as dramatic as the movement from maintenance to mission. In addressing this difficult issue, a higher question assumes special significance: What is the role of the Church in such a situation: to support the status quo, or to proclaim the Gospel to a hurting world? All kinds of support should be made available to the faithful, but ultimately the vision of disciples making disciples must be served. Bishop Payne has said, "I don't give a lot of energy to resistance. I focus on what's good and let the miracles work things out."

The experience of the Diocese of Texas has been that, with enough time and evidence of the vision's power, most people will come around. In some cases, however, it may take years. For example, four years after the vision was adopted in the Diocese of Texas, one of the missionary outposts was out of worship space and needed additional rooms for the many ministries that had developed. A long-time member of the congregation objected to the changes planned for the building and asked the diocese to intervene to stop them. When he realized that the diocesan office was unwilling to do so, he withheld his pledge to the capital funds drive and encouraged his friends to do likewise. No rancor developed within the congregation, and there was no condemnation of the lack of support by this wealthy family and its friends. Rather, the clergy and the lay leaders of the congregation continued to pursue the planned expansion as a necessary expression of living out the vision. The focus remained on mission, on community, and on miraculous expectation. In the end, this individual caught the vision and made a six-figure gift for the planned expansion, encouraging his friends to do likewise. The congregation had waited, prayed, and held steadfastly to the vision of reaching out and changing lives. The glorious transformation occurred.

It is crucial to deal effectively with the divisive issues that threaten to fracture a diocese or a denomination. The strategy for doing so is to hold to the vision and train staff people to do likewise. As Episcopal Presiding Bishop Frank Griswold has said, "Issues don't dominate where people are engaged in mission" (Barnwell, 1999). Nevertheless, some people would rather fight over internal issues than rebuild the Church. Fighting is easier, and it often makes people feel extremely righteous, justified, prophetic, and holy, regardless of which side they support. In the contemporary Church, such people use a "just war" theology, fight with enormous creativity and zeal, brutalize those with whom they disagree, and leave the general body of the faithful disillusioned, demoralized, and depressed. It is no wonder that the mainline membership declines as the faithful flee the battle and the unchurched refuse to engage in it.

Stage 6: Generating Short-Term Wins

GOAL: *Plan specifically to create visible improvements, or wins, within six to eighteen months of launching the change effort and to give public recognition and rewards to people who have participated in the wins.*

TYPICAL ERROR: *Failing to create short-term wins*

Because real organizational transformation take time, it is important to set short-term goals that can be achieved and celebrated. Without this form of encouragement, people may abandon a change effort or ally themselves with those who are resisting it. It is a mistake to hope for short-term wins instead of planning them.

COMMENTARY. Kotter describes an effective short-term win as one that is clearly related to the change effort, unambiguous, and visible enough for large numbers of people to see and believe it. Such a win reinforces the change effort by providing evidence that the sacrifices were worthwhile. It rewards those who have participated in the change, tests the vision against reality, undermines cynics, blocks self-serving resisters, keeps key people on board, and builds momentum for further change.

Although it is important to plan short-term wins in the Church, the Church has an advantage that is unavailable to a corporate leader using Kotter's model. The Church's advantage is its knowledge that short-term wins are inevitable because the missionary model brings the work and presence of the Holy Spirit into play. In the Church, therefore, the challenge is not so much to plan for short-term wins as to identify and report them.

APPLICATION. From the beginning, the Bishop of Texas sought to discover what he called "resurrection stories" or "resurrection experiences" occurring in the diocese—that is, stories of individual or congregational transformation resulting from the new vision. Ironically, the Gathering itself was such a story. It was a monumental short-term win because it convinced many of those present that significant changes were possible in the Diocese of Texas. Many of those who attended were inspired by the experience, motivated to change, and determined to pursue the vision. In turn, they created virtually immediate wins in the congregations of the diocese. For example, one woman went back to her small church after the Gathering and convinced the other members of her congregation to begin a ministry to the schools on either side of the church. What was needed, the principals of these schools advised, was an after-school program for the latchkey children in this economically deprived area. The proposed program was started by the congregation and continues to this day. Another example took more time. St. Albans, a dying Anglo-American congregation, successfully made the transition to a growing Anglo-Hispanic congregation through appointment of a bilingual vicar. Between these extremes in time, literally thousands of stories surfaced, some dramatic and bold, others subtle and quiet, some repeated to many, and others kept for close friends or the confines of the heart. But stories there were, and many were repeated, inspiring still others to come forward with the transformations occurring in their lives and congregations.

In addition to the resurrection stories, the bishop and diocesan staff sought to identify islands of health and wellness in the diocese, places where things were already going well and where lives were already being changed in line with the vision. Congregations with extraordinary growth were spotlighted and praised. Those with successful outreach programs or extraordinary offerings in Christian education or inspiring youth ministries were singled out for recognition and congratulations. Accomplishments related to the vision were acclaimed wherever they occurred and in whatever form they took. Instead of focusing on what was not working, the bishop and his staff highlighted what was working. Speakers at the Diocesan Council told about the glorious transformation of their lives and about their expectation of miracles. Members of the diocese began to see the deep involvement of the Holy Spirit in their midst and came to understand that they had a great deal to share with others. Every means of communication was used to celebrate and report these transformations. The number of resurrection stories grew, and the stories themselves were repeated.

The diocese also reported on its own faithfulness to the vision and its commitment to the missionary model. Diocesan staff members kept their promises, followed through on their offers to help, and continued to serve as a resource to the congregations, all the while reporting these activities through all the channels of communication available to the diocese. In subtle and dramatic ways, the bishop and diocesan staff lived the vision and reported the results. For example, the diocesan vision called for evangelism, growth, and reaching out to all sorts and conditions of people. Therefore, the diocese built the church of Santa Maria Virgen from the ground up, the first new Hispanic church building constructed within the Episcopal Church in America. Bishop Payne learned Spanish so that he could deliver his sermons in Spanish in the Spanish-speaking congregations. In these cases and others, the bishop understood the power of symbolism and the necessity of reporting on diocesan and congregational achievements. In essence, his strategy was to focus continually on accomplishments and possibilities rather than on resistance.

Stage 7: Consolidating Gains and Producing More Change

GOAL: *Use the increased credibility derived from earlier successes to drive deeper change.*

Alter all systems, structures, and policies that are not aligned and integrated with the vision. At the same time, hire, promote, and develop people who embrace the vision and can effectively implement it.

TYPICAL ERROR: *Declaring victory too soon*

Although it takes three to ten years for major changes to become embedded in a corporate culture, many leaders are tempted to declare victory after the first evidence of improved performance. If the momentum ends prematurely, however, powerful forces associated with tradition will reassert themselves and reverse the earlier gains, stalling change and defeating the vision.

COMMENTARY. In stage 7, the change effort kicks into high gear. Kotter describes five characteristics of this stage:

1. As the momentum for change continues to build on the success of short-term wins, the guiding coalition uses its credibility to initiate even greater change projects, driving change deeper and deeper into the organization.

2. As the change expands and deepens, more and more people are enlisted and developed to help bring about change.

3. Change leaders appear throughout the organization, especially at the lower levels, and take charge of specific projects involved in the change.

4. At this point, the role of the senior leaders is to maintain the high profile of the vision and the shared sense of purpose it provides, and to keep the sense of urgency strong.

5. Unnecessary dependence among various parts of the organization (in the form of redundant reports, unnecessary authorizations, obsolete reporting requirements, and so on) is eliminated in order to facilitate change for the long term as well as for the short term.

As we have seen, Lewin's model of change involves three processes: unfreezing, changing, and refreezing. At stage 7 in Kotter's model, the organization is still changing but (to extend the metaphor) the water is beginning to thicken. If a change leader abandons the effort by celebrating victory before the new cultural change is frozen, momentum will be lost and regression will occur. Resistance to change never fully disappears. Therefore, the change effort cannot be declared successful until the changes have been incorporated into the culture and frozen.

APPLICATION. As the bishop and diocesan staff emerged from the maintenance mind-set and lived the vision at ever deeper levels, they identified even greater changes that needed to be made. One such change involved the congregations' participation in decisions about mission funding (see Chapter Seven). In order for the missionary vision to be lived, more youth ministers were necessary. At first the diocese encouraged the congregations to hire or develop youth ministers, but the shortage continued. To meet the need, the diocese began to offer training programs in youth ministry to those who were willing to take up this calling. The provision of specialized training for the congregations was expanded beyond the department of youth ministry to include the departments of Christian education and communications. The department of communications, for example, now trains the laity in media networking at the local level. The diocese has even opened specialized schools to meet the training needs of its congregations. For instance, the new Center for Youth Ministry trains youth ministers for congregations. The department of Christian education offers regular training for Christian education leaders for deployment in the congregations.

The bishop and diocesan staff continue to use every possible avenue of judicatory life to keep the congregations focused on the vision, treating it

not as something that will be but as something that already is. One of the
rectors of a congregation in the Diocese of Texas confessed, "When the
bishop first started talking about the diocese as 'one church,' we all said,
'What?' Then he presented the idea of 'miraculous expectation,' which
seemed quite foreign. Finally, the notion that we could actually grow to
two hundred thousand members was, of course, out of the question. But,
the bishop kept talking about the one church of the diocese, miraculous
expectation, and glorious transformation, about making disciples, and
about reaching all sorts and conditions of people, and gradually something begin to change in us and in the diocese. And I got on board, although I wouldn't have thought I would. With repetition, the ideas and
the slogans of the vision do work, but the first thought of them is surprising. In fact, I was surprised that I began to be responsive to them. It's
been a remarkable process. We've grown into the vision."

Stage 8: Anchoring New Approaches in the Culture

GOAL: *Anchor change (new goals, attitudes, behaviors) in the culture of
the organization (that is, in its social norms and shared values).*

TYPICAL ERROR: *Neglecting to anchor changes firmly in the culture*

The only change that endures is change that has been embedded in the
organization's culture. In Lewin's terminology, the change must be re-
frozen. Until new goals, behaviors, and attitudes have become rooted in
the social norms and shared values of the organization, they are subject
to degradation and reversal by traditional forces.

COMMENTARY. More than half a century of research confirms that individual behavior in groups and organizations is highly influenced by the
norms of behavior and the shared values of the group or organization.
Norms determine what behavior is acceptable to the group and what behavior is not. Whether subtle or blatant, norms are very powerful in determining group behavior and attitudes, and they cover everything from
appropriate dress to how hard to work to appropriate communication
channels. Group norms may override individual motivation, preferences,
and desires. A group enforces its norms by rewarding those who comply
with them and punishing those who do not.

In a congregation, norms will largely determine the type of dress that
is considered appropriate for Sunday, whether newcomers are warmly
welcomed, participation in the coffee social after the Sunday service, how

enthusiastically the congregation joins in the singing, the importance given to volunteering, and so forth. Norms themselves are based on shared values of the group. Values, like norms, are taught and enforced by group members and may endure despite changes in group membership. Shared values will determine the priority of evangelism, the expected quality of the sermon, the extent of community outreach, the number of small groups established in the congregation, and so forth.

For the most part, behavioral norms and shared values are self-perpetuating. They are self-perpetuating because the group reinforces them through rewards and punishments, sometimes without even being aware of it. Furthermore, they are virtually invisible and so are difficult to confront directly and change. Finally, group members hire—or, in the case of congregations, attract—other members like themselves and so perpetuate the established culture. Because this culture affects and is affected by hundreds, thousands, or hundreds of thousands of people who must change their norms and shared values, cultural change is very difficult and time-consuming.

Kotter describes three general methods for anchoring change in an organizational culture (that is, "refreezing" the culture with a different set of norms and values):

1. Articulate the connection between the new behaviors and the success of the organization. Show people how changes in specific behaviors and attitudes have improved organizational effectiveness and performance. Do not ask people to make the link themselves. Regularly remind people of the benefits of the change effort.

2. Reinvigorate the change process with new projects, themes, and change agents.

3. Create ways to ensure leadership development and succession that will support the change. Revise promotion criteria, as necessary, to be sure that the next generation of leaders will personify the new approach and further the vision.

APPLICATION. Five years into the missionary model in the Diocese of Texas, the bishop and the guiding coalition continue to articulate, affirm, and support the vision in everything they say and do. They highlight breakthroughs, discoveries, and good work, and they continually report on the benefits that the model's implementation has brought. Members of the guiding coalition maintain an emphasis on the goals and themes of the vision: evangelism, community building, miraculous expectation, and personal transformation. There has been no letup in the drumbeat that supports the vision, and the number of people at the drum continues to grow from those who have experienced the rewards of living the vision. As the diocesan culture slowly changes, the vision itself seems more and more natural to the diocese and so wins more and more adherents.

New programs are continually developed that further the vision and drive it deeper into the culture of the diocese. Some of these programs are developed intentionally to serve this purpose, but others arise spontaneously from the model itself as a natural expansion of its vision. When denominations have operated in the maintenance mode as long as those in the mainline, it is difficult for their members to envision at the outset what it would mean to live out the Great Commandment and the Great Commission. As church members become more familiar with the missionary model and live its potential, they grow hungrier for its fruits. From such hunger new programs grow naturally, generated by the model itself.

It is important to remember that there is a big difference between a change model developed from an analysis of corporate America and a change model developed for application to the Christian Church. The primary difference is the role of God. Once launched, the process of changing to a missionary focus in the Church becomes the province of the Holy Spirit, and so the change effort expands and strengthens with a power that is not encountered in business enterprises. There is no comparable dimension in business that can broaden, deepen, and drive a change effort, transforming its participants and leading them to ever-broadening horizons and opportunities.

For example, one new program that has grown out of the vision in the Diocese of Texas is the Community of Hope, a spiritual resource for training lay chaplains. As a result of this program, spiritual training is offered at more and more locations in the diocese and even in other dioceses. Chaplaincy programs at universities within the diocesan boundaries, programs that once served university Episcopalians, now recruit and train clergy to become missionary leaders who are training Episcopal university students and faculty to be missionaries to the entire university body. As a result of these and other initiatives (such as the new youth ministry training program), the Diocese of Texas is experiencing an increase in the number of young adults offering themselves for the ordination track. This development is a crucial one for the future of the diocese and the Episcopal Church.

New leaders in the Diocese of Texas are being groomed in the tradition of the missionary model. The annual conference for new vestry and wardens, for example, trains lay leaders in understanding and implementing the vision. When congregations need new clergy because of vacancies or expansions, the diocese works with the congregations to help them find missionary leaders who support the vision. As the vision becomes more and more part of the diocesan "DNA," search committees of congregations seeking new clergy look increasingly for candidates whose unique gifts can be used to sustain and expand the vision within the congregation and within the diocese. To ensure that the next generation of leaders embraces the missionary model, the diocese has enhanced its internship program for new seminary graduates. These graduates are put through a one-year program with the diocesan staff in which they study the vision and its application as part of developing their ministerial skills. This internship program provides on-the-job training in the missionary model during the first year of ministry. Commitment to the vision has become a major criterion for clergy selection and transfer within the diocese.

Managing Resistance to Evangelism and Church Growth

The missionary model is grounded in evangelism and leads naturally to church growth. Unfortunately, evangelism and church growth are not automatically looked on with favor by all congregations, denominations, and clergy. Evangelism is often a disturbing topic that elicits strong ambivalence if not outright resistance from many church members. The legacy of the maintenance church—neglect of evangelism—has come home to roost.

For example, growth may be stated as an objective that is given cursory attention, pro forma support as an ideal, or short-term commitment via some special program, but it is not often conceived as an enduring goal of the Church. In fact, the opposite is frequently the case. Lip service is paid to the need to evangelize and grow, but continuous, wholehearted, involved support for growth is generally lacking. The reality is that maintenance church members favor the status quo and look on growth with disfavor. The maintenance mind-set views an interest in membership numbers as unseemly, inappropriate, and even ugly because the maintenance church thinks in terms of members rather than in terms of disciples, the unchurched, and the Great Commandment and the Great Commission.

In maintenance mode, church members have many reasons for opposing evangelism and growth. For some members, resistance to growth stems from a misunderstanding of the meaning of evangelism and biblical ignorance of the Great Commission. Many mainline Church members do not know what evangelism really is and imagine it to be more aggressive and intrusive than it is. For them, it smacks of excess, intrusive behavior, or door-to-door witnessing, which many mainline churchgoers find offensive. Others resist the effort that evangelism requires, both individual effort and the collective effort of the congregation. For still others, evangelism is merely new and different and therefore frightening. It is not something that they have imagined for themselves or their church, and they must be led patiently through the experience in order to understand and accept it.

For yet other members, the idea of too many new people is disconcerting. Church growth may mean the end of a familial atmosphere in the church, or a lessening of the old members' sense of belonging. It may require members who are comfortable with each other and with the norms of the congregation to assimilate strangers who will bring change and uncertainty. Growth may mean sharing power with newcomers, and so it may also mean potential reductions in the perceived importance and status of established members. Yet another deterrent to growth is the fear that new people will bring with them uncertainties and attitudes that may raise troubling questions about faith and doctrine, causing repressed doubts to surface in a congregation. An emphasis on evangelism will also mean less attention to other valued activities, and those who favor them may resist evangelism as an unwelcome competitor for time and funding.

Moreover, a commitment to the experience of evangelism is often perceived as risky because it tests our beliefs and forces us to articulate those beliefs. Evangelism requires ongoing, conscious reflection on our words and actions. Discipleship is a way of life that makes us vulnerable because our words and deeds become self-implicating in this self-examination. Evangelism can be perceived as a frightening process because it forces us to be accountable to ourselves and to others for our beliefs, motives, and behavior. But precisely because the process of evangelism does require these actions, it is a powerful tool of spiritual growth that can create a Christian community that is richer in spirit and in deed.

The missionary church, by contrast, is concerned with its membership numbers, not because they represent the number of members in the church, but because they represent the number of disciples of Jesus Christ. For the missionary church, membership numbers are not distasteful; they are inspiring. To some degree, they measure the success of the evangelistic efforts and of the members' commitment to the Great Commission to make disciples. Increased membership is a goal that is clearly stated and openly avowed as an important aspect of the work of the Church, especially in the New Apostolic Age, with great spiritual hunger in the nation. One of the ways to judge the extent to which a denomination, judicatory, or congregation is operating in maintenance or missionary mode is to assess the attitude of its members toward church growth. For the great evangelists in the Diocese of Texas, the goal of two hundred thousand disciples by the year 2005 is woefully low.

Nevertheless, membership numbers are recognized as only one measurement of the success of the missionary church. Although they are important, they are not complete in and of themselves. Other criteria must also be considered in assessing the quality and extent of evangelism. These criteria are related both to individual disciples and to their community. An intention to include all sorts and conditions of people in the evangelistic effort is a significant criterion. Disciples in a missionary church experience a sense of the miraculous, of the transforming power and presence of the Holy Spirit in their lives. They embrace the power of prayer and recognize divine involvement, encounter the holy in daily life, and live with the confidence of experiencing miracles in their lives and God's ever-faithful care. They are committed to following the will of God and to carrying the Christian life forth into their relationships with family members, friends, and co-workers. Thus, in addition to the number of disciples, the quality of their discipleship is important.

Any congregation, judicatory, or denomination that is not growing has reason to be deeply concerned. Our Lord's command to make disciples of all nations is very clear, and so is His command to love one's neighbor as oneself. Any congregation, diocese, or denomination that is not growing is not communicating the transformational power of the Christian faith to an unchurched world in spiritual pain. It is not sharing the blessings of the Gospel with others; it is not stepping out in faith and miraculous expectation. The Christian Church is fundamentally a missionary church. Any congregation or denomination that is not missionary in its outlook should pause to consider whether it has strayed from the Great Commission to make disciples and thus change lives and bring people into harmony with God and their fellow human beings.

Transferability of the Missionary Model

Can the missionary model implemented in the Diocese of Texas and its congregations be adopted by other judicatories and other denominations of the mainline Church? In other words, is the model transferable? Or is it a singular phenomenon that cannot be replicated?

We believe that the model is universal and can be adapted successfully by any mainline denomination, its judicatories, and its congregations. We hold this view while acknowledging that substantial differences exist among denominations, judicatories, and congregations in terms of culture, resources, structure, and history. It is not possible to prove this transferability with examples from other denominations because the missionary model is too new. Therefore, proof has to be constructed logically on the basis of the universality of the needs, solutions, and principles involved in denominational implementation. Although serious differences do exist among denominations, no such difference is fatal to the model's transfer. The differences among denominations are not as significant as the profound similarities that override them. Furthermore, the model used in the Diocese of Texas is an ancient one. It is the same model used by the first-century Church, but it has been adapted to contemporary times. Its success has been demonstrated.

The basic transferability of the model rests on several factors:

○ The universality of the mainline denominations' problems and opportunities (see Chapter Four), which serve as motivating factors for denominational transformation

○ The proposed solution, which takes the form of the missionary vision and the change strategy designed to achieve it

○ The management and leadership principles for implementing that vision and that strategy

This universality is not dependent on denominational similarity in terms of financial resources, culture, tradition, history, or demographics.

There are impediments to the implementation of the model, but, again, they do not derive from differences among the denominations. Rather, they derive from entrenched attitudes that occur in all the mainline denominations and that make change difficult, especially the type of change called for by the missionary model. Several of these impediments are described in the passages that follow. They represent real challenges to those who would change the Church, but they are not insurmountable. The vision is a powerful means of overriding objections and corralling the forces necessary to bring about change. Nevertheless, it is important to recognize these impediments because they are more insidious than the more obvious obstacles to change that have already been addressed.

Elitism

Assumption: Principles of management developed from research on corporations and business enterprises should not be applied to the Church. The Church is not a business, and it is nontheological to treat it as one. Any effort to make the Church entrepreneurial is unseemly and inappropriate.

Reality: The Church is at once part of the world and separate from it. Like Christians themselves, the Church has a divine origin and a divine calling, but it operates in the context of the material world and has material responsibilities. In a sense, it uses the God-given material world to serve the spiritual ends for which materiality was created. Every mainline denomination is a multimillion-dollar nonprofit organization with human and financial resources that must be well managed if the denomination is to fulfill its mission of ministering to the needs of God's people. Some church members shy away from talking about the church as a business with services to offer, and yet this conceptualization, within limits, is useful.

Conceiving of the Church as a spiritually based, divinely inspired nonprofit organization can be beneficial in effectively confronting the very real problems of marketing, provision of services, human resource management, goal setting, motivation, communication, and accountability that management experts have been addressing for decades. The Church is not a business in the usual sense, but neither is it immune to the problems that necessitate the use of sound management principles. For that matter, a family is not a business, either, nor is a family immune to situations that call for such sound business practices as budgeting, planning, and using resources in the most effective ways. Elitists who disdain the ideas, principles, and lessons associated with entrepreneurism and sound management do a disservice to the Church. The word *entrepreneurial* has a negative connotation for some in the Church because it is usually associated with business organizations, and yet the heart of entrepreneurism is envisioning, innovation, and hard work.

Accountability for the quality of one's work is a principle that is assumed in business and in families but is often ignored in the Church. In this sense, the Church should be more businesslike. Setting goals, providing feedback, and establishing performance standards are well-accepted ways of enhancing the performance of an organization. Clergy who have not been held accountable for how well they serve their congregations may bristle at the thought, but the rest of us should be buoyed by the idea that the goal of the Church is to be as effective as possible in the lives of its members. For very good reasons, the possibility that keeping our jobs will depend on the quality of our performance is an everyday experience for most of us. Historically, this kind of accountability, whereby the clergy accept responsibility for performing well in their assignments, ultimately to the benefit of their congregations, has been lacking in the maintenance church, but not in the missionary church.

If the Church is to meet the challenges of the New Apostolic Age, it will have to become more entrepreneurial in its visioning, its willingness to innovate, and its commitment to change. Elitist attitudes, which disdain these aspects of the future Church as nontheological or inappropriate, are simply unrealistic and counterproductive and can be pointed out as such.

Prejudice Against Evangelism

Assumption: Evangelism belongs to the evangelicals, evangelists, and the fundamentalists, not to the mainline denominations; it is not the sort of thing "we" do.

Reality: Just as some elitists scorn anything that smacks of entrepreneurism, others spurn any concept popularly associated with evangelical and fundamentalist churches. In the last three decades, dedication to mission has played a more central role in the evangelical and fundamentalist churches than in the mainline churches (hence the growth in fundamentalist congregations and the decline in mainline congregations). Now that the concept of evangelism has been "tarred" with fundamentalist associations, some reject evangelism as a proper focus for the mainline Church, despite the Great Commandment and the Great Commission. As a result, mainline churchgoers find it difficult to understand evangelism outside a fundamentalist context.

A further complication stems from the association of a central principle of evangelism with fundamentalist churches. In the mainline denominations, evangelism ultimately (although not initially) involves talking about what it means to be a disciple of Christ. It means talking, in a personal way, about one's relationship with God and how that relationship has affected one's life. Active discipleship (and there is no other form) uses numerous concepts that have been co-opted, to some degree, by the fundamentalists and so have earned the disfavor and disdain of many in the mainline. When these ideas are then suggested as crucial elements in reaching the unchurched, they are often dismissed. For example, the idea of expecting God to do the unexpected (that is, to perform miracles), or of helping the unchurched realize that God wants to be present in their lives in a meaningful and transformational way, too often seems to be the province of the evangelicals and the fundamentalists, and yet these ideas of miraculous expectation and glorious transformation are at the core of the Christian faith. One can hardly talk about evangelism and discipleship, much less about the Good News, without talking about these potentialities. The concept of cultivating a faith that is disciplined, life-changing, and central to a person's life is an essential aspect of the mainline Church, regardless of how close this concept may seem to the proselytizing words of the fundamentalists.

Evangelism, community, and personal transformation played a nuclear role in the growth of the Christian Church for the first thousand years of its existence. Those who disdain these aspects of the faith, because of the popular association of these elements with evangelicals and fundamentalists, do not serve the Church well.

Fatal Differences

Assumption: There are differences between the Diocese of Texas and other denominations, judicatories, or congregations that will prevent the missionary model from being transferable.

Reality: It is true that denominations, judicatories, and congregations can differ significantly according to many criteria (relative homogeneity, education, racial makeup, income, age, politics, social status, culture, history, denominational loyalty, and so forth). Judicatories and their congregations may be urban or rural. They may be reservoirs of executive talent or may be composed of people with little management experience. They may be in areas that are steeped in religious tradition (for example, the so-called Bible Belt) or in areas that are not. They may be wealthy or not wealthy.

Regardless of the criteria that are used to distinguish one denomination from another or one congregation from another, there is no difference that is fatal to the transferability of the model. The reason is straightforward: the model is not dependent on demographics, education, social status, racial makeup, religious tradition, numerical size, financial base, political positions, or denominational loyalty for its successful implementation in a denomination, judicatory, or congregation. It is dependent on a missionary vision embraced by the people and inspired by the Holy Spirit. In other words, differences do not prevent the transference of the model; rather, overriding similarities enable its transference. The missionary model described in this book can be transferred to any denomination, judicatory, or congregation willing to embrace its vision and implement its principles.

Financial Resources

Assumption: The Diocese of Texas was able to implement the missionary model because it is a large and relatively wealthy diocese. Other judicatories and their congregations could never do so because they do not have the financial resources.

Reality: The Diocese of Texas has been a large and relatively wealthy diocese for many years because it has chosen not to divide itself into smaller dioceses and thereby reduce its resources. For decades, however, there was no guiding vision. The financial resources of the Diocese of Texas did not create the vision, and the funding ability of the diocese does not sustain the vision. Any diocese or denomination, even if it is not wealthy, can adopt and implement the vision. The Christian Church had no extraordinary financial base in the first century, but it grew throughout the Roman Empire.

Some of the most dramatic changes in the Diocese of Texas have occurred in mission congregations that have very little money. Christ Church, in Matagorda (see Chapter Ten), is one such example. It was the vision, the new lay vicar, and the commitment of the people of the congregation that transformed the church, led it to reach out to the community, and caused its remarkable growth in size and influence. That congregation has always been a poor one in terms of financial resources, and yet it boldly adopted the vision and made extraordinary things happen. Another example is the coalition of congregations in East Texas that banded together as "one church" to support activities that none could support alone. All these congregations are little churches doing big things because of the vision, not because of ample financial resources.

It also happens that the vision itself will inspire new giving. As one rector of a Houston parish said, "There has been a transformation in stewardship in this parish with the new vision. There is a better sense of stewardship, a greater commitment to the diocese as a whole, and a broader and deeper generosity." The amount of money given for missionary funding by the congregations of the diocese increased by 15 percent in the first year after adoption of a more participatory process for making funding decisions, a process inspired by the vision. Because analysis of and accountability for resource allocation are also reflections of the vision, funds that for years were being used with little effectiveness can be converted to more productive purposes. In this way, the effects of funding can be enhanced even if the dollar amount of the funding stays the same. Finally, the concept of living in miraculous expectation also applies to the financial area of the Church. The vision calls people and resources to it, manifesting in extraordinary ways what can barely be imagined at the outset.

The claim that the missionary model cannot be adopted without substantial resources reflects the secular preoccupation with money as the means of getting things done. The vision is inspirational precisely because it offers what money cannot buy, but it also demands the same kind of currency from congregational members: their time and talents, their love and compassion, their effort and dedication, and whatever funds they can provide. Lack of adequate resources as a justification for not implementing the missionary model is simply an excuse; it is not a reason.

Clergy and Lay Resistance

Assumption: Because the missionary model is a dramatically different variation on what is already being done, the reaction to it will be predictable. Resistance will too great to overcome. There are too many vested interests who do not want anything to change and who even see that the way things are is good.

Reality: The missionary model is not a dramatically different variation on what is already being done. It is not a variation on the maintenance model at all. It is completely different. The missionary model is transformational. The results of its implementation are the work of the Holy Spirit, and so they exceed and even contradict human expectations. The end cannot be imagined at the beginning. It is rather like trying to explain to someone what it would be like to have a relationship with Jesus Christ. One simply cannot understand what it means until one has experienced it.

Implementation of the model unfolds as a self-authenticating process. There will be resistance, but the resistance can be overcome through the positive results of the model and through the kind of orchestrated change effort described in this chapter. What happens (and this is what may not be predicted) is that a profound sense of need on the part of the people washes over resistance. The Holy Spirit moves among them, and they embrace the model and the change it brings. The common vision of a missionary church fundamentally alters the attitudes and behavior of the people in a judicatory and its congregations. It touches their relationships to one another and to their Church. Unless this phenomenon has been experienced, it is difficult to believe that it can occur. On the basis of logic and our contemporary past experience, it is virtually impossible to predict. One of the contributions of the Diocese of Texas is its having tested the theory of the missionary church in its contemporary incarnation, providing proof that the model does work, that it does overcome the resistance of both clergy and laity, and that it is transformational for a diocese and its congregations.

9

MAKING DISCIPLES

Lord, I believe.

—John 9:38

THE EPISCOPAL CHURCH declared the 1990s the "decade of evangelism," thereby suggesting that evangelism was a temporary program worthy of the church's attention for ten years. It was a classic error of the maintenance church. In this effort to address declining membership, however, the Episcopal Church was not alone but merely tardy; the United Church of Christ had already made evangelism a priority—from 1989 to 1993 (Hadaway and Roozen, 1995). Because the mainline churches have followed the maintenance model for so long, there is confusion in the Church today about what evangelism is, and there is considerable resistance to its practice as an inherent part of the Christian faith.

The Process of Making Disciples

Yet the guiding principles of evangelism remain today as they have been for almost twenty centuries. William Temple, Archbishop of Canterbury, developed the classic definition of evangelism—the presentation of Jesus Christ in the power of the Holy Spirit so that seekers are led to put their trust in God, accept Christ as their Savior, and serve Him as Lord in the fellowship of the Church—and the principles of Anglican evangelism, to take one example, fit that definition well:

- ○ Evangelism is the process of making disciples (not the event of announcing new members), and it informs all activities of the Church.

o Evangelism is empowered by the Holy Spirit. Evangelists carry the Good News, but the Holy Spirit brings about the conversion.

o Evangelism is based in the congregation and is achieved by means of personal witnessing, which leads to the explicit presentation of Jesus Christ in the power of the Holy Spirit through the worship service. Each congregation, therefore, is a missionary outpost.

o The Christian message must be conveyed in words and forms that the target audiences can grasp, a process that Jesus began and that the apostles continued after His death. Churches, therefore, must understand the secular people whom they seek to reach and must rearticulate the Christian understanding of life and death in words and images that are meaningful to them.

Evangelical Protestants and many independent churches think of the conversion moment, the altar call, or the membership card as the ultimate moment of evangelism. For such churches, the result of evangelism is primarily a single decision or event, and the effectiveness of evangelism is measured by the conversion occurrence. The emphasis in biblical evangelism, and in evangelism in the mainline denominations, is on making disciples, not on conversion moments. Evangelism in the mainline Church is not the inducement of one decision. It is a process made up of many decisions that lead the unchurched to membership and then to discipleship. Evangelism is not complete until the new person has become fully integrated into the Church and has become a disciple of Christ. Even then, the evangelistic process is not complete because it is the responsibility of that person to make other disciples. And so the process of evangelism continues, the Good News passed on from one person to another, from one generation to another.

According to the Great Commission, the disciple-making process is carried out through baptism and through teaching new disciples to obey Christ's commandments. Its focus is on the individual, and its goal is changed attitudes and behavior—spiritual transformation—leading to a richer and more productive life. Evangelism is not about recruitment but about transformation. Every Christian is a disciple in progress who participates in a process from which no one graduates. Each new spiritual discovery leads to another discovery, each quickening of the soul to a greater quickening, each joy to a greater joy.

The First Apostolic Age was characterized by a strong perception of the presence and work of the Holy Spirit. The Great Commission makes it clear that those who were to be made disciples were to be baptized "in the name of the Father and of the Son and of the Holy Spirit." Jesus promised, "You will receive power when the Holy Spirit has come upon you; and you will be my witnesses in Jerusalem, in all Judea and Samaria, and to the ends of the earth" (Acts 1:8). Thus the Holy Spirit is the key to evangelism: "The Holy Spirit empowers us as witnessing Christians for outreach, gives us the gift of transparent compassion, and gives us the words to say. This Spirit speaks God's living Word through our caring, listening, and speaking, and is the agent in conversion" (Hunter, 1992, p. 120). This idea has two important ramifications, as Dunnam has observed (1992, p. 14): "We cannot do evangelism effectively without the power and presence of the Holy Spirit. Likewise, if we are following the Spirit, we will be evangelizing—not just talking about it but doing it." And the second ramification is equally important: "If the power to evangelize comes from the Holy Spirit, so does the result" (p. 14). It is our responsibility as disciples to evangelize, but the result of that effort is left to the Holy Spirit. We carry the word, but the Holy Spirit converts. Our emphasis should be on carrying the Good News rather than on the way in which it is received. True evangelism is centered in humility, through which the Good News is offered without hope of personal credit.

Dunnam (1992, p. 42) has written that evangelism is

> centered in Jesus Christ, empowered by the Holy Spirit, and ultimately grounded in the God of all creation. The power and purpose of this God—alive and active throughout history, named in scripture and worshiped today as Father, Son, and Holy Spirit—is what finally accounts theologically for the kind of evangelism that we have been exploring. An evangelism born in the vital connection of word and deed, nurtured in the life of discipleship, and reaching toward maturity in the fellowship of the gathered community and its service in the world, is—theologically speaking—an evangelism properly tuned to the praise, power, and purpose of the triune God.

The Hourglass Model

Various models have been developed to illustrate the manner in which secular people become Christians. John Wesley's "order of salvation" is one such model, as is the traditional evangelical model of a single confrontational conversation in which the seeker makes a commitment to Jesus Christ. As Hunter reports (1996), Saddleback Community Church uses the model of a baseball diamond: first base is membership ("knowing Christ"), second base is maturity-directed ("growing in Christ"), third base is ministry ("serving Christ"), and fourth base is mission ("sharing Christ"). Other Christian models exist, but perhaps the most effective one for illustrating the complete process of evangelism is the hourglass model, so called because it starts with a broad opening through which to attract the seeker, narrows in its preparation of the disciple, and expands again to send the disciple back into the world. The hourglass model consists of six stages, each building on the one that precedes it:

1. Attraction
2. Worship
3. Discovery
4. Initiation
5. Assimilation
6. Discipleship

The model is appropriate for any mainline denomination and is particularly powerful in its description of the components, sequencing, and individual roles involved in missionary work. This model clearly shows that evangelism is a process that begins with the efforts of the laity, ultimately involves the whole congregation, and is centered in worship. It also clearly shows that disciples are created individually in community, just as Christ converted individually in community. In this sense, seekers in the process of becoming disciples are like grains of sand that must make their way through an hourglass, one at a time. The hourglass model is shown in Figure 9.1.

Figure 9.1. The Hourglass Model of Evangelism.

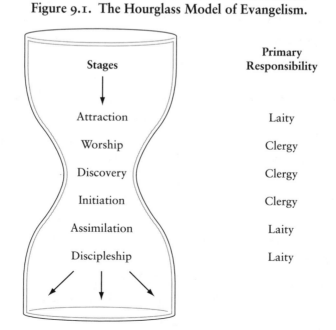

Stages	Primary Responsibility
Attraction	Laity
Worship	Clergy
Discovery	Clergy
Initiation	Clergy
Assimilation	Laity
Discipleship	Laity

Attraction

A critical premise underlies the hourglass model of evangelism: that the laity will engage unchurched people whom they already know. Disciples in the mainline denominations are not called on to carry the Good News to strangers (although they can) but rather to acquaintances, family members, and friends. The hourglass model assumes that the good and faithful Christian who is following the Great Commandment and the Great Commission will engage the nonbelievers whom he or she knows by extending to them an invitation to attend a worship service or church event. It also assumes that this invitation to enter into a conscious relationship with Jesus Christ will be made from the Christian perspective, which presumes an existing divine presence in the nonbeliever (because he or she is made in the image and likeness of God). Such an invitation must be grounded in love of the Great Commandment and in respect for the dignity of the nonbeliever; otherwise, the Christian risks exhibiting the patronizing attitude that was often present in nineteenth-century evangelism and is present in some evangelical churches today.

The first step in the hourglass model, then, is attraction—that is, drawing the unchurched person to a church activity or to a worship service that will lead to his or her attending another worship service. This first step in evangelism is the responsibility of every member of the congregation. Understanding of this step may be facilitated by examination of three of its aspects:

1. The question of who should be attracted
2. The question of why seekers might be attracted
3. The question of how seekers can be attracted

WHO SHOULD BE ATTRACTED. Evangelism in the mainline denominations is directed toward the unchurched and is focused on three categories of individuals:

1. Unchurched non-Christians (that is, secular individuals with no formal religious background)
2. Unchurched Christians (that is, Christian dropouts who no longer attend any Christian church)
3. Dropouts from religions other than Christianity (that is, individuals who no longer practice a faith, whatever it may have been)

Two other categories of the unchurched deserve mention because books on evangelism sometimes include them as appropriate objects of evangelistic efforts. People in the first of these two categories—*churched nonbelievers* (that is, those who attend worship services but are untouched by the Gospel)—are not properly the focus of evangelism but rather of renewal movements within the Church. Renewal movements, designed to deepen and strengthen a Christian's faith, can be considered a form of internal evangelism but are not, strictly speaking, evangelism per se. Renewal is inner-directed (that is, aimed at active or nominal church members), whereas evangelism is outer-directed (that is, aimed at people who are not church members). This distinction is important because it is easy to confuse the two concepts, particularly when a judicatory links them in a single department of "renewal and evangelism." The purpose of renewal programs in the maintenance church is to refresh the faithful. In the missionary church, however, renewal programs engage members in the work of the Church, advance their spiritual growth, and equip them for evangelism. A missionary church focused on an evangelistic vision of miraculous expectation seeks renewal in preparation for, and as a result of, its efforts to make new disciples. In the missionary church, renewal programs are not add-ons; they are an integral, continuing part of what the Church does. The second category of unchurched people who are not considered appropriate objects of evangelistic efforts in the mainline Church is the category of *churched Christians* (that is, Christians from other denominations or congregations). The effort to recruit churched Christians is not considered evangelism. It is proselytism, and the mainline Church does not proselytize.

It is possible for a denomination to evangelize all three categories—unchurched non-Christians, unchurched Christians, and dropouts from other religions—but it is not necessarily possible for a single congregation to do so. This point is crucial to the design and development of effective congregational, judicatory, and denominational efforts at evangelism. Although the Gospel itself does not vary, the way in which it is most effectively communicated depends on the audience destined to receive it. Some congregations are more attuned to one category of the unchurched than to another. When the judicatory perceives of itself as one church, it can encourage each of its congregations to evangelize those individuals and those categories of unchurched people with whom it is most comfortable.

Some congregations are enthusiastic about seeker services—rock music, off-site worship, and other elements that may appeal to a segment of unchurched people who have no experience with the mainline or who have had a bad experience of it. Other congregations prefer traditional hymns, organ music, and on-site church services that are attractive to people who want to return to a church experience they remember. Some congregations appeal more to the young and others to the old, some are more formal and some are more casual, and so forth. Through its various congregations, the one church of the diocese can truly reach all sorts and conditions of people and rejoice in its diversity.

The process of attracting seekers begins with identifying who the seekers are, where they are, and how they can most effectively be reached. The best candidates are people who are members of one's social network and who can therefore be approached through that network of relatives, friends, neighbors, and colleagues; indeed, according to Dunnam (1992, p. 48), "Approximately 77 percent of the persons who become Christian disciples do so because of the testimony, deeds, and encouragement of someone they trust." In our actions we are all witnesses to our faith, whether we realize it or not and whether we intend to be or not. But we must still speak out from that faith in explaining the path to its acquisition. We must speak out to those whom we know. We must evangelize.

WHY SEEKERS MIGHT BE ATTRACTED. On the subject of effective evangelism, the experience of the early Christian Church is instructive. The sociologist Rodney Stark, having studied the evangelism of the early Church, in addition to conversions in the contemporary Mormon Church and in various religious cults, has formulated several hypotheses about the nature of religious conversions. These hypotheses are specifically related to the Christian Church in its first centuries and to its rate of growth, which he estimates at 40 percent per decade:

> Although several other factors are also involved in the conversion process, the central sociological proposition about conversion is this: Conversion to new, deviant religious groups occurs when, other things being equal, people have or develop stronger attachments to members of the group than they have to nonmembers.
>
> Data based on records kept by a Mormon mission president give powerful support to this proposition. When missionaries make cold calls, knock on the doors of strangers, this eventually leads to a conversion once out of a thousand calls. However, when missionaries make their first contact with a person in the home of a Mormon friend or relative of that person, this results in conversion 50 percent of the time [Stark, 1996, p. 18].

Research also indicates that most converts credit their experiences of conversion to theology, even though theology is not actually a motivating factor in conversion; in fact, many converts initially view their new reli-

gion's theology as quite odd (Stark, 1996). Rather, the determining factor
is social networks. According to Brown (cited in Stark, 1996, p. 20), "ties
of family, marriages, and loyalties to heads of households [were] the most
effective means of recruiting members of the church," a comment to
which Stark adds (p. 20) that "the basis for successful conversion movements is growth through social networks, through a structure of direct
and intimate interpersonal attachments. Most new religious movements
fail because they quickly become closed, or semiclosed networks. That is,
they fail to keep forming and sustaining attachments to outsiders and
thereby lose the capacity to grow. Successful movements discover techniques for remaining open networks, able to reach out and into new adjacent social networks. And therein lies the capacity of movements to
sustain exponential rates of growth over a long period of time."

When the Christian Church abandoned its missionary role in favor of a
maintenance posture, it closed the social networks that reached beyond
the Church. Membership began to decline with the closing of the networks because fewer church members talked about their faith with their
family and friends. As Stark has observed (1996, p. 56), the unchurched
who are most likely to be reached are those one already knows:

> The fact is that typically people do not seek a faith; they encounter one
> through their ties to other people who already accept this faith. In the
> end, accepting a new religion is part of conforming to the expectations
> and examples of one's family and friends. This limits avenues by which
> movements can recruit. . . . Many new religions have become skilled
> in making attachments with newcomers and others [in the big cities
> who are] deficient in interpersonal attachments. Movements can also
> recruit by spreading through preexisting social networks, as converts
> bring in their families and friends. This pattern has the potential for
> much faster growth than the one-by-one conversion of social iso-
> lates. . . . It is network growth that so distinguishes the Mormon rate
> of growth—meanwhile, other contemporary religious movements will
> count their growth in thousands, not millions, for lack of a network
> pattern of growth.

With the social networks of the mainline churches closed, those who
would ordinarily be drawn to the faith by evangelistic activities look elsewhere for the answers to their spiritual questions. "Elsewhere" often takes
the form of new religious movements—generally sects that are variants of
the standard religious culture. Stark writes, "People are more willing to
adopt a new religion to the extent that it retains cultural continuity with

conventional religion(s) with which they are already familiar" (Stark, 1996, p. 55). It should not be surprising, therefore, that many fast-growing sects and independent churches present themselves as Christian, nor should it be surprising that "new religious movements do best in places where there is the greatest amount of apparent secularization—for example, in places with low rates of church membership such as the east coast of the United States and Canada, and northern Europe" (Stark, 1996, p. 54).

Stark postulates a second important reason for the growth of Christianity in its first three centuries: the response of Christians to the plagues that struck the Roman Empire in 165 and 251, decimating its population. The first plague was probably smallpox, and during its fifteen-year duration it killed between one-quarter and one-third of the entire population, a cohort that included the emperor himself, who died in 180. The second plague was probably measles and had a similarly devastating effect on the previously unexposed population. In both cases, the Christians had a better explanation for the crisis than did the pagans (who had none), and the Christians were less afraid of death because of the promise of eternal life. Furthermore, the Christians ministered to the sick, whereas the pagans and their priests fled the city to get away from the sick. Christian ministration, to sick pagans and sick Christians alike, not only improved the Christian survival rate (which must have been persuasive to the pagans) but also showed the Christians' love and compassion in a convincing way. By living their faith, the Christians provided a powerful example to non-Christians of what it meant to be Christian.

Christianity grew at a phenomenal rate in the first century because the early Christians made effective and dramatic use of their social networks to attract new adherents to Christianity. They evangelized family members, friends, acquaintances, and friends of friends. They were open, accepting, and, ultimately, externally focused. Their enthusiasm for the Good News and the transformations it had wrought in their lives carried them out into the world. Praising and giving thanks for the newness of the life they had been given, they spread the joyous news to their families and friends and thus to the Roman Empire.

HOW SEEKERS ARE ATTRACTED. The hourglass model of evangelism reflects the practices of the early Church and is therefore highly effective. Mainline churches rarely train people for one-to-one evangelism leading to direct conversion; rather, mainline church members lead seekers into a system in which they can experience transformation. That system is the community of faith. The mainline is largely a ministry of encouragement, spiritual development, support, and hospitality. As such, its evangelism is nonthreatening to the person approached, but the nonverbal communication that takes place through the expression of hospitality is profound. Therefore, evangelism in the mainline Church begins with attracting an unchurched person to a church event or worship service. The process starts with a question posed to someone who is already known, perhaps even a recent acquaintance. The question is whether the friend or new acquaintance has a church or attends church regularly. If not, the disciple issues an invitation to attend a church service or event.

This simple act of invitation is the first stage of evangelism. It can be much like a parent's or grandparent's offer to show a new baby's photograph. It is low-key, respectful, and nonintrusive. It is an overture, not a demand, that says, "My church has made a difference in my life, a difference for which I am grateful. If you do not attend a church, you are welcome to come with me to see what I have found." This invitation communicates three distinct but powerful nonverbal messages to the unchurched person:

1. I have a faith by which I live.
2. I am part of a community of faith.
3. I am proud of my community of faith and believe that you could benefit from being part of it.

Extension of the invitation is a natural expression of the desire to share good news with another and to help one's fellow human being in need. It is very different from the stereotypical evangelical images of knocking on a stranger's door, standing on a street corner, or demanding confessions of faith from the unchurched and the startled.

Attraction, in this model, consists of a gentle sharing of one's faith commitment and its promise of hope and transformation, in the context of an invitation to attend a worship service. So understood, the first stage of evangelism is possible for all church members. Indeed, it is a natural extension of their faith. The word *evangelism* carries a negative, burdensome connotation to many. Too often, members of the mainline do not understand the process of evangelism in their churches and so imagine all manner of difficult requirements associated with it, most of them onerous. As denominations, we have not done a good job of making clear to our members what evangelism entails and how straightforward this first stage is. The later stages of mainline evangelism involve the clergy and other members of the laity. But the first stage involves only an individual member—a single Christian on whose shoulders rests the responsibility of initiating the process of evangelism, reaching out to a man or a woman seeking God and not knowing where to turn.

Worship

In the mainline, the structures of the Episcopal, Roman Catholic, and Orthodox Churches are most similar, retaining as they do links to the apostolic Church that gave rise to all three. Evangelism in this tradition is accomplished primarily through worship, with the presentation of Jesus Christ in the power of the Holy Spirit. Although Protestant denominations in the mainline have somewhat different structures, they share many of the same elements of worship that achieve the evangelistic objective: praising God, praying for humanity, hearing and expounding on the Holy Word, making a confession of sin and receiving God's absolution, exchanging the Lord's peace, and gathering at the Lord's table for the Eucharist. The metaphors and symbols that make up the liturgy help evoke an experience of the presence of the transcendent God. The totality of the various parts of the service, following the ancient order developed by the early Church, is far more powerful and engaging than any single element alone. Form in and of itself does not precipitate the presence of the Holy Spirit, but the gathering of the faithful in prayer is a medium for encountering the presence of God.

The quality of the worship service has a major impact on church attendance and therefore on the power of the evangelistic experience for newcomers and disciples alike. How well the worship service is planned, executed, and supported will determine, in part, whether the seeker returns and moves through the hourglass to the next stage of discipleship. Worship should be so ordered that all the elements of the service (music, sermon, prayers, announcements, and participants) maximize recognition and acceptance of the seeker and convey a sense of joy for his or her presence. Each element of the worship service is important and deserving of thoughtful attention and effort.

The homily or sermon is a critical element of the worship service because it represents an opportunity for the preacher to apply the Christian message to contemporary situations important in the lives of the assembled. Sermons should address the visitor, the new member, and the unchurched as well as disciples, offering principles and interpretations of the Christian faith that are useful to them. Sermons that help people discover their dignity and self-worth as creatures made in the image of a loving God fortify members as well as seekers, as do sermons that deal with

God's transformational power and with the hope of miracles. Sermons that answer questions, help listeners apply their Christian faith to daily life, and address the trials of a life of the cross are also meaningful. Well-prepared, relevant sermons attract disciples and can provide deep Christian insights sought by members and seekers alike. Sermons that disappoint drive seekers and newcomers away and reduce the meaningfulness of the service for disciples.

Music constitutes a unique dimension of the worship service, one that can be inspiring and deeply moving. Music seems to touch our souls; it moves our emotions, and it puts us in touch with something greater and grander than ourselves. Hymns and songs unite our voices, channel our feelings, and lead us to transcendent experiences. Music witnesses to life's beauty and elegance. It acknowledges that the triune God is beyond words, beyond intellectual understanding. Music is an experience that allows us to recognize what we cannot express, to feel the joy and power of God, which is beyond description, and to experience a moment of oneness that breaks down the artificial boundaries of material life.

Prayers that acknowledge visitors, newcomers, the unchurched, and those still seeking God are inclusive and meaningful to all present. Opportunities for silent prayer reinforce the intimate relationship between worshipers and their Creator, permit private intercessions, and provide practice in listening for divine inspiration. "Be still, and know that I am God," reads Psalms 46:10. Announcements that welcome visitors, embrace seekers, and steer newcomers toward greater involvement in the life of the congregation strengthen community and mission. Seekers are impressed by services that capture the joy of Christianity, project a sense of the presence of God, and inspire confidence of divine involvement in the struggles and joys of daily life.

Every member present has an evangelistic responsibility to make seekers and newcomers feel welcome before, during, and after the service and to participate mightily and faithfully in the joy of worship. The hourglass model of evangelism relies on each member to initiate the discipleship process by attracting the seeker to church, but it relies on all the members of the congregation to create a meaningful worship service that will move that seeker through the hourglass of evangelism to discipleship.

Discovery

Once a newcomer has been invited to church, has attended, and, over time, has experienced the power and presence of the Holy Spirit in worship, he or she is led to a more intimate relationship with God. This stage is the third in the process of evangelism in the hourglass model: discovery. It takes place through discovery classes, in which the seeker is led to accept Christ as Savior and follow him as Lord in the fellowship of the Church. These classes are also called *inquirers' classes, confirmation classes, explorers' classes,* or *new members' classes.*

Discovery classes play a pivotal role in making disciples; their importance cannot be overemphasized. The design of the discovery classes determines the degree of their effectiveness. Effective discovery classes go beyond teaching the basics of the Christian faith and denominational tradition (although these components are crucial); they are involving and transformational. The Diocese of Texas has prepared a videotape on the content and design of discovery classes that models best practices for the congregations. The structure of the classes (that is, how often the classes meet and for how long) may be modified by each congregation, but the process and the content are expected to remain virtually the same throughout the diocese. This diocesan model emphasizes the vision of the diocese and ensures that the discovery of the Episcopal Church, the Episcopal faith, and the Episcopal experience is comprehensive and well presented throughout the congregations of the Diocese of Texas.

Because of the importance of the discovery classes to the making of disciples, the Diocese of Texas has set a goal of developing an in-house videotape series for the use of clergy in the congregations. The twelve-part series will feature some of the diocese's outstanding preachers, who will provide the lecture portion of the sessions. Clergy in each congregation will be able to choose to use all or none of the videos, but each video will contain the standard by which to judge content and performance for each of the twelve sessions. By developing its own videotape series, the Diocese of Texas will ensure high-quality discovery classes across all its congregations. The principle of ensuring uniform quality and comprehensiveness of presentation while providing for individual congregational differences is applicable to all mainline denominations. It makes sense, when a denomination or judicatory is viewed as part of one church, for the various missionary outposts to be provided with the best resources that the denomination as a whole can provide for the making of disciples. This element of the hourglass model of evangelism is so critical that it should not be left to the vagaries of individual congregational resources.

A model for twelve weekly discovery classes, along with suggested themes and topics for small-group sessions, is shown in Exhibit 9.1. It can be adapted, of course, for use by any denomination or judicatory. The process component is grounded in a small-group experience complemented by introductory and concluding lectures on the Christian faith and the denominational tradition. According to the denomination, these lecture/discussions sessions might include such topics as scripture, reason, tradition, the Trinity, the creeds, the sacraments, Church history, and the individual's place in the Body of Christ. These sessions are often taught by the laity as well as by clergy.

Exhibit 9.1. Model for Discovery Classes.

1. *Forming a Community and Addressing Fears*

    Week 1: Sharing basic personal data and fears, to build community in the group and create an atmosphere of safety

    Week 2: Sharing what drew the seekers to church initially and why they made the decision to return

2. *Basic Christianity*

    Week 3: Exploring whether the seekers have made the commitment to follow Jesus Christ as Savior and Lord, and, if so, when (some group members may have made such a commitment to Christ in the past)

    Week 4: Sharing personal experiences of divine power

    Week 5: Sharing personal experiences of answered prayers

3. *Life as a Disciple*

    Week 6: Exploring and discussing the rule of life that seekers have followed or would like to follow as members of the Christian community

    Week 7: Exploring and discussing crosses used for growth

    Week 8: Exploring and discussing the meaning and roots of stewardship

4. *Toward Discipleship*

    Week 9: Making decisions about initiation

    Week 10: Looking beyond initiation to what seekers' own ministries might be in congregations, judicatories, and denominations

    Week 11: Exploring and discussing how one becomes an evangelist, and how new members can contribute to and benefit from evangelism once they have become active in the church

    Week 12: Living discipleship

An important element of the discovery process, both in these classes and afterward, is finding answers to the spiritual questions that have led the unchurched to the congregations in the first place. If the Church cannot satisfy the spiritual hunger of those who come to its table, then it will lose them to someone else's offering. One of the reasons why the early Church triumphed over paganism in the first centuries was that it had credible answers for the profound questions raised by the plagues that were decimating the Roman Empire, and paganism did not. In congregations, judicatories, and denominations, newcomers should be led to opportunities through which they can grow spiritually. In the Diocese of Texas, for example, spiritual development is enhanced through many different Bible-study classes, faith-sharing small groups, weekend experiences such as Cursillo, and programs offered by the Division of Spiritual Development.

What the discovery classes make clear is that spiritual development is a journey of discovery. A powerful faith relationship with God is developed through study, prayer, and practice. Because secular people (and many church members) are ignorant of the basic precepts and principles of Christianity, ministries of instruction for the laity, beginning with the discovery classes, are a crucial part of discipleship. Secular people need help finding meaning and purpose in life, abandoning false gods, and focusing on the eternal truths of the faith. In the process, they need to find acceptance; be able to tell their stories of fear, alienation, and suffering; and be heard without judgment. Seekers come to church as flawed individuals in search of wholeness. To help them prepare for their new life in Christ, compassion for their plight is important, as is the willingness to listen to them. Seekers are friends and allies to be encouraged and mentored, not adversaries to be won. They need time to respond to the love of the Christian community and the influence of the Holy Spirit. Each person moves through the hourglass according to his or her unique timetable.

Discovery classes are key to making disciples because each person who participates has the potential for a transformational experience that will lead him or her to the next stage of discipleship. It is during the discovery classes in particular that one is likely to experience a sense of the divine, of intimacy with the Transcendent, that is compelling, vivifying, and redirecting. Discovery classes provide a setting in which lay disciples can share their faith experiences with seekers in a way that is nonthreatening to themselves and to the seekers and that is in fact powerful for both. There is not much opportunity in the mainline Church to reveal a divine encounter, talk about a transcendent experience, or recount a story of answered prayers. Discovery classes provide these opportunities for seekers and members alike. Out of such experiences come new disciples—individuals who have experienced, in an immediate and contemporary way, the same fruits of a relationship with Jesus that compelled fishermen and tax collectors to become disciples two thousand years ago.

Initiation

When the discovery classes have been completed, and when the seeker has been led to experience a life of Christian faith in greater depth, it is time for the fourth stage of the evangelism process: initiation. Initiation is celebrated through baptism (in the case of non-Christians), confirmation (for those who were baptized in infancy but who have never made an adult profession of faith), and reception (for those Christians who have been baptized and who have already made a profession of faith). Initiation formally recognizes the individual as a member of the Body of Christ and celebrates his or her becoming an active disciple of the Church.

Assimilation

Assimilation is the process through which the new member becomes an active and involved participant in the life of the congregation, offering his or her time, talents, and treasure to the Church. Through assimilation, the new member becomes an established member of the one church of the judicatory and the denomination. By deepening their involvement in the work of the congregation, members deepen their faith and commitment to the Christian life. Assimilation is facilitated by involvement in small groups, lay ministries, volunteer work, prayer, and Bible study.

Discipleship

Discipleship is the ultimate goal and final stage of effective evangelism. Once assimilated into the congregation, new members have an opportunity to experience the richness of a community of miraculous expectation, the meaningfulness of personal transformation, and the joy of a life in Christ. After such an encounter with the divine, the new disciple is led to carry the Good News to others—to make disciples in turn. Disciples can be identified as having the following characteristics:

- They have knowledge about the content and depth of the Christian faith.
- They have knowledge about the denomination and its beliefs.

○ They are willing to share their Christian faith with others.

○ They witness to Christ by word and deed through familial, community, and work relationships as well as through Christian service.

Prayerful contemplation of the Great Commandment and the Great Commission and of our own role in evangelism may facilitate adoption of the missionary vision. There are many ways to be an evangelist, many ways for introverts and extroverts alike to make disciples—by attracting seekers, participating enthusiastically in worship services, greeting newcomers, engaging visitors, teaching discovery classes, helping newcomers be assimilated into the congregation, serving in outreach or small-group ministries, acting as an usher, participating in a prayer group, sharing faith experiences, and helping new Christians move through the hourglass in dozens of other ways. For example, any form of hospitality on the premises of a church is an affirmative witness to the community of faith; the way a person lives can also be a powerful witness to faith. Evangelism is highly personal, and affirmative person-to-person contact is essential. Actively approaching friends, neighbors, and acquaintances and inviting them to worship services or to church activities is a nonthreatening yet assertive way to touch potential disciples.

None of us is comfortable in every role in the evangelism process; some of us are better suited to certain activities, but all of us are suited to some activity. We are called to consider how God can best use us and to assume whatever role in evangelism the Holy Spirit leads us to take. We are also called to support, through prayer and other means, the evangelistic activities of our fellow disciples.

10

DEVELOPING CONGREGATIONS

*You did not choose me but I chose you. And appointed you to go
and bear fruit, fruit that will last. . . .*

—John 12:16

ANY DENOMINATION, JUDICATORY, or congregation that is serious
about evangelism is serious about congregational development. Every missionary outpost, whether a start-up with a hundred members or an established congregation of thousands, has a congregational development
challenge and opportunity. Congregational development is critical to disciples making disciples and is therefore a top priority of the missionary
church.

In the 1950s, planting new churches was a major priority in all mainline denominations, and rates of new-church development were much
higher than they are today. In the 1960s, evangelism, as practiced in the
maintenance model of attracting nominal Christians, was a high-profile
denominational program that received a significant share of total program
dollars (Hadaway and Roozen, 1995). By the 1980s, however, the situation had changed dramatically, and although mainline churches were still
claiming, into the early 1990s, that church growth was a priority, funding levels for church growth did not keep pace with inflation (Hadaway
and Roozen, 1995). Many other programs competed for the available
money, and the resulting staff cuts reduced congregational development
efforts to minimal levels.

In the maintenance model, congregational development is not considered
critical, and when it is implemented, it is generally limited to the starting

of new congregations. There is little or no effort to grow existing congregations. In denominations with episcopal polity, the bishop generally chooses the site for the new congregation and selects a member of the clergy to provide leadership. Decision making is top-down, and existing congregations are not usually involved in the development of the new churches.

In the missionary church, by contrast, congregational development is deemed critical and includes both start-up congregations and the growth of existing congregations. The strategy for congregational development is threefold: to plant new congregations, to build on islands of health and strength in the judiciary by growing healthy congregations, and to reverse the trend of declining or stagnant congregations. This three-part strategy recognizes that interaction with the unchurched takes place in the missionary outposts, not at the level of the judicatory. No one joins a judicatory; people join congregations. Because church growth is the result of congregational evangelism, the primary role of the judicatory should be to serve as a resource for the congregations. In particular, it should provide the unifying, missionary vision for the one church of the judicatory, as well as the resources and services that the congregations need to fulfill that vision.

Implementation of this three-part congregational development strategy in the Diocese of Texas began with an analysis of all the congregations in the diocese. Members of the diocesan ministry staff were asked to identify those congregations that were thought to have significant growth potential. A subsequent analysis was conducted to determine why congregations with growth potential were not growing, and what it would take to make them grow. For example, was the lay leadership conflicted? Would additional funding be of significant help, and if so, how? These congregations were then targeted for assistance and were offered additional support by diocesan staff or outside consultants.

The bishop and his staff conferred with the Houston and Austin regional planning groups (discussed later in the chapter) to gather as much information as possible for decisions about planting and support in metropolitan areas. They also used cluster conferences and the new warden and vestry conferences as a communication tool for engaging local leadership. The bishop and his staff began by asking themselves what they should be doing, as a ministry staff and as a diocese, to support congregational development. In answering this question, they found that a large share of the diocese's resources was focused where these resources were not producing the greatest results, and it became clear that better resource allocation was needed.

The Congregational Development Team

Three members of the ministry staff of the Diocese of Texas are directly involved in congregational development: Kevin Martin, Canon for Mission and Congregational Development; Ronald Null, diocesan treasurer; and Joel Shannon, director of resource development. Working together, they constitute the congregational development team, which functions as a diocesan resource for missionary outposts. In addition, the coordinators for the diocesan departments of youth, Christian education, outreach, and communication are all involved with congregational development even though it is not their primary focus.

Canon Martin's position is rare if not unique in the Episcopal Church. As leader of the congregational development team, he works with the missionary outposts to train their leaders and facilitate their growth. Mr. Null helps congregations with their financial planning and leads them toward a better understanding of budgeting as an active way to support mission and ensure accountability. Mr. Shannon's position is new and is unprecedented in the Diocese of Texas. He is responsible for assisting congregations in their development, by consulting with their vestries and with their building and finance committees and by helping them assemble the resources they need to grow. He is also responsible for raising funds to help each new congregation build its first building. He says, "We've raised the expectations of our missionary outposts, and now we're trying to meet and exceed them. They see that the diocese has something important to offer them—that we are a unique resource they can use." In all cases, the ministry staff involves and works with highly talented and experienced lay leaders who have been inspired by the vision and called to diocesan service. The bishop's management style with these teams is to be specific about their following the vision, but not about their approach or their tasks. He "turns his teams loose" (in the words of one staff member) to serve the leadership of the congregations and to fulfill the vision.

Canon for Mission and Congregational Development

The idea of having one individual directly responsible for congregational development, someone whose focus is training and growth, is rare in the mainline Protestant denominations. The Canon for Mission and Congregational Development has several key responsibilities:

○ Consulting with and training lay leaders, with an emphasis on growing congregations

○ Working with the Houston and Austin regional planning groups to find new sites and bring together the initial clergyperson and leadership team, in addition to serving as staff person to the Austin Regional Planning Group, the task force that helps plan the start-up congregations in the Austin area

○ Providing resources to congregations so that they become more effective in attracting the unchurched

○ Conducting direct interventions in congregations with conflicts or other problems, to restore their health, vitality, and growth

○ Providing appropriate support to missions, according to their potential

○ Along with the diocesan treasurer and the director of resource development, furnishing staff support to the Quin Foundation (named for the late Bishop Quin, and created to provide financing for new buildings in the diocese) and helping the foundation analyze the most effective uses of its funds in furtherance of the diocesan vision

Director of Resource Development

This is a new position in the Diocese of Texas and is unusual in the mainline church because of its focus on funding for congregational development. This position has the following key responsibilities:

○ Providing start-up congregations with a list of architects and fundraising consultants (after average Sunday attendance has stabilized at three hundred), in addition to helping new missionary outposts raise funds, acquire land (if it has not already been acquired), design their facilities, and deal with their construction contractors

○ Developing building programs, acquiring land, raising money, and envisioning the future in order to help plan the growth of congregations that want to grow, no matter what their size

○ Serving as staff person to the Houston Regional Planning Group, the task force that works to determine where to start new congregations in the Houston area

○ Along with the diocesan treasurer and the Canon for Mission and Congregational Development, furnishing staff support to the Quin Foundation and helping it analyze the most effective uses of its funds

○ Serving as staff person to Partners in Mission, a new funding program for congregational development (discussed later in the chapter)

○ Developing a new diocesan planned-giving program (called "legacy stewardship") for congregations to use in talking with their members about planned giving (capital-asset bequests as a form of stewardship have not been much discussed in the church, which speaks of the Resurrection but not often about death and choosing a "successor steward" for one's earthly possessions)

Principles of Congregational Development

Congregational development is an area in which the mainline church has an advantage over nondenominational entities because of its structure. The vision of the judicatory as one church is powerful because it creates a shared responsibility with the congregations for the development of new congregations. Whether congregational or episcopal in polity, a judicatory has the framework to provide resources and coordination for congregational development in its geographical region. Congregational development is most effective at the judicatory level because judicatory resources, planning, and coordination can be brought to bear. Judicatory planning can be initiated at the congregational level, however. When farsighted clergy and laity make strategic alliances with neighboring missionary outposts of their judicatory, they lay the groundwork for a coordinated program of congregational development, which at the judicatory level is guided by six principles, discussed in the passages that follow.

Principle 1: Classification of Congregations According to Size and Culture

This is the most important principle of congregational development. A congregation's particular size, as measured by its average Sunday attendance, produces its distinct culture. Its size also determines its needs; therefore, congregations of different sizes have different needs. It is a critical strategic error for a judicatory to treat congregations of different sizes as if they had similar needs, structures, and cultures. The size-classification categories used by the Diocese of Texas are shown in Table 10.1. They were developed by Canon Martin, who expanded on an earlier model proposed by Rothauge (1986).

Principle 2: Size-Appropriate Information and Training

A judicatory should provide each congregation with information and training that are appropriate and specific to its size. Most small congregations cannot use the programmatic information that transition and program missionary outposts want, and that is generally provided by the judicatory, whereas resource congregations are not interested in programs

Table 10.1 Diocese of Texas Congregational Classification System.

Congregational Category	Average Sunday Attendance	Culture
Family	7–75	Dominated by one to four families
Pastoral	76–140	Dominated by the clergyperson
Transitional	141–225	In transition; larger than pastoral, not yet program; developing staff
Program	226–400	Programmatic and staff-driven
Resource	400+	Many resources for members; multiple staff; serves as resource for other missionary outposts and for the judicatory as one church

at all but rather in training and personnel. A congregation with fifty people in attendance on Sunday cannot use a Christian-education curriculum that assumes grade-level distinctions, because its single Christian-education class will include students who are in a mixture of grades. By contrast, a congregation with five hundred in attendance on Sunday does not need another youth event; it needs a trained youth pastor.

Principle 3: Maximum Return on Judicatory Resources

The judicatory can have a greater impact on some congregations than on others, and it should concentrate its resources on congregations in the size categories where it can do the most good. Among all its congregations, a judicatory can have the greatest impact on new starts; among its established congregations, a judicatory can have the greatest impact on (in order of influence) transitional congregations and family congregations.

When the idea of categorizing congregations on the basis of their size was first conceived, no provision was made for transitional congregations. After the Diocese of Texas conferred with laity and clergy from these congregations, however, it became clear that a special category was needed in order to describe congregations that were somewhere between the pastoral and program categories. The most serious problem with transitional congregations is that they do not know how to become program churches, and so they tend to guess. They do not know what a program-size congregation is like in terms of staff operations, program offerings, or the behavior of the ordained leader. Teaching these congregations how to make this transition is the single greatest contribution that the judiciary can make to their growth.

The Diocese of Texas has developed a curriculum designed to achieve this purpose. It includes a new vocabulary, with new concepts, to help transitional churches identify what is happening in their congregations (for example, "emotional terrorists" can sabotage a transitional church). Through this specialized curriculum, the clergy and laity of transitional congregations learn about the unique obstacles that their churches face and how they can network with other transitional congregations to overcome them. The diocese also provides needed encouragement to its transitional congregations.

Principle 4: Culture Change as a Tool of Growth

Growth within a given size category is comfortable for congregation members, but growth beyond that category and into the next is not. Therefore, the most effective way in which the judiciary itself can grow is to facilitate the passage of each congregation into its next appropriate size category by helping the congregation change its organizational culture so as to embrace this growth.

Principle 5: Empowerment of Laity

Empowerment of laity is accomplished chiefly through leadership training, provision of resources, and support. The judiciary itself cannot build its congregations. It must have the support, involvement, and dedicated effort of its laity.

Principle 6: Use of Congregational and Demographic Analyses

A comprehensive analysis of all the congregations in the judiciary is a critical first step in recognizing that all the congregations are different and in developing responsive and productive strategies for them. Such an analysis should include an estimate of each congregation's potential for growth. In essence, this analysis identifies congregations that need help, those that do not, and those that for now cannot be helped. When this analysis was conducted in the Diocese of Texas, it revealed counterproductive strategies and long-standing practices that did not support the diocesan vision (these are discussed in later passages). The results of the analysis produced a new strategic approach to congregational development in the Diocese of Texas.

In conjunction with the congregational analysis, an extensive demographic analysis of the judicatory's geographical area should be prepared. In the Diocese of Texas, the demographic analysis centered on the following questions:

○ Demographically, who are the people of the diocese?

○ Demographically, where are the people of the diocese?

○ Can existing congregations serve these people?

○ If the diocese had just been created, where would it start its new missionary outposts?

These data and the analysis of them have been extremely important in the process of evaluating and planning congregational development. Missionary outposts use the data to determine the most effective activities and programs for their parishes, particularly in transitional neighborhoods, and to identify potential locations for new congregations.

Conferences to Grow Existing Churches

A missionary church concerned with making new disciples pays considerable attention to helping existing congregations grow. The Diocese of Texas has developed several new conference programs to help its missionary outposts achieve their growth objectives. These programs are described in the following sections.

Cluster Conferences

Because congregations in each size category have their own characteristic organizational cultures, and because each size of congregation grows in a different way, the most effective approach to growth planning and development is to hold cluster conferences, which are annual meetings of clergy and laity drawn from congregations of similar size throughout the judicatory. Their purpose is to provide the training and networking necessary to make the vision a reality in the missionary outposts.

Cluster conferences include both clergy and lay leaders of the congregations so that clergy do not have to "sell" the ideas they glean from the conferences to congregational leaders. The experience of the Diocese of Texas has been that clergy and laity are hungry for what they discover at these conferences. When people devoted to evangelism, discipleship, and church growth are put together in a room, synergy develops. Affirming, praising, and highlighting those congregations that have most effectively pursued evangelism is all it takes to provoke spirited discussions. The result is a powerful environment of peer learning.

Each cluster conference meets from noon of one day to noon of the next day and overlaps at lunch with the next cluster conference; thus there can be some interaction between congregations of different sizes. Half of what is presented at the conference is theoretical, and half is a take-home to-do list. Benchmarking of each size category allows the high-performing missionary outposts to set standards for the category, to share the factors that have contributed to their success, and to recognize their leadership. Cluster conferences champion innovative congregations.

As part of the conference, attendees are divided into small groups and assigned this question: "What do you need from your judiciary?" The results of the first cluster conferences in the Diocese of Texas yielded six major lessons for the staff:

1. Congregations want judiciary help and are eager to tell the staff what they need. Historically, one of the serious communication problems in the dioceses of the Episcopal Church has been limited feedback from the missionary outposts. The cluster conferences are one means of rectifying this weakness.

2. Each size category needs dramatically different resources. Therefore, judicatories have to customize the resources they provide to the specific needs of each category.

3. Cluster conferences provide direct contact between the judiciary staff and lay leaders of the congregations, with no filtering by clergy. This kind of direct contact is important in inaugurating a new vision, which may arouse a degree of caution among some clergy but is often initially grasped and supported by the laity. More important, lay leaders of the visionary congregations have direct and meaningful contact with one another and can explore common issues.

4. Many judiciary-designed programs distributed to small congregations are ignored by those congregations. The time, effort, and money invested in creating such programs are therefore wasted.

5. Congregations of program size want and need training in how to design and implement different programs, and they want training in how to deal with the unchurched.

6. As mentioned earlier, churches in the transitional category do not know how to become program churches, and they need help growing.

By coming together in conferences of like-sized congregations, clergy and lay leaders are able to identify and concentrate on the dynamics that are characteristic of their congregations. To name a demon is often a way of gaining control over it. Understanding that churches of similar size have similar problems, clergy and leaders are better able to articulate effective responses. Conversely, a source of liberation and renewal is the fact that particular opportunities are available to congregations of a certain size. By discussing the risks and opportunities that characterize their congregations, clergy and lay leaders experience less isolation, more confidence, and greater inspiration. They also have the opportunity to discuss the vision and its meaning for their congregations, to get better acquainted with the judicatory staff, and to hear concrete suggestions regarding congregational development. These twenty-four-hour conferences promote networking opportunities among clergy and laity of different congregations and facilitate sharing at a deeper and more significant level.

Perhaps the most exciting development from the conferences in the Diocese of Texas is that revitalized congregations are increasingly taking a leadership role in the conferences themselves, furnishing more of the material and posing more of the challenges to be addressed. In coming together to share their spiritual treasure, growing congregations are showing the way for others. This transfer of conference leadership, from the diocese to the missionary outposts, is thrilling and crucial: the congregations are the ones with the experience of what works on the front lines of mission. The transfer of leadership evidences a further flattening of the diocesan hierarchy and is another result of the diocesan vision.

Lay Leadership Conferences

All mainstream Protestant congregations have lay boards, with varying degrees of power, that are responsible for managing the congregations. In the Episcopal Church, the governing board of a congregation is called a *vestry,* and its head is called the *senior warden.* In the Methodist Church, the governing body is called the *board of stewards,* and its head is called the *chair.* In the Presbyterian Church, the governing board is called the *session* (composed of *elders*) and its head is the *moderator* (who is either the pastor or someone appointed by the presbytery to serve in his or her absence). Often the members of these boards receive very little preparation and training for their work, but their responsibilities can be substantial and frequently require specialized knowledge. Therefore, the Diocese of Texas initiated annual conferences for new wardens and for all the members of the vestry of every missionary outpost. These conferences have proved extremely valuable and are highly recommended for congregations of all the mainline denominations. The purposes of the conference are to permit direct communication between the judicatory staff and elected lay leaders and to train the laity in serving as senior officers and members of the governing boards of congregations. Election to such boards is not training enough; teaching lay leaders about the job they are called to do is crucial to the growth of the congregation.

Annual Stewardship Conference

The purpose of the annual stewardship conference is to teach members of the judicatory about good stewardship and about how to ask their congregations for money. The conference emphasizes the biblical principle that everything each of us possesses has come from God and belongs to God. As the parable of the talents makes clear, Christians are not to be considered owners of what they have but merely stewards, and only for a period of time. A portion of what has been given by God should be used for God's work in the world. The ministry of the Church is free to everyone, but it still requires funding. When this fundamental principle of the Christian faith is lived, worthwhile endeavors are funded.

Good stewardship is not just about money, however. It is also about devoting one's time and talent to the Church and its work. Stewardship is an important aspect of discipleship because it involves sharing with others what has been given to us. All our gifts are just that: they came from God and are properly used in God's service. Deuteronomy 7:17 reminds us, "Do not say to yourself, 'My power and the might of my own hand have gotten me this wealth.'" What we have been given is not meant to be hoarded but rather shared so that it can be multiplied. Therefore, "It is more blessed to give than to receive" (Acts 20:35). Of everything we can share with others and the Church, the most precious thing is our time because it is what is most limited.

Convocations

The Diocese of Texas is divided into ten convocations, each of which is headed by a dean and represents a geographical region of the diocese. The clergy in the convocations meet periodically to address issues, topics, and programs that promote their common ministry. The diocese sends a weekly letter to each dean via fax or e-mail. Each dean adds specific convocational news and forwards the newsletter to all canonical and licensed clergy in the convocation and to the spouses of deceased clergy. The newsletter includes lists of events, clergy changes, hospitalized and bereaved people, and job opportunities, in addition to anything else of potential interest to the greater diocesan clergy family. This weekly letter has been an effective pastoral tool, and it has brought the diocese together, in a tangible way, as one church.

Growing the Judicatory and Its Congregations

As already described, the Diocese of Texas uses a threefold congregational development strategy. The following passages discuss its implementation.

Planting New Congregations

New congregations are crucial to the missionary church because they offer the fastest way of reaching the unchurched. They also provide the quickest route to ethnic and generational diversity. An analysis of new starts in the Diocese of Texas over the past quarter-century indicates that the diocese has not employed the most effective process for developing new congregations. Although the diocese did purchase land and subsidize new congregations through the start-up phase, the long-term results were mediocre. For example, one new start consumed $850,000 in diocesan funds over fifteen years while declining from the one hundred members who founded it to seventy-eight members by the end of that decade and a half. There are multiple reasons why new starts failed to achieve their membership goals, and these reasons are straightforward:

○ The land for the new churches was purchased by the diocese without adequate financial or strategic analysis and without sufficient congregational involvement, and so the properties were often inadequate in size or poorly located.
○ Because the new congregations had to borrow money to build facilities, they were forced to construct buildings that were too small and to take on too much debt. The inadequate facilities and the heavy debt load constrained their ability to hire the additional staff they needed, and these factors seriously retarded growth and crippled what had once been potentially large congregations.

○ The initial funding was generally also the end of diocesan assistance. As soon as a congregation attained self-sufficiency, it was left to grow on its own and to raise its own funds. Unfortunately, however, the new congregations usually attained financial self-sufficiency at the expense of programmatic spending.

○ The finances of the new congregations were further constrained by the congregations' having to pay assessments to both the diocese and the national church.

○ As the congregations grew slowly or failed to grow at all, the diocese made little effort to evaluate their progress but periodically provided resources in the areas of Christian education, youth, and stewardship.

In line with its vision, the Diocese of Texas has adopted new policies regarding start-up congregations in metropolitan areas. These policies are applicable to all mainline denominations with episcopal polity, and in denominations with congressional polity they can serve as guidelines for developing analogous polices:

○ In the absence of a compelling reason, property for new congregations is not purchased until it is actually needed.

○ In metropolitan areas, only those congregations that have the potential to become resource-size missionary outposts are started.

○ A congregation is not started until there are at least two hundred people for an initial Sunday service.

○ The judicatory as one church purchases the land, helps build an adequate first facility, and funds a ministry team for the first three to five years. In this way, the judicatory can support its newest congregations and avoid placing serious financial constraints on them.

○ The Canon for Mission and Congregational Development conducts workshops on planning and progress evaluation for all new congregations. He or she also trains a cadre of laity to assist in providing this kind of specialized ministry.

○ Founding clergy are chosen who can build a missionary team.

○ Regardless of their economic success, new congregations remain missions for the first five years of their existence and so remain under the direct supervision of the bishop. This practice permits new congregations to benefit from the experience of the bishop and the diocesan staff in making their critical early decisions.

○ In order to pay for new congregations in the Diocese of Texas, the bishop has challenged one thousand diocesan members to contribute $1,000 each per year to the Partners in Mission program, which yields $1 million annually.

Austin offers a good example of how a new congregation can be successfully planted as the child of all the congregations in an area when the diocese is perceived as one church. The Austin Regional Planning Group was created to consider the question of where in the greater Austin metropolitan area the diocese should build its new churches. More specifically, the group was asked to take the following actions:

○ Evaluate existing congregations in the greater Austin area, including the growth potential of each, based on current size as measured by average Sunday attendance

○ Identify sites for new missionary outposts and project the size of the congregation that could be expected for the site

○ Build multicultural initiatives into the plans

○ Investigate whether institutional development (for example, expansion of Episcopal schools) could be integrated into the effort to start new congregations

The planning group was asked to survey the Austin congregations, use demographic data, and make recommendations concerning new-congregational development in Austin. The group met monthly (and sometimes more often) for eighteen months. After completing its study, the group held three meetings at different locations, to discuss its conclusions with the Austin congregations and to obtain feedback. Afterward, the group identified three locations that it believed were the best sites for new congregations. The bishop asked the group to continue meeting in order to provide oversight for these new congregations.

The results of this highly cooperative, interactive approach between the diocese and its Austin congregations were many and important. The planning group had been created in the belief that the most effective way for the diocese to tie in to the civic, social, economic, and political roots of a community was through the laity in that community. Talented laity bring their own networks, and often their own staffs, and so make it possible to significantly leverage the power and resources of the diocese and its missionary outposts. Just as important, laity from different congregations take ownership of congregational development and the decisions that are made. In concert, their actions reflect the vision of one church and reinforce that vision in the minds of disciples. Empowerment of the congregations to assess their own missionary situations and to make decisions that concern them sends a clear message of diocesan trust and is evidence of the less hierarchical approach to management that Bishop Payne has introduced.

The Austin Regional Planning Group proposed a new mission for northwest Austin. As a result of its work, no opposition emerged from any existing congregation. The vicar of the new missionary outpost was invited to preach at eleven of the twenty Austin congregations, and on that occasion he asked for their help in providing continuing prayer support for the new mission, for money to help the mission get started, for personnel to staff a phone bank to make calls to thirty-two thousand potential members, and for a core group of people who would found the new congregation.

On the Wednesday after the Sunday service, the vicar met with those people who were interested in further discussion or in some form of involvement. The results of this new approach to founding missions were astonishing. Austin provided a clear example of the diocese responding as one church of miraculous expectation rather than as a group of isolated congregations in competition with one another.

Declining or Conflicted Congregations

Working with declining or conflicted congregations is a matter of supreme importance to any judicatory that is serious about mission. Part of the Diocese of Texas's congregational work has been to help declining congregations conduct a comprehensive self-analysis and to explore new ways to achieve revitalization. This process has led to the restarting of some congregations that have been in the most serious decline. One such example is a small, one-hundred-year-old congregation in Tyler that is predominantly African American and that was down to an average Sunday attendance of six. The diocese identified a native son of this congregation who had maintained a medical practice in Tyler for over sixteen years, but who had moved away from the congregation. The bishop asked him to consider returning to the missionary outpost as a member of the clergy. The physician agreed and began a special training course, independent of the seminary process, that led to his ordination under a special provision of the Episcopal Church. As a result, the congregation has made a remarkable leap forward, growing from a Sunday attendance of six to an attendance that numbers in the thirties to the fifties.

Not all declining congregations can be helped. For some, the organizational culture is too locked in the past, and the changes that would be required are too threatening. But when the members are willing, there is hope. A good example is St. Alban's, in Houston, which changed its demographics from a predominantly Anglo-American congregation to a Hispanic one.

Missions

The shift from a maintenance model to a missionary model required the Diocese of Texas to change its approach to missions. For more than ten years, the diocese had supported some missions with seminary-trained vicars who cost $300,000 annually, and yet the missions had experienced little growth. No analysis had ever been conducted to determine why the missions had not grown, and it was generally accepted that small rural congregations would not grow. Little serious thought was given to whether the chosen vicar was the right person for the particular mission, and once the vicars were ensconced, the diocese did not check on them again to see what they were doing. To correct this situation, all the missions were analyzed and divided into six different categories:

1. *New plants* are missions that have never existed before, are generally aimed at the dominant economic culture, have the potential to gain economic self-sufficiency within a relatively short period, and are expected to grow fairly rapidly into resource-size congregations. New plants remain as missions under the direct supervision of the bishop for at least five years, regardless of their self-sufficiency.

2. *Potential parishes* are existing missions that are growing, moving toward financial self-sufficiency in accordance with preset plans and timetables, and are expected to reach full status as parishes.

3. *Restarts* are missions that are not growing, or that are declining, in which the bishop intervenes so that there will be a possibility for growth. For example, an Anglo-American mission may be redeveloped into a Hispanic mission.

4. *Multicultural missions* are begun in order to appeal to specific ethnic constituencies (Hispanic, Asian, or racially mixed to a significant degree) that are composed primarily of lower-income people and that may or may not reach self-sufficiency soon. The diocese is committed to multicultural missions even when they are not projected to be self-supporting for a long time. Nevertheless, some of these missions have also achieved the greatest growth.

5. *Self-supporting missions* are those that once were subsidized, or that were stagnant, sometimes dysfunctional, and often served by clergy who did not want to be there and who were not well suited to the needs of these missions. These missions are no longer served by full-time clergy but rather by other leaders, who are more suited to the specific missions and are much less costly. The use of lay vic-

ars and bivocational clergy is one form of alternate leadership that has proved effective in these missions.

6. *Chaplaincies* are subsidized missions that are not growing and that employ seminary-trained clergy. Chaplaincy missions do not represent the highest and best use of diocesan funds and are candidates to become parishes or self-supporting missions. By 1999, the number of chaplaincy missions in the Diocese of Texas had been reduced to two, each of which is on a plan to become self-supporting. The bishop found it necessary to close only two chaplaincy missions, and these were closed by local request. Such decisions are potentially difficult, but the diocese has a responsibility to use its funds in the best interests of the diocese as one church, and in accordance with its vision.

Christ Church, in tiny and economically depressed Matagorda, is a good example of a chaplaincy mission that became a self-supporting mission as a result of the new diocesan approach. Founded in 1838, when Texas was still a republic, Christ Church is the mother church of the Diocese of Texas. For the past few years, Christ Church has had about twenty members, with an average of twelve in attendance, and has been linked to St. John's Church, in nearby Palacios. Together, the two missions have constituted what is called a *cure* (a single position held by one clergyperson, who is in charge of both congregations). Even so, Christ Church had to be subsidized at an annual cost of $34,000, to support the resident seminary-trained vicar.

When the vicar left to take another position, the bishop appointed Harley Savage as lay vicar. Mr. Savage, who serves without a stipend, is a rice farmer and lifelong resident of Matagorda County; his great-grandfather was married in Christ Church at the turn of the century. After training, he was ordained under Canon 9, a church provision that allows him to become a priest for the locality of Christ Church only.

In the first six months after the vicar arrived, church attendance increased by 400 percent. The vicar offered the congregation a new meaning of miraculous expectation by proposing an unprecedented outreach program. One of his parishioners admitted, "When the vicar mentioned an outreach lunch program to meet the [hunger] needs of the Matagorda community, I never thought it would work. We didn't know if anyone would come, and we didn't think we could pay for it for very long." But the outreach has been extraordinarily successful in the little Gulf Coast town:

Each Wednesday more than 40 guests settle in at family style tables to greet old friends and a spontaneous assortment of visitors [several months after this story was written, the number of visitors had increased to an average of 150]. Many of the town's elderly are regulars, joined by businessmen with polished shoes and creased pants who are in town for a meeting. Sitting next to them are several not-so-neatly-clad pipeline workers, the Methodist minister and some of her flock. Recently, a group of cowboys driving a herd of cattle through town stopped in to have a bite [Barnwell, 1998, p. 16].

Hutchinson (1998, p. 16) describes the scene this way:

One of the regular diners is Roy (not his real name). Roy can be seen all over town pushing the old lawn mower that he uses as a walker. He would be a 'street person' in any other town, but in Matagorda he comes and goes, conversing with everyone, carrying an extra lunch to his brother in a pail attached to handle of his mower. He is always in church on Sunday.

When somebody suggested that an offering basket be placed next to the iced tea so that diners could make a freewill offering for their meal, the result was a basket overflowing. The lunch program is now self-supporting and sometimes earns a modest profit. One of the guests was overheard to say, "I put in $5.00 when it's something I really like; otherwise I just put in $3.00."

According to Barnwell (1998, p. 16), "The energy generated by this outreach program manifests itself in many ways [within the congregation]. It's no longer only a few who do all the work at Christ Church. The number of acolytes and lay readers continues to grow." The congregation has a new choir director (with a master's degree in music education) and plans soon to build a larger parish hall and more rooms for Sunday school. Fundraising projects have enabled Christ Church to send five children to Episcopal camp in the summer and four senior high students on a summer home-repair mission trip to Colorado. Through a foundation grant, a new mobile medical clinic has been acquired to serve Matagorda County, providing much needed free medical care that was previously nonexistent.

Harley Savage says, "We're out of the 'keep the church open' stage to the 'we have to spread the Gospel' stage, and we can't do that by keeping it in the building!" These changes at Christ Church have all been made possible by living in miraculous expectation. They are examples of what can be accomplished with love, enthusiasm, and the help of the Holy

Spirit. "The Gospel is about really touching people," Mr. Savage says. "It's about giving them something they can hold on to!" It is also about a diocese of miraculous expectation that allocates its resources in accordance with its vision.

All Saints' Church, in Cameron, is another example of a chaplaincy mission that achieved self-supporting status when its last seminary-trained vicar received a new position and was replaced with a lay vicar. The new vicar, who serves without pay, increased weekly attendance at the tiny church from fifteen to forty. The congregation has added midweek church services, Bible study classes, couples groups, and Sunday school classes. Younger couples with children who had never been to the church before started attending services, and the unchurched without children also came.

St. John's Episcopal Church, in Palacios, formerly linked with the Matagorda Church, has experienced the same kind of growth under its new lay vicar. Other small churches have also grown as a result of the vision, careful analysis of the mission's situation, and the appointment of a missionary leader. Congregations that are led by a lay vicar engage "supply priests," who come as sacramentalists to maintain the sacramental life of these missionary outposts.

The decision to stop subsidizing nongrowth missions took place only because there was a vision (and because resident seminary-trained vicars were not displaced until their next moves had been accomplished). The vision guided the diocese to a better use of its resources as one church. In contrasting new opportunities to the old way, which had left both clergy and laity frustrated, the new measures were deemed acceptable, and the diocese reaffirmed the wisdom of its vision.

In each of these cases, the tiny missions exhibited remarkable growth with a new vicar. In none of these cases was funding the reason for that growth. In all these cases, a new missionary leader tapped the deep inner resources of the congregation and enabled its members to bring forth their unique talents in pursuit of the missionary vision. The success of these missions is a direct result of the vision, and they illustrate an important principle: implementation of the missionary model is not a function of financial wealth; it is an activity of the Holy Spirit.

Another important principle that emerged from the diocesan study of missions was the principle of reallocating resources from nongrowth missions to missions and congregations that have growth potential. In making resource-allocation decisions, the investment criterion became the number of lives that could be affected. Is it morally right or a proper exercise of fiduciary responsibility to spend $20,000 to maintain a full-time ordained person in a mission of twenty people? Or should that money be spent on a new congregation of four hundred people? Which alternative is more in accordance with the diocesan vision?

In the Diocese of Texas, small-town missions that are not growing are assigned lay vicars, bivocational priests, nonstipendiary clergy, non-stipendiary vocational clergy, Canon 9 priests, or retired clergy. Through such deployments, the diocese can provide the same coverage as before and still meet these congregations' needs. This strategy has resulted, through 1998, in a reallocation of $300,000 from missions to start-up congregations, without the closure of a single church. Ironically and miraculously, some of these nongrowth congregations are now growing as a result of the new arrangement, and some have taken on more funding responsibility themselves. In summary, the primary strategy used in deploying clergy to mission congregations is to find missionary leaders, whether they are seminary graduates or not, who are suited to these particular missions and who can work to make these missions grow.

Intentional Multiculturalism

Part of the vision of the Diocese of Texas is to include as disciples "all sorts and conditions of people, bringing joy to those who are reaching out and to those who are reached." The diocese is intentional in its efforts to break down the cultural, ethnic, and socioeconomic barriers that have separated the members of its congregations from other people within its geographical borders. Toward this end, it is committed to subsidizing Hispanic, African American, and Asian ministries in order to facilitate their development.

One of the fruits of evangelism is that it promotes expansive diversity and therefore counters racism. As an invitation to all people to join the Body of Christ (there can be no exceptions), it requires those in the dominant culture to gain some understanding of other cultures in order to reach their unchurched members. Evangelism encourages us to consider the special gifts that different cultures have to offer. It also promotes an appreciation of people as individuals rather than as stereotypical groupings, and it leads us to identify with the similarities between people rather than with the differences between cultures.

Exclusionary policies are particularly hideous when they occur within the Church. Leopoldo Alard, Bishop Suffragan of Texas, fled Cuba as a nineteen-year-old in the aftermath of Castro's revolution. He had been president of Episcopal Youth in Cuba, his grandmother had been a member of Cuba's first Episcopal confirmation class (in the 1890s), and the

Episcopal faith had played an important role in his life. The young man arrived in Miami on a Wednesday and on Friday morning went to services at an Episcopal church near the city center. Entering the church, he explained to a priest, in passable English and with great expectation and joy, that he had just arrived as a refugee from Cuba, that he had been active in the Episcopal Church there, and that he was seeking a church home in his new country.

As he was telling his story, the priest took his hand and ushered him outside the church. Standing on the steps, the priest pointed toward a Roman Catholic church down the street. Thinking that the priest was confused, the young man said, "But I'm an Episcopalian." He pulled out his Cuban Episcopal Church card and showed it to the priest. Having lost his belongings, his country, and his family, the teenager was determined not to lose the only thing he had left—his church. But the priest was firm. Some other church was where the youth belonged. He was not even permitted to stay for the service.

Though devastated by the rejection, racism, and apparent abandonment by his church, the determined teenager did not give up. On Sunday, he went to another Episcopal church in Miami where he was not turned away. Two weeks later, he allied himself with other Spanish-speaking Episcopalians, and together they founded the first Spanish-language Episcopal congregation in Miami.

In the Diocese of Texas, multiculturalism is seen as an asset, not a liability. One of the bright spots of the diocese's multicultural ministry is the progress it has made among Hispanic people. The Diocese of Texas now has eight congregations that use Spanish in their worship services; three of these congregations use Spanish exclusively. The third-largest missionary outpost in the diocese (as measured by average Sunday attendance) is a Hispanic congregation with over eleven hundred members. The number of clergy in the diocese who are fluent in Spanish (in addition to the Hispanic clergy) has increased, and more and more seminary students are choosing to study Spanish as a second language. Bishop Leopoldo Alard's election as Bishop Suffragan was a recognition of the importance of this ministry to the diocese and an affirmation of the diocesan vision. Before his election, Bishop Alard had served ably as the Canon for Hispanic Ministry.

The Diocese of Texas has six predominantly African American congregations. They are older congregations, formed in the late nineteenth and early twentieth centuries, that have been static in recent years. The diocese is committed to increasing the size, strength, and number of its African American congregations. A good example is St. James's, in Houston, which has been rapidly growing (by about 50 percent in four years) and has experimented with contemporary services. With the help of the diocese, another congregation in a racially mixed area has purchased a 27,000-square-foot building to serve as a parish hall and health care center for the neighboring high school.

In 1998, the Diocese of Texas began working with Asians for the first time, bringing an Asian priest to one of its mission congregations. The diocese is committed to its vision of one church that includes all people.

PART THREE

LEADERS IN THE
NEW APOSTOLIC AGE

MISSIONARY CONGREGATIONS

I have become all things to all people, that I might by all means save some.

—I Corinthians 9:22

CONGREGATIONS ARE THE missionary outposts of a judicatory or denomination conceived of as one church. How well these missionary outposts prepare their disciples for the great call to evangelism will determine how successful they are in reaching the unchurched and in fulfilling the Christian vision of community, miraculous expectation, and personal transformation. This chapter describes some of the characteristics of a missionary outpost, a congregation cast in the missionary model that is dedicated to and driven by this vision. It explores what it means to live the missionary vision "in the field," where new disciples are made and old disciples are strengthened. Because the chapter deals with individual congregations, its principles are applicable to all mainline denominations. The examples are taken from the Diocese of Texas, but the missionary principles are universal in the mainline Church.

Factors in Church Growth

Church growth is intimately and inevitably linked to evangelism. One cannot speak meaningfully of one without the other. Church growth is a natural result of evangelism and one of the measures and objectives of evangelistic activities. A life in Christ is contagious. It moves believers to share the transformational power of their spiritual strength with those who are of value to them. Church growth is an admirable and desirable Christian goal, not for the sake of growth itself but because growth means an increased number of lives committed to Jesus Christ. The growth or decline of our church family should be of great importance and great interest to each of us, not in our pride but in our humility.

As an example, the Diocese of Texas has set as its goal a membership of 200,000 disciples by the year 2005, an increase of 120,000 disciples within a decade. Such spectacular growth is unprecedented in the Diocese of Texas, much less in the Episcopal Church, but it sets a worthy goal for the evangelistic efforts of the missionary outposts. Such growth would mean 120,000 fewer Texans suffering from spiritual hunger. Of course, it would take a miracle to achieve. But the Diocese of Texas is a community of miraculous expectation, and so there is nothing impossible about this vision. In fact, if each member of the diocese attracted only one person to worship every five years, someone who then became a disciple, the growth of the diocese would far exceed this visionary goal.

Research has identified two interrelated sets of factors that have a significant impact on church growth: internal factors (for example, such factors within a congregation as adequacy of facilities, availability of parking, quality of the pastoral leadership, involvement of the laity, average age of the congregation), and external factors (for example, circumstances in the environment where the church operates, such as social, political, demographic, and economic factors). According to Hadaway and Roozen (1995), congregations that are not in growing communities or among receptive populations (that is, congregations without favorable external factors) must work on identity, direction, purpose, and openness (that is, on their internal factors) if they want to grow. Although positive internal factors, such as a strong sense of mission, will enable some churches to overcome their negative external factors, no congregation can entirely escape the influence of its community and its environment. Even so, evangelistic outreach is the single most important factor in church growth, eclipsing even high-quality worship, Christian education, and other programmatic elements that have some relationship to increased membership.

For a congregation to grow, it must embrace evangelism as fundamental to its ministry, and church growth as a desirable result. It is not sufficient to add a "program" of evangelism to the slate of church activities. Evangelism is not a program. It is an ethos. It infuses all the activities of the church and represents a redirection of mind and spirit. A church that wants to grow has a spiritual excitement and a sense of community that make it qualitatively different from one that is stagnant in membership or that is in decline. Visitors find an "open to growth" church friendlier and more welcoming than a church with a closed membership. An open church creates a contagious spirit and a tangible sense of value that visitors find attractive and want to experience. In a growing, evangelistic church, "there is a strong sense of purpose that flows from a distinct identity and vision" (Hadaway and Roozen, 1995, p. 66). The congregation has a mission, knows what its mission is, and goes about changing lives through that mission.

Characteristics of Missionary Congregations

Those to whom the mainline denominations seek to carry the Gospel can be divided into three categories: secular people with no religious background, lapsed Christians who have no church, and former members of other religious traditions. The extent to which a congregation is effective with these categories of the unchurched will determine its success as a missionary outpost in making disciples. Effective missionary outposts are not accidental, of course. They emerge as a result of an intentional pursuit of the missionary vision, and they exhibit a number of characteristics that distinguish them from congregations in the maintenance model. In general, missionary congregations exhibit the characteristics described in the following passages (the first four characteristics apply directly to denominations as well). Table 11.1 summarizes some of the different characteristics of congregations in the missionary and maintenance models.

They embrace evangelism as fundamental to their ministry, and church growth as a natural and desirable result.

In the missionary congregation, evangelism is not a program, a part-time activity, or a department tended by specialists. It is the work of the whole church and all its members. Evangelism pervades everything that the congregation does. The missionary vision—making disciples as one church, through a community of miraculous expectation and glorious transformation achieved by the power of the Holy Spirit—drives all decisions. The rector of a Houston church says, "We are absolutely more aware of people trying to reach the unchurched—in this parish and in others—as a result of the vision. Although hesitant at first, we really are gung-ho about it now. In the beginning, people in the congregation didn't want to grow, but they have since developed a real enthusiasm for it. It takes a transformation of the parish to accept the vision and the growth it brings, and that takes time—but it does come."

When a congregation embraces evangelism, all groups in the church have an evangelical dimension. They are all reaching out to the unchurched.

Table 11.1. Comparison of Characteristics of Congregations
in the Maintenance and Missionary Models.

Characteristic	Maintenance Model	Missionary Model
Terminology	Church	Church, but as a missionary outpost of the one church of the judicatory
Goals	Maintenance of status quo, with some improvement	Making disciples; growth in membership; spiritual development of members; glorious transformation; miraculous expectation
Focus	Church members	Community (church members) and mission (the unchurched); all church groups have an evangelical dimension
Discovery	Confirmation or inquirer's classes, with varying content	Discovery classes, with a clear content that leads the seeker to accept Christ as Savior and to follow Him in the fellowship of the church
Language	Christian jargon (that is, phrases that are confusing or meaningless to the unchurched despite their powerful effect on the churched)	Language that is meaningful to the unchurched
Relevance	Requires the individual parishioner to dig it out	Church and faith made relevant to everyday life of members, seekers, and the unchurched through sermons, Christian education, small groups, and other activities of the missionary outpost
Acceptance of doubt and disbelief	Discouraged	Encouraged
Meaningful worship with a spiritual component	Occasional	Consistent, meaningful worship emphasized; people participate joyfully in the service; a palpable feeling of the presence of God; all members aware of visitors, newcomers, and the unchurched and strive to include them in the community

Table 11.1. Comparison of Characteristics of Congregations in the Maintenance and Missionary Models, Cont'd.

Characteristic	Maintenance Model	Missionary Model
Sermon quality	Not as important as other other factors	Crucial; powerful sermons directly relevant to joys and struggles of daily life, useful to visitors, newcomers, disciples
Signage	Inadequate signage so that visitors are easily lost or intimidated while finding their way around	Clear signs and maps that welcome visitors and newcomers and that point the way to all possible destinations in the church; large signs that provide the hours of worship service; reserved parking spaces for visitors
Biblical studies	Some Bible study	Biblical teaching; regular Sunday Bible study classes; Bible study in other Sunday school classes; weekday Bible study groups; special Bible studies, such as the year-long Bethel, Navigator, Trinity, or Disciple Bible Studies
Prayer	Limited opportunities for participation in prayer with others	Emphasis on prayer and praying, especially with and for others; many opportunities to pray or be prayed for (prayer meetings, teams, events, retreats, ministries, chains, groups, walks, and so forth)
Small groups	Some, but not emphasized	Emphasis placed on small groups through which to experience community, fellowship, and faith; many small groups that attract visitors and involve newcomers
Lay ministries	Some lay ministries involving a few members	Many and varied lay ministries; developed to meet the needs of church members and the unchurched; involve the vast majority of the congregation

Table 11.1. Comparison of Characteristics of Congregations in the Maintenance and Missionary Models, Cont'd.

Characteristic	Maintenance Model	Missionary Model
Welcome to visitors	Cold to warm reception	Enthusiastic reception; seekers acknowledged and celebrated; mentors and guides available; special packets offered to visitors; follow-up

What is often surprising about secular people is how many of them are friends. Yet we are not aware of them as "secular" because the topic of faith has never come up. The missionary field in contemporary America is made up of neighbors, co-workers, and fellow volunteers, not strangers. The field consists of parents we encounter through the lives of our children, friends we make in clubs and civic organizations, and acquaintances who comment on and inquire about the quality of our lives. The field is rich indeed, and it is easily accessed.

They communicate the Good News in clear language that is devoid of Christian jargon and that is meaningful to the unchurched.

As has been the case for two thousand years, a missionary outpost must love and understand the people to whom its message is targeted. St. Paul became "all things to all people that some could be saved." If the Church is to make disciples of the unchurched, it will have to develop some understanding of what they are like, just as St. Paul had to develop an understanding of the Gentiles and others to whom he carried the Gospel in the first century. Biblical illiteracy in America, especially among the young, is now so great that Christian expressions and references are either largely meaningless or burdened with negative connotations.

Hunter (1992, pp. 42–54) has identified some of the characteristics of secular people that help explain how to approach them evangelistically:

○ Secular people are often spiritual and even "religious," but not in the Christian sense. As in the days of St. Paul, people are affected by a variety of religions and philosophies that lead them to pose important religious questions and to try to answer them. It is not that unchurched people have no philosophy of life, but rather that their philosophy or worldview is not Christian.

○ Unchurched people struggle with many of the same moral choices that Christians do, but they do not use Christian terms and explicitly Christian criteria when they analyze alternatives and make choices. They are more likely than Christians to rely on moral philosophies, peers, pop culture, or their parents in making moral decisions.

○ Secular people are characterized by doubt rather than by guilt, which does not motivate them. (Christians who do wrestle with guilt and remorse find forgiveness and therefore can deal with them.)

○ Many secular people have a negative image of the Church, doubting its relevance and credibility. They believe science more than religion and many of them have had an indifferent or unproductive experience with church. On the other hand, they are curious about Christianity and Christians. Also, their confidence in reason alone to provide meaning, explanation, and purpose in life seems to be fading.

By studying the culture of the unchurched to whom they are reaching out, disciples in the missionary outposts can gain valuable insights for the evangelistic work ahead. Just as important, they are likely to develop an empathetic understanding and compassion for the plight of the unchurched. Secular people face a frightening world without the assurance of the love of God, the power of the Holy Spirit, the support of divine strength, or the promise of new and abundant life amid the chaos and suffering. In their spiritual isolation, they lead lonely and often desperate lives. Their suffering is a call to the Church. They are not to be judged, but to be reached.

They make the Church and the Christian faith relevant to everyday life, especially as a source of meaning, spiritual growth, and glorious transformation.

The key to the contemporary missionary message is the relevance of the Christian faith to daily life. What difference does it make whether one is or is not a Christian? What does the Church have to offer a hurting human being that no other group, no other organization, and no other institution can provide? The redemptive power of Jesus Christ made manifest in a Christian life is awesome beyond measure. But how can that hope be communicated to the unchurched? Meaning, purpose, joy, love, community, fulfillment, and satisfaction are fruits of the faith. The Church must step out in relevance to be recognized as the primary source of meaning and spiritual growth in the New Apostolic Age.

At the most basic level, people attend church when they find it relevant to their lives, and they do not attend church when they find it irrelevant. In the missionary model of evangelism, it is the responsibility of all members of the congregation to help make the Church relevant. Through participation in worship and other activities, members have an opportunity to interact with seekers and newcomers—to make their own experiences of Christian life pertinent and powerful to others. In the moment of attracting a seeker to the congregation for the first time, the church member enriches his or her own experience of the Christian faith.

The unchurched go to church when they perceive some kind of void or unmet need within themselves that they hope the Church will fill. It may be that a new year, a new baby, or some kind of tragedy has brought them to the realization that they are suffering from feelings of emptiness, loneliness, or alienation. Whatever the longing, they are looking for satisfaction and, in their moment of suffering, are open to new answers and new possibilities. In such moments, the yearning of the human soul for a relationship with its Creator comes to the fore and is made conscious, paving the way for actions that were once rejected. When seekers are readied for the Gospel by the pain of living without it, they will seek out a church that offers a vision of the Gospel that is meaningful to them.

The central communication question in reaching the unchurched is how the Good News can be expressed in nonchurch language—that is, in language devoid of Christian jargon. To put this another way, how can the Gospel be couched in the cultural terms of its targeted audience and yet retain the power and beauty of its Christian heritage? To someone unschooled in Christianity, what can it mean to "become part of the Body of Christ," or to "drink His blood," or even to "accept Jesus Christ as Lord and Savior?" Christian phrases and concepts that inspire, comfort, and persuade Christians have no effect on non-Christians who have had no religious training and who cannot appreciate the power of the words. The translation from "churchese" to nonchurch language can be difficult for church members who are familiar with the Bible and its stories.

An Episcopal church in a small town in the Diocese of Texas sent letters to twelve thousand residents, inviting them to the town's civic center for a free dinner and a talk titled "Is God Boring, Untrue or Unnecessary?" According to the rector, the goal of the mailing was to reach "those people who, for whatever reason, are not involved actively in a church. Maybe they don't know about God; maybe they have just slipped away or are inactive for whatever reason." After dinner and the brief talk by the rector, those present heard a short introduction to a program on Christianity that would begin a week later in the congregation's parish hall. More than 225 individuals attended, of whom only 100 were from the church.

They explain the uniqueness of the denomination's religious tradition.

Each denomination has a responsibility to teach its members and explain to the unchurched the unique elements of its faith. Within the set of beliefs that define the Christian Church, each tradition has its own perspectives that sustain its members and offer hope and meaning to the unchurched. In the Episcopal Church, for example, the cornerstones of the faith are Scripture, tradition, and reason. Disciples have a hard time explaining the faith if they do not understand it themselves. Many Christians, in fact, are amazed to discover the intricacies of their faith, the richness of its components, and the power of its principles when they encounter them in Sunday classes or through conversations with more knowledgeable disciples. For many years, the mainline Church has done a disservice to its members and made their exit easier by failing to teach them much more than the very rudiments of the faith. As one church member told another after a lesson on the meaning of the Resurrection, "I had no idea this was what we were about. It's beautiful."

They emphasize the power and importance of prayer and provide multiple opportunities for individual and group prayer.

Prayer is central to the Christian life and is a powerful tool for seekers and newcomers, who may be unfamiliar with what it can accomplish. Missionary congregations emphasize prayer, especially to newcomers, and they provide many opportunities to practice it in both structured and unstructured settings. As has been the case in the Diocese of Texas, such an emphasis can lead to new prayer ministries, such as the intercessory prayer ministry that has emerged at Palmer Episcopal Church, in Houston. It has also led to greater curiosity about the Church's traditional forms of prayer, a growing acceptance of extemporaneous prayer, and deeper involvement in the study and practice of prayer. Prayer lines, prayer chains, contemplative prayer sessions, silent prayer, prayers for the sick, and study groups based in prayer have all blossomed in the Diocese of Texas as a result of its missionary vision.

They create many small groups within the congregation through which individuals can experience community, meet personal and spiritual needs, and share their faith and fears.

Small groups provide a sense of belonging, a chance for intimacy, and an opportunity to be oneself that is often lacking in the isolating, fractured world of the new century. In the setting of a small group, people can explore their lives in a profound way, seeking meaning from their faith, finding strength in their relationships, and discovering answers to their deepest questions. Small groups also provide an opportunity for experiencing the spiritual, an essential part of the Christian faith. Such groups sustain their members and the congregations to which they belong, and they often play transformational roles in the lives of seekers, newcomers, and established members.

One such group in a Texas congregation embraced a "private person," who had started attending the group and who finally revealed that she was a cancer patient. Over time, she became more trusting of the group and more honest about her life and fears. Said one group member, "Very gradually, she taught us how to ask for the care we each need and how to offer it to others. She shared her feelings, her frustration, her anger, and, obviously, her trust in us and her faith in God. Her funeral was a celebration, not only of her life but of our newly found relationship with her and our newly formed community. She taught us how to admit our weakness and how to live and die with dignity and love."

A women's spirituality group in a Houston congregation was begun by three women and quickly grew to more than twenty. The group has been together for two years and remains well attended, with newcomers joining in and commenting that they have found it a "safe place to be real." It continues to be a refuge, a source of strength and hope, and a spiritual oasis for its members.

They provide many educational opportunities for both adults and children to learn more about the Christian faith, spiritual growth, and the work of the Church.

People are hungry for God's Word. Sunday school, outreach groups, Bible study, spiritual retreats, renewal weekends, seminars, and a variety of other educational programs can enrich disciples' and newcomers' understanding of the power and depth of the Christian faith. Congregations in the Diocese of Texas have seen these classes grow beyond their expectations when they were offered to tap this hidden hunger. One congregation in the Diocese of Texas has become so focused on biblical study that it has placed Bibles in the pew racks as an outward sign of its commitment to know the Scriptures.

They offer multiple lay ministries to teach service and discipleship and to involve members in Christian service.

A missionary congregation develops a comprehensive array of lay-based ministries to serve many purposes. Ministries meet the individual and social needs of disciples, provide a training ground for new leaders, and involve members in the work of the Church. As bridges to the unchurched, they attract seekers and help integrate them into the life of the congregation. Ministries are often aimed at uplifting the poor and underserved and, as such, are avenues to faith and opportunities for Christian service.

Wherever there is a perceived ministerial need, the missionary church tries to meet it.

Missionary congregations encourage the formation of new ministries (groups, classes, choirs, and so forth), not only because they meet emerging needs but also because new groups grow faster than old ones. Ministries add to the value of church membership by allowing current and potential members to build relationships, make contributions to others, be recognized, cope with loneliness, belong to something larger, and find meaning. Some ministries are designed to build community within the church and to minister to its members, whereas others are designed to make disciples and so minister to the spiritually hungry, the seekers, the unchurched, and those in pain or trouble. Ministries—whether youth programs, college ministries, courses in Bible study, child care facilities, prayer teams, training programs for spiritual directors, exercise classes, bowling adventures, seminars on ethics, or pastoral care that uses both clergy and trained laity—form the heart of the work of the Church. Through outreach ministries (see Chapter Sixteen), congregations exhibit God's love and healing power for the unchurched and set an example of Christian conduct. For example, the James Ministry, in the Diocese of Texas, was developed to meet the practical needs of those who are ill, housebound, unable to drive, or otherwise in need of physical assistance. In addition to serving the needs of those it reaches, the ministry also helps the congregation maintain a small church–family atmosphere of caring. It is also through such ministries that members grow in their faith, are strengthened in life, and discover new talents to use in God's service.

As reported by Hunter (1992), Frazer Memorial United Methodist Church, in Montgomery, Alabama, involves over 83 percent of its 7,500 resident members in more than 190 lay ministries, some of which are focused on the community of believers and some of which are focused on the unchurched. Willow Creek Community Church, in the greater Chicago area, involves six thousand people in ninety ministries. It is no coincidence that these large and growing churches make use of a strong lay ministry that uses the unique gifts of each member to reach nonmembers who are like themselves. If a church is to fulfill the biblical ideal of a "priesthood of all believers," it must empower and involve its laity in the ministry of the church.

They accept doubt and disbelief as part of faith and are tolerant of disciples in the making.

A missionary church is prepared to accept into its fellowship those who do not yet believe in the Gospel but who are seeking meaning, purpose, or spirituality in their lives. The only requirement for attending church services ought to be a desire to learn something about God. The role of the Church is to accept nonbelievers into its fellowship and transform them into believers. Too often, the Church is perceived as a place for people who believe rather than as a place for people who have come in order to believe. Evangelism is about attracting people who do not believe and then bringing them into the Body of Christ as new disciples. The attitude that one has to be a Christian in order to attend a Christian church creates a barrier of entry that discourages discovery.

They encourage honest sharing among members about their faith and its effect on their lives.

A church based on the missionary model, remembering that Christianity is "more caught than taught," will provide opportunities for secular people to meet creditable Christians within the Church. Laypeople who share their own experiences, struggles, and discoveries as they carry on the experiment of faith are persuasive to the unchurched. In their honesty, these evangelists admit to their own doubts and so address secular people's doubts and questions. Doubt has always been part of faith, especially for seekers and newcomers. Unless doubt is dealt with openly, it will corrode a developing faith and undermine seekers' efforts to align themselves with a congregation. Therefore, the church's ministries must affirm secular people, even in their expressions of distrust and disbelief.

"Seek first to understand, then to be understood" is the petition offered in the Prayer of St. Francis and is a potent principle for highly effective living. By listening first and then seeking to understand the unchurched, we are better positioned to explain our Christian lives to them. However, the first stage of evangelism remains attraction—that is, asking someone to come to church with us. Through this simple act of faith, we bring that person into the presence of the Holy Spirit, where forces more powerful than we could muster assist in the disciple-making process. The gift of personal transformation made possible by a life of faith begins with the movement of the Holy Spirit within us, and it is our responsibility to offer such a gift to those we know.

They provide meaningful experiences of worship that offer an encounter with God and a message that is relevant to the struggles and joys of daily life.

The quality of the worship service is critical to retaining visitors and newcomers as well as established church members. A vibrant congregation, through music, joyous participation, and its enthusiastic response, brings a sense of the presence of God to the worship service. It is the responsibility of each church member to contribute his or her part to the fullness of the worship experience.

They enthusiastically welcome visitors and newcomers and attempt to integrate them rapidly and deeply into the life of the church.

Because evangelism in the mainline Church begins with an invitation to worship, the manner in which visitors are received at the worship service is crucial to the success of the evangelistic effort. Congregations that truly welcome visitors, make them feel at home, and follow up on their visits grow faster than those that do not. Name tags for everyone, regular members included, make newcomers feel welcome and make it possible for them to learn the names of those they meet. "Visitor Sundays," designed to encourage the faithful to bring visitors, are effective as long as it is understood that every Sunday is a visitor Sunday, and as long as something exciting is happening for the visitor to experience. Many churches have special packets for visitors to carry away with them. Some reserve special parking places close to the church, and others assign mentors to help newcomers through what may be an unfamiliar service.

St. Francis Episcopal Church, in College Station, is a mission in the Diocese of Texas that exhibits these characteristics of a missionary congregation and that illustrates the transformation of a small congregation from a maintenance model to a missionary model. A mission is a small congregation that is not yet financially self-supporting; its clergyperson is a vicar (rather than a rector) who is appointed directly by the bishop. The growth and metamorphosis of St. Francis under its new vicar, Father Andrew Doyle, has resulted directly from the implementation of the diocesan vision, which is now lived out in the life and work of the congregation.

Father Doyle was in Bishop Payne's first seminary graduating class (that is, he was in the first class whose members the bishop would place in positions within the Diocese of Texas). Father Doyle spent the first two years of his ministry impressed by the diocesan vision, and he tried to figure out how to implement it at the congregational level, in the small, struggling parish to which he was assigned before moving to St. Francis. During this period, he found that the new Bishop of Texas and the Canon for Mission and Congregational Development were willing to provide companionship to the newly ordained, that they were intent on each person's finding his or her own special gifts, and that they were committed to the vision of one church in mission, community, and miraculous expectation. Father Doyle began looking for a church to dynamically embrace what the bishop was trying to do: reach the unchurched. He decided that he wanted to be a companion to the unchurched just as the bishop had been a companion to him, and so he attended a meeting at Camp Allen, the conference center of the Diocese of Texas, to study church plants. There he was given his opportunity: to serve as the new vicar of St. Francis. He felt, at that moment, that he had been freed to make the right personal choice, rather than forced to take the right career step, and that his ministry was being served by the diocese, rather than vice versa. The diocesan vision, with its emphasis on mission and community, had led him to a new place, where he believed he could do exciting things.

St. Francis had been founded in 1984 as one of the first attempts by the Diocese of Texas to make a modern "plant" (that is, to begin a congregation from scratch). Thirteen years later, the congregation's mission status had not changed because of critical errors made in the start-up period. Among the primary mistakes were that the diocese had purchased land before consulting with the founding members of the mission, had saddled the new mission with a large debt, and had provided a parish hall but not enough parking space. As a result, the mission was struggling. It was unable to pay its debt or enlarge its parking space, and it was deeply alienated from the diocese. When Bishop Payne began his episcopate, he made St. Francis one of his restarts.

One year after the new vicar was installed, the mission's annual budget had increased by 50 percent (from $98,000 to $150,000), its pledges by 64 percent (from 28 to 46), its communicants by 66 percent (from 87 to 144, with another 28 ready for the spring's discovery classes), and Easter Sunday attendance by 113 percent (from 103 to 219).

In support of the mission, the diocese provided funding for an expanded parking lot (now filled) and assisted in paying the salary of the vicar and a staff member. It also worked hard to mend fences with the mission. Diocesan actions took the pressure off the congregation. The purpose of the mission changed from the effort to become a financially self-supporting parish to the experience of becoming a thriving Christian community, with parish status as the byproduct rather than the goal. The mission was thus freed to focus on meeting the needs of the unchurched, serving the spirituality of its members, and responding to the demands of a healthy community.

Through all these changes, the diocesan vision provided the guiding standard. Being clear and honest about goals is empowering, the new vicar found. It allowed the mission members to determine what they wanted to achieve and how they could achieve it. They identified what they could do, in addition to the resources that the diocese could provide. In turn, the mission's success made it a resource for the diocese. St. Francis is no longer an isolated congregation. It shares with other churches what has proved effective, participating fully as a missionary outpost of the one church of the Diocese of Texas.

The vicar says, "I have used the diocesan vision and the bishop's planning in my own congregation. In the first two years, we have concentrated on our infrastructure, equipping ourselves for mission. We haven't even really begun yet. Basically, we've just been cleaning the house and dusting off the furniture and getting ready for everyone to come in." During this period, the vicar and the other members of the congregation have concentrated on three basic areas of change to create a fertile field in which newcomers would feel welcome: worship, community life, and buildings. "We paid special attention to those changes that would be attractive to our young married couples," the vicar says.

The principles of a missionary congregation are in evidence in the steps taken by St. Francis to prepare itself to invite and receive the unchurched. Among the most important principles are those that have found expression in the following ways:

○ The Sunday worship service is smoother, more accessible, and more expressive of its members. When the vicar arrived, the congregation was using four books, a bulletin filled with tiny print, handouts, and a music sheet. Following the example of St. David's, in Austin, the congregation now combines everything needed for the service into one bulletin.

○ The layout of the worship space in the parish hall has been changed to accommodate a larger music ensemble, which promptly grew from four to twelve members. A choir was added, there have been experiments with newer music from Oregon Catholic Press, and a jazz setting was created for the Eucharistic celebration. Three other seasonal mass settings were added, along with another service, and the music ensemble has inaugurated unaccompanied chant and Taize music with contemplative prayer.

○ There is now a soft space where children can play and where parents can rock babies while still participating in the worship service.

○ Community life has changed dramatically. "When I arrived at St. Francis," the vicar recounts, "the vestry had been cleaning the church. When we stepped out in faith and hired a sexton, we were able to start three new home groups. We also came in under budget on the sexton, so we hired a part-time youth director. We beefed up the greeter's ministry, began a hospitality ministry, and started Sunday morning education classes for all ages. We saw that we needed a nursery, so we hired attendants. We had one child in the nursery last spring; a year later, we have some fifteen families making use of the quality trained nursery care we provide." All these actions were in service to the vision.

○ A leadership team was planted to coach the ministries and empower people to be creative in getting together.

○ A group for people in their twenties and thirties was begun and grew so large that it split and is about to split again, for a total of three groups in eleven months.

○ Money was raised to finish the first phase of the education wing by adding three new rooms.

○ The use of space was reconsidered. The music ministry, said to be important, had been meeting in a closet. It was given a room.

○ Twenty-seven new parking spaces were added, thanks to a gift from the diocese, and a more effective church sign was installed.

○ The chapel had been a classroom and a storage room. It was converted back to a chapel and has become a permanent sacred space, not shared with any other activity.

○ New baby-changing tables were installed in both the men's and the women's bathrooms.

○ A garden project was initiated, to include an outdoor labyrinth, given the congregation's interest in spirituality, prayer, and contemplation.

○ A director of lay ministry was hired.

○ Planning was begun for a 500-seat church, with room for expansion to 700 seats, that will free the parish hall to serve as a parish hall.

○ Plans were laid to develop visitation teams and pastoral-care groups, to help with inreach and outreach as the congregation grows to program size and continues to move away from a centralized clerical model of ministry.

○ Planning was begun for alternative worship times, community outreach (family care, finance workshops, a family pet clinic), and a "basics of the faith" class.

"For all the dramatic changes at St. Francis," the vicar says, "the real miracle is revealed by those who have said, 'I never thought I would find a place that would meet my spiritual needs and that would be a companion for me on my pilgrimage.' How did so many new people come to be here? Because we were welcoming and caring, because we fed them spiritually and offered them a place in community. Perhaps the greatest gift for our established members has been in helping them determine how they can best serve one another."

APOSTOLATE OF THE LAITY

Come to him, to that living stone, rejected by humankind but in
God's sight chosen and precious; and like living stones be
yourselves built into a spiritual house, to be a holy priesthood, to
offer spiritual sacrifices acceptable to God through Jesus Christ.

—I Peter 2:4–5

AN APOSTOLATE CAN BE DEFINED as a group of individuals who carry out, individually and together, the duties or mission of an apostle. In the missionary church, the laity form an apostolate, and on their shoulders falls the primary responsibility for evangelism. Christianity is, in its essence, a lay religious movement—a historical fact that is sometimes forgotten. Christianity began as a lay movement, and it was as a lay movement that it first had an impact on the Roman Empire. Martin Luther recovered the apostolic truth of "the priesthood of all believers." John Wesley demonstrated the evangelistic power of the laity by building Methodism on the shoulders of lay preachers and class leaders.

According to the Scriptures, each person has a unique ministry to perform in the Church. St. Paul writes that the Holy Spirit has given each person different gifts to use in the Lord's work. These spiritual gifts allow some to become healers, others miracle workers (I Corinthians 12:9–11), still others apostles, prophets, evangelists, pastors, and teachers, "to equip the saints for the work of ministry, for building up the Body of Christ" (Ephesians 4:11–12). An apostolate of the laity develops from and is driven by this missionary vision of building up the Body of Christ. Each disciple in each congregation accepts personal responsibility for evangelism, recognizing his or her responsibility to participate in the Great Commission and to live out the Great Commandment: "I heard the voice of the Lord, saying, 'Whom shall I send, and who will go for us?' Then said I, 'Here am I; send me'" (Isaiah 6:8). Clergy in the missionary church call the laity to service, provide the training necessary to prepare them as disciples, and facilitate their deployment to the ministries for which they are most suited. As communicators of the vision, the clergy inspire, encourage, support, and recognize the laity, but they are not the chief evangelists. It is the laity who witness and serve, using their spiritual gifts, and thus, by example and the power of the Holy Spirit, make disciples of the unchurched.

The missionary success of large independent churches, such as Saddleback Valley Community Church (in Orange County, California), Willow Creek Community Church (in the greater Chicago area), and the Crystal Cathedral (in California), is a testament to the evangelistic prowess of the laity when it is properly recognized and channeled. Perhaps of even greater significance to the mainline Church, as a convincing precedent of the power of a lay apostolate, was the creation of Methodism. Of necessity and conviction, John Wesley entrusted the Church's ministry to the laity, and Methodism in its founding years was essentially a lay movement. As Hunter writes (1996, p. 122), "Laypeople did virtually all the ministry that took place in, and out from, every Methodist society. There were class leaders, and band leaders, and other kinds of small group leaders, as well as local preachers and those so-called 'assistants' who took de facto charge of societies and circuits—all laypersons. Other laypeople visited sick and hospitalized people, others worked with children and their families; others visited poor people, widows, and single parent families; still others engaged in conversations with undiscipled people and started new classes for seekers." In Wesley's Methodism, those who ministered also evangelized, and the movement grew. This distinctive feature of the lay apostolate was ultimately abandoned, and Methodism evolved into a mainline denomination, with evangelism relegated to professional ministers. Nevertheless, the eighteenth-century model of the lay apostolate was solid enough to endure for generations and create the foundation for Methodism as a mainline denomination.

Laity are often the first to catch the missionary vision and to appreciate the transformative potential of the missionary model. That has been the case in the Diocese of Texas. Although the missionary model was initiated at the judicatory level, it can also be initiated by the laity at the congregational level of any denomination. Lay leaders who want more than the status quo for their congregations are moved to work with other members of their congregations, with their clergy, and with the laity of other congregations to develop a missionary vision for their congregations, their judicatory, and their denomination. In so doing, they create the foundation for a lay apostolate.

A lay apostolate is more than an involved laity. It is a community of disciples committed to making other disciples. An apostolate manifests the dialectic of the Church—internal community and external mission—in a tangible way that has meaning and substance for the unchurched. The passages that follow describe the characteristics of a lay apostolate in the mainline Church. This is not a complete description of the lay apostolate's characteristics, but it is a comprehensive one. The principles discussed here provide a conceptual blueprint that can be modified by a congregation as that congregation seeks to use the unique human, spiritual, and material resources available to it.

A lay apostolate is rare in the mainline Church; Frazier Memorial United Methodist Church (in Montgomery, Alabama) is an exception. The transition from maintenance to mission, from laity to lay apostolate, is not an easy one to make. Training and education are necessary. Fortunately, there are books, training programs, consultants, specialists, judicatories, denominations, apostolic congregations, and other resources to which the faithful can turn in order to develop the strategies, methods, and means of creating a lay apostolate in their own congregations.

Although the lay apostolate operates at the congregational level, where new disciples are made, it is a reflection of the values and vision of the missionary church. Therefore, the characteristics of the lay apostolate are also characteristics of the missionary denominations of the New Apostolic Age. Table 12.1 compares the perspective and functions of the laity in the maintenance church to the perspective and functions of the lay apostolate in the missionary church.

Members of the lay apostolate accept individual responsibility for evangelism, making disciples within their social networks.

In accordance with the Great Commission, members of the congregation who form a lay apostolate accept responsibility for evangelism instead of trying to assign it to clergy, specialized programs, or designated teams. These disciples have committed themselves to making other disciples, primarily through their networks of family members, friends, and acquaintances. As members of the apostolate, they recognize that evangelism is a process, not an event—a journey that begins with attraction and ends with discipleship (except that discipleship itself never ends but only deepens). They are aware that evangelism begins with an invitation

Table 12.1. Comparison of the Laity in the Maintenance Model and the Lay Apostolate in the Missionary Model.

Laity's Function or Perspective	Maintenance Model: Laity	Missionary Model: Lay Apostolate
Primary role	Churchgoers	Apostles: disciples making disciples
Other roles	Volunteers	Living examples of the power of the Christian life; service to others through lay ministries; providers of pastoral care; communicators of the missionary vision
Congregational identity	As a congregation, separate from other congregations in the judicatory, isolated, and sometimes in competition with them	As a missionary outpost of the one church of the judicatory and denomination, networked to other congregations, cooperative with them, and synergistic
Responsibility for evangelism	Very little; most responsibility rests with clergy	Primary responsibility for evangelism; passionate about the unchurched
Relationship to the clergy	Reactive	Proactive
Lay Ministries	Few	Many, based on needs of unchurched and disciples; ministries are lay-driven
Pastoral duties	Limited	Extensive
Training of laity	Little or none	Extensive and comprehensive training and educational program to prepare the laity for lay ministries, pastoral duties, and evangelism
Testimony	Largely nonexistent	Frequent
Management of volunteers	Rudimentary	Sophisticated; extensive training
Educational programs	Design programs to inform and challenge congregations and serve church members	Design programs to inform and empower congregations to achieve vision; programs serve church members and the unchurched

Table 12.1. Comparison of the Laity in the Maintenance Model
and the Lay Apostolate in the Missionary Model, Cont'd.

Laity's Function or Perspective	Maintenance Model: Laity	Missionary Model: Lay Apostolate
Use of Christian jargon	Extensive	Nonexistent, or limited to educational contexts
Acceptance of doubt and disbelief	Little acceptance	Great acceptance; Christianity more "caught than taught"
Small groups	Few	Many; lay-driven and based on needs of members and the unchurched
Role of the miraculous	Miraculous sometimes experienced but not expected	Miraculous expected and experienced
Expectation of glorious transformation	Occasional at best	Glorious transformation expected and experienced
Visitors and newcomers	Perfunctorily welcomed	Warmly welcomed and accepted; acknowledged and assisted; assimilated into the congregation as quickly and personally as possible
Congregational growth	Lip service only; indifferent; growth actually feared or resisted	Committed to growth and passionate about making disciples
Church membership	Restricted to "as is"	Inclusive and intentionally multicultural

to worship, and they are dedicated to vigilantly extending that invitation whenever the opportunity appropriately presents itself.

Members of the lay apostolate participate in comprehensive education and training programs.

Comprehensive training and education programs are necessary to prepare the lay apostolate for its missionary work. The maintenance model is deeply embedded in the mainline Church. Without education and training of newcomers and disciples, the missionary model cannot be implemented effectively. Training in evangelism, Scripture, prayer, service to others, and the meaning and relevance of Christianity to the triumphs and tragedies of life are important aspects of preparation for effective evangelism and pastoring. The lay apostolate understands the necessity of such education and training, supports its introduction into the Church, and participates enthusiastically.

Members of the lay apostolate understand, support, and are passionate about the missionary vision.

Members of the lay apostolate live the vision and thus become exemplars of the Christian life. They witness to the Church's transformative power, its caring community, and its spiritual offerings. They serve in their missionary congregations as part of the one church of the judicatory—committed to mission as a passion of their souls and to carrying the message of hope and transformation to the spiritually hungry and the spiritually bereft. As a result, miracles occur and are recognized. For example, in one congregation in the Diocese of Texas, one guest of the program to feed the homeless (he slept in a car in the parking lot) was so encouraged by the compassion and love of those who ministered to him that he found new hope, which led him to dramatically changed circumstances. Over time, this man found a job, a place to live, and a new life. At his confirmation, more than twenty parishioners stepped forward to be with him as the bishop laid hands on him. It was a miracle for the congregation as well as for this soul.

Miracles come in many forms, and sometimes one miracle is in fact many miracles. That was the situation in the Diocese of Texas when one member of a congregation reached out to an unchurched individual who was in her circle of acquaintances. It turned out that her acquaintance was having serious problems with his second child, a six-month-old boy, who was experiencing four or five seizures a day and was heavily medicated. The problem was an extremely abnormal EEG for which no apparent cause (for example, a tumor) had been found. Because the burden of dealing with this child was so great, the man was greatly distressed, and so the church member reached out to him and his wife and invited them to attend a worship service. After some time, they did come to a morning service. As one of the parishioners who was present said, "One could immediately sense the congregation's compassion and concern for this family, as it was obvious that the little boy was in trouble. He was very medicated to prevent the seizures and his eyes were glassy. Really, he was like a sack of potatoes—just there."

The nature of the service was such that there was a great deal of prayer for the family. After the service, one of the priests invited the family back to his office and offered to pray for the family and anoint the child with oil. The family was very receptive to that idea. The priest and his wife laid their hands on the baby and prayed for him—just a simple prayer that the Lord Jesus Christ would touch him and heal him. The room filled with a tremendous outpouring of spirit, and there were many tears and much compassion for this little boy.

The following Sunday, the family came back to church. The boy was brighter and more alert, pointing at the lights on the ceiling and playing with members of the church during the service. Something was going on. When the priest inquired about what had happened, the father responded that the boy had experienced only one seizure during the entire week after the Sunday when he had been anointed. The parents were excited, with a great sense of relief in their faces and also a tremendous joy. The priest encouraged them in their decision to take the boy back to the doctor to find out what was happening. A specialist examined the child the next day and found that the boy's EEG was normal. There was no accounting for the change on a medical basis. Deeply moved, happy, and quite surprised, the physician playfully accused the parents of switching babies. The child was weaned off the antiseizure medications and has had no seizures since.

The miracles encompassed in the story began with one person reaching out to another—a disciple inviting an unchurched acquaintance and his family to attend a worship service. This first step in the hourglass model of evangelism led to the family's attending the service, to the prayer and anointing, and to the healing. Many lives were touched as a result of this first, simple invitation: the lives of the sick child, his parents, the disciple who befriended them, the physician, the priest who anointed the child, and the members of the congregation who witnessed the events. Out of the vision of the diocese as one church, committed to making disciples and living in miraculous expectation, came a series of miracles involving these family members and the congregation that loved them.

Members of the lay apostolate participate in at least one lay ministry and create new ministries when they perceive that new needs have arisen.

Through lay ministries, congregational members contribute to community and mission, furthering their own spiritual growth and serving others. Each member of the lay apostolate participates in at least one of the many ministries developed to serve the needs of disciples and the unchurched, to build the church community, and to make disciples. Several ministry models are available. For example, Frazier Memorial United Methodist Church uses a volunteer system, whereby members of the congregation simply volunteer for the specific ministries in which they want to participate; Saddleback Valley and Willow Creek Community Churches follow a discernment system, in which self-assessment tools and training are used to identify the most appropriate ministries for church members (Hunter, 1996, pp. 124–129). The lay apostolate also creates new ministries, as necessary, to meet emerging requirements. There are two criteria for judging proposals for new programs and ministries: the extent to which they meet the needs of disciples and the unchurched, and the degree of effectiveness they are expected to have in making disciples.

The blessings of lay ministries in the Diocese of Texas have proven bountiful for the ministering and the ministered alike. For example, a shy, withdrawn man in deep emotional pain began participating in ministries that allowed him to remain quietly in the background. He blossomed as he continued in service, touched by the return of the gifts he had offered, and so grew bolder in expressing his special talent for music. He began leading songs, calling out to parishioners by name, and including them in the singing. He has since volunteered in multiple programs and has brought much happiness and inspiration to many.

Members of the lay apostolate welcome seekers and newcomers.

Members of the lay apostolate accept, identify with, and warmly welcome seekers, newcomers, and the unchurched to the congregation, making them feel comfortable, assisting them in worship, and asking them to return. The lay apostolate is cognizant that visitors and seekers have come to the Church by holy invitation, and that they are to be received with gladness of heart, as sheep who were lost and now are found. Members of the lay apostolate involve newcomers, seekers, and visitors as soon as possible, and as personally as possible, in the life and work of the Church. Extensive research (available through diverse sources) has been conducted on the most effective means of welcoming visitors and newcomers to a congregation and making them feel at home. Members of the lay apostolate use this research to develop effective programs in their congregations. The Diocese of Texas, for example, offers a hospitality checklist to those who want more information on hospitality and greeting visitors.

Several years ago, a clergy member in the Diocese of Texas visited, incognito, a congregation that described itself as "one of the friendliest churches around." Without his wife, children, or clerical collar, he appeared to be a single middle-aged man visiting the congregation for the first time. The worship, he said, was terrific, the music was excellent, the congregation was involved, and the sermon was inspirational. But the warm, friendly welcomes that would have made him feel at home were reserved for church members who already knew each other. At the coffee social after the service, no one spoke to him. He spotted another visitor, a woman who also had been omitted from the enthusiastic greetings and the morning conversation. He watched as she stepped from the coffee table to the guest book. She picked up a pen to sign the book, studied the page for a moment, and then put the pen down without writing. She looked around, set down her half-filled coffee cup, and left for the parking lot. No one spoke to her. She did not come back to "one of the friendliest churches around"! Hospitality, as Canon Martin of the Diocese of Texas has pointed out, is not a function of being friendly to friends but of learning how to be good hosts and hostesses to the strangers and the seekers who come to church in search of something they do not have.

By contrast, in another congregation a new member of the confirmation class was called forward to be confirmed but had no family or friends to stand with her. When the acolytes and lay ministers saw this situation, which was in stark contrast to what was true for the large number of supporters whom other new members had gathered around them, they quickly and with quiet grace stepped forward to surround her with her new parish family. This revealing moment of kindness and community created by the newcomer, the young acolytes, and the middle-aged lay ministers was shared by the whole congregation as a testament to the power of mission and the vision of a community of miraculous expectation.

The assimilation process through which newcomers emerge as disciples is critical in the missionary church. When it is thorough, comprehensive, and grounded in genuine welcoming and relishing of new disciples, it can be quite powerful. One couple came to Houston for medical treatment, visited one of the congregations in the Diocese of Texas, and was warmly welcomed. During the husband's stay for treatment, he was cared for by members of the congregation. After returning to their country, which was overseas, the couple decided to return permanently to the Diocese of Texas and to this congregation. The former newcomer is now a member of the vestry, or governing body.

Members of the lay apostolate make extensive use of small groups.

Small groups provide support, build community, and aid spiritual development. They are a means of fortifying the faithful and of attracting the unchurched. Small groups are handled in different ways by different churches, and many excellent resources are available to guide the laity (and clergy) in the development of small groups. By offering a loving, sharing community, a small group provides one of the great missing pieces of life in twenty-first-century America. As such, it is vitally important to the Church. In fact, the early Church was built around small groups ("house churches"), to which there are multiple references in the Bible. John Wesley built Methodism through small groups, which he called "classes." Some large independent churches even describe themselves as collections of small groups.

Members of the lay apostolate participate in pastoral care.

Whether it is encouragement, spiritual development, prayer, comfort of the sick, support for the bereaved, listening, or empathizing, the lay apostolate can fulfill a variety of pastoral roles in the congregation. Lay pastors, when they are properly trained and when their efforts are coordinated, can provide deeper and more extensive pastoral care than would otherwise be possible, enriching their own lives and the lives of those they touch. The lay apostolate recognizes the opportunities in pastoral care, and its members are intentional about developing and supporting programs for pastoral care in which they can participate.

Members of the lay apostolate emphasize the relevance of the Christian faith.

Members of a lay apostolate communicate the relevance of Christianity to the joys and struggles of daily life. They extend the promise of personal transformation to those who enter into an intimate relationship with God, and they offer the hope of miraculous expectation to the unchurched. Jesus Christ was in the world, fully human as well as fully divine. His works and miracles reflected His profound compassion for the human condition. The lay apostolate recognizes that Christianity is not an abstract, theoretical religion devoid of capacity to comfort, guide, and inspire. Quite the opposite: it is a vibrant religion, alive with the power and workings of the Holy Spirit and profoundly relevant to daily life. Members of the lay apostolate transmit the joy of Christianity as well as its hope.

Members of the lay apostolate appreciate that in the New Apostolic Age, America is a mission field.

The lay apostolate feels deeply about the membership decline of the mainline Church in America and recognizes the extraordinary mission field that the post-Christian era has created. The lay apostolate also accepts a basic tenet of missionary work: the Good News must be spread by means of language and forms that are culturally and personally meaningful to those approached. The challenge to the contemporary Church is to speak to the unchurched in terms that they can understand and to which they will respond. One of the advantages of perceiving of a judicatory as one church is that it can support different congregations within its boundaries to meet the different needs, cultures, and generations of the unchurched it is called to reach.

Members of the lay apostolate work at identifying and understanding the target populations they want to reach.

Through the millennia, for purposes of evangelism, the Church has modified both the form and the content of its message. Each generation requires a different approach; what is meaningful to one generation is not necessarily meaningful to another. Evangelism aimed at the unchurched is more difficult in this generation because of the lack of biblical knowledge among many Americans, the reduced social pressure to join a church, and the perception that the Church is insular and out of touch with the needs of people in the workplace and in their neighborhoods.

Members of the lay apostolate appreciate that they must speak to the unchurched in language that the unchurched can understand. To that end, the laity seek to learn about their target populations. Each generation in America has its own set of characteristics and preferences (as do the immigrants who come here). A great deal of sociological research is available to help the lay apostolate identify the needs and desires of each generation. The lay apostolate makes an effort to speak to the unchurched in their own language—to speak, that is, to their needs, in words they can understand rather than in Christian phrases that have no meaning for them.

Members of the lay apostolate acknowledge that the missionary church requires more time and effort than the maintenance church.

There is no question that it takes more time and effort on the part of the laity to create a lay apostolate than to uphold the status quo of the maintenance church. Members of the lay apostolate acknowledge that discipleship is more work than mere membership, but they also recognize that the rewards are worth it. They are grateful for and challenged by the opportunity that the apostolate offers. For example, a member of one of the vestries of a congregation in the Diocese of Texas said, "The first time I served on the vestry, I celebrated my retirement with a small group of friends who knew how pleased I was to be leaving. This time, I dreaded leaving the vestry and actually had to grieve the loss of that service and community. Obviously, something had changed. What had changed was the congregation and the diocese and their commitment to service and to mission. As a result, I changed, too."

Members of the lay apostolate accept responsibility for creating the apostolate.

The lay apostolate is created by the laity, not by the clergy. Its creation may be inspired by the clergy or suggested by the laity, but its development is the responsibility of the laity. In their passion for mission and Christian service, lay members are moved to act in concert, in their own congregation and even across congregations, to create a body of men and women committed to Christian discipleship.

13

APOSTOLATE OF THE CLERGY

According to the grace of God given to me, like a skilled master builder I laid a foundation, and someone else is building on it. Each builder must choose with care how to build on it.

—I Corinthians 3:10

LIKE THE LAITY, THE CLERGY have an apostolate in the missionary church of the new century. That apostolate is based on acknowledging the centrality of the Great Commandment and the Great Commission in Christian life and the value of church growth and transformation. The clergy apostolate finds expression through the missionary vision that can unite the congregations of a judicatory and return them to the apostolic passion and power of first-century Christianity. The term *apostolate* captures this missionary role of the clergy in the new apostolic denominations. Like St. Peter and St. Paul, clergy are apostles to the unchurched, serving as missionaries, teachers, pastors, and administrators who inspire and coordinate the disciple-making efforts of the laity. By embracing the missionary model, clergy can initiate its implementation in their own congregations. On a broader scale, they can initiate its implementation in the judicatory by working with other congregations or with the judicatory leader.

In the missionary model, the role of a clergy apostolate is more comprehensive than the role of the clergy in the maintenance model. It requires less effort in some areas but more in others. On the one hand, a clergy apostolate transfers more of the Church's work in pastoring, community building, and mission to the laity. Its focus is on guiding and coordinating lay efforts and on teaching and inspiring laypeople rather than on carrying out the work personally. On the other hand, an apostolate of the clergy demands more. It requires that clergy serve as missionaries as well as managers and preachers. It is an exciting and demanding role, in keeping with the turbulent environment and rapid change of the new century. Table 13.1 compares the perspective and functions of the clergy in the maintenance church to the perspective and functions of the clergy apostolate in the missionary church.

Ultimately, the apostolate is deeply rewarding for the clergy who accept it as their way of ministering. Apostolic clergy in the Diocese of Texas have reported a resurgence of passion for their work, a more productive connection to their congregations, and a stronger sense of the Holy Spirit working in them and through them, and all of this has led to their personal and spiritual renewal. The apostolate has meant different church assignments for some and revitalized congregations for others. It has resulted in innovative programs, more powerful worship services, and greater lay involvement for congregations. Evangelism and the vision have also brought a powerful sense of God's will that has propelled some clergy to a richer appreciation of mission, a deeper faith, and a greater awe of God's work in the world.

One lay member of the Diocese of Texas said, "I have seen the clergy change. They were very wary initially and couldn't believe that the bishop would do what he said he was going to do. But he did. I would say that 85 to 90 percent of the clergy are now getting out of their boxes and are on board with the program. It has been terribly exciting for me personally. The vision of one church, of making disciples, of a community of miraculous expectation and glorious transformation, has taken hold. Church is no longer a spectator sport for us. People in the diocese are involved, discovering their gifts, being changed. Instead of watching the priests celebrate the Eucharist, we are joining in that celebration right along with them. I am so grateful for all that has happened."

Some of the qualities that characterize the clergy apostolate in the missionary church are described in the following paragraphs. The list is comprehensive but not exhaustive. It is meant to summarize the central concepts that distinguish the role of the clergy apostolate in the missionary church from the role of the clergy in the maintenance church. For some members of the clergy, these characteristics will be welcome and will resonate with what is already being done. For others, they will seem different but intriguing, even attractive. For still others, they will seem foreign and unattractive. Education and training play a large part in the acceptance and thoughtful development of a clergy apostolate. When the apostolate is

Table 13.1. Comparison of Clergy in the Maintenance Model
and the Clergy Apostolate in the Missionary Model.

Clergy's Function or Perspective	Maintenance Model	Missionary Model: Clergy Apostolate
Primary role	Pastor	Missionary, teacher, evangelist, leader, vision communicator; develops a pastoring system
Congregational identity	As a congregation, separate from other congregations in the judicatory, isolated, and sometimes in competition with them	As a missionary outpost of the one church of the judicatory, networked to other congregations, cooperative with them, and synergistic
Outward focus	Little or none	Disciples making disciples
Inward focus	The congregation as an association of individuals; ministering to congregation members; concern with internal issues, which are sometimes divisive; maintaining or improving the church	The congregation as a community of miraculous expectations and personal transformation, part of the one church of the judicatory; making disciples; developing effective structures to build community and further mission; living in miraculous expectation; glorious transformation of lives
Leadership style	Hierarchical model; loyalty expected	Servant-leadership model; participatory; trust-driven; loyalty earned
Communication style	Top-down; dictate; lecture; little feedback is sought	Two-way; listen; teach; feedback solicited
Responsibility for evangelism	Primary responsibility	Primary responsibility for evangelism rests with the laity; provides support, encouragement, and resources to the lay apostolate; passionate about the unchurched
Use of language	Christian jargon	Language understood by the unchurched
Music in the worship service	Quality not a top priority; traditional music only	High-quality music that may be traditional or contemporary or a combination, as needs dictate

Table 13.1. Comparison of Clergy in the Maintenance Model and the Clergy Apostolate in the Missionary Model, Cont'd.

Clergy's Function or Perspective	Maintenance Model	Missionary Model: Clergy Apostolate
Sermons	Not necessarily relevant to daily life; not necessarily powerful; aimed primarily at church members	Powerful and instructive; inspiring; explain Christian principles that are relevant to daily life; aimed at church members and the unchurched
Prayers	Prayers important	Many opportunities for prayer in the church and the worship service, including time for silent prayer
Accountability	Loyalty to the judicatory leader or denomination	Loyalty to the doctrine, discipline, and worship of Christ; accountability for meeting clear performance objectives based on the denominational vision
Congregational growth	Lip service only; indifferent; growth actually feared or resisted	Committed to growth and passionate about making disciples
Committee and other appointments	Reward active, visible members with appointments, regardless of their skills or community leadership roles	Seek leaders who endorse the vision, are themselves visionary and talented, and who are leaders in their communities
Lay ministries	Some lay ministries; focused primarily on members and congregational maintenance	Many lay ministries, based on needs; focused on members as well as on the unchurched; lay-driven
Budgeting and finance	Develop a budget based on the previous year's	Analyze the allocation of financial resources; develop accountability for results; reallocate resources to support the vision; maximize return in accordance with the vision
Planning	Top-down, with minimal lay input; usually programmatic or maintenance planning; few if any strategies or tactics	Solicit input from those to be served; critique the present system on the basis of the vision; re-create the system, as necessary; establish goals, strategies, tactics

Table 13.1. Comparison of Clergy in the Maintenance Model
and the Clergy Apostolate in the Missionary Model, Cont'd.

Clergy's Function or Perspective	Maintenance Model	Missionary Model: Clergy Apostolate
Christian education	Goals: encouragement and knowledge	Goals: discipleship; teach what evangelism is and how to accomplish it; stress spiritual formation; teach the basics as well as the richness of the Christian faith; make Christianity relevant to everyday life
Youth ministry	Youth viewed as church of tomorrow; form youth groups	Youth viewed as church of today; make disciples; train youth for evangelism; train and use youth ministers
Communications	Newspaper or newsletter; pew cards	Newspaper or newsletter that supports the vision and focuses on the miraculous; pew cards and brochures; videos; web page and e-mail; work with local newspaper; contribute to judicatory newspaper
Role of the miraculous	Miraculous sometimes experienced but not expected	Miraculous expected, experienced, and shared
Expectation of glorious transformation	Occasional at best	Glorious transformation expected, experienced, and shared
Membership	Restricted to "as is"	Inclusive and intentionally multicultural; faithful understand themselves to be disciples as contrasted to members

proposed at the judicatory level, it is the responsibility of the judicatory to provide such training. When it is proposed at the congregational level, it is the responsibility of the judicatory to support its development through the provision of whatever resources and training are appropriate.

Apostolic clergy embrace the missionary model and its vision.
   The clergy apostolate embraces the missionary vision of one church as a community of miraculous expectation—it is, in fact, passionate about

it—and glorious transformation guides judicatory and congregational change. One of the remarkable manifestations of the power of the vision in the Diocese of Texas was the decision of the Right Reverend Don Wimberly, Fifth Bishop of Lexington, to accept the position of Missioner for East Texas within the Diocese of Texas. Bishop Wimberly was one of five nominees for the office of Presiding Bishop and Primate of the Episcopal Church in the United States in 1997. His decision to leave the Diocese of Lexington after a decade and a half of service was based on the excitement he felt at participating in the vision of the Diocese of Texas. Bishop Wimberly's enthusiasm for mission is fundamental to the Diocese of Texas as the diocese reclaims its missionary roots. He has described his opportunity to serve in Texas as an "interruption from Heaven" that allowed him to return to hands-on ministry and participate in the re-creation of the diocese as one church in miraculous expectation.

Apostolic clergy examine their beliefs about the laity and the goals they have set for them.

Members of the clergy apostolate undertake a rigorous self-examination of their beliefs about the laity, the goals they have set for them, and the degree to which they are willing to relinquish control to the laity in building their congregations. What do the clergy think of the faith, gifts, and abilities of the laity? Is the view too limited and too constricting and thus counter-productive? Will the clergy trust the laity to be guided by the vision rather than directed by tight control? The clergy apostolate releases control and grants authority to empower the laity to assume a much more active role in the church and its evangelistic activities.

Apostolic clergy encourage the creation of many lay ministries and small groups, and they are committed to helping the laity discover their gifts and their ministries.

Lay ministries are an integral part of the missionary church, as are small groups that involve newcomers, attract seekers, and fortify disciples. Whenever a perceived need of the churched or unchurched can be met by a lay ministry or small group, the clergy apostolate encourages creation of that ministry or group. To make such activities as effective as possible, the clergy apostolate is committed to helping lay members discover their gifts and ministries. There are several effective models for a gifts-discovery program, and in this area there has been a significant amount of academic research, to which clergy can turn for assistance. By supporting such a program, the clergy can increase the number of volunteers in the congregation while helping them discover the joy that comes from serving others.

One Houston congregation offers a course called "Popcorn Theology" as a means of reaching the unchurched. (The church did not originate this term but has used it successfully to advertise the course in the local press.) During each class session, members watch a movie and eat popcorn. A local film critic discusses the motion picture, and then the class members talk about it together, looking for what it means in spiritual terms and in terms of the Christian faith. Among the films they have viewed are *Babette's Feast, The Apostle,* and *Dead Man Walking,* all of which speak to deeply spiritual issues.

Apostolic clergy encourage and support the development of a lay apostolate.

The clergy apostolate surrenders primary responsibility for evangelism and encourages the development of a lay apostolate to build the Church. With this vision as the guide, the laity is empowered to take a more active role in the congregations and the judicatory, making the decisions that they are most qualified to make and participating on the basis of their gifts and talents. The whole congregation functions as a team rather than as a hierarchy, and the clergy encourage the laity's enhanced role in the work of the Church.

Apostolic clergy encourage and support the development of a comprehensive program for recruiting, training, and managing volunteers.

The extensive lay involvement that is necessary for building a lay apostolate requires a well-planned and well-coordinated program for recruiting, training, and managing volunteers. The volunteers themselves can run the programs, but they still have to be trained and coordinated. Apostolic clergy provide support, encouragement, and, as appropriate, staff or outside resources to assist the laity in the development of programs for recruiting and managing volunteers.

Apostolic clergy understand that the missionary church is primarily relational.

Clergy in the maintenance church focus on religious doctrine, church structure, institutional concerns, controversial issues, and maintenance of the status quo. The clergy apostolate focuses on relationships. The missionary church is primarily concerned with fostering three categories of relationships involving its disciples: their relationships with God, their relationships with themselves, and their relationships with other people. In fact, the three are inseparable; the development of one facilitates development of the others. For example, community (disciples' relationship with others and with themselves) facilitates the development of spirituality (disciples' relationships with themselves, with God, and with others), and vice versa; mission (disciples' relationships with others, with themselves, and with God) deepens faith (disciples' relationships with God, with themselves, and with others); and so on. The activities of the church intentionally address and foster these relationships, whether in worship services, small groups, lay ministries, programs for Christian education and outreach, or other areas.

Apostolic clergy design worship services to be highly effective for both the churched and the unchurched.

Members of the apostolic clergy carefully plan worship services to maximize the services' effectiveness for visitors, newcomers, and established members. Particular attention is paid to the relevance of sermons to the joys, disappointments, and spiritual questions of life, as well as to Christian beliefs that fortify, sustain, and inspire. Attention is also be paid to the quality of music and to the welcoming of visitors and newcomers. Research indicates that those who attend church still regard the sermon as the single most important factor in the worship service. It is the sermon that facilitates the application of Christianity to daily life and that fosters an understanding of the richness, depth, and power of the Christian faith. A sermon that is poorly organized, without relevance to daily life, or trivial in its subject matter disappoints, disheartens, and drives away disciples and potential disciples. Christ Church, in Alexandria, Virginia, a pre–Revolutionary War Episcopal church where George Washington worshiped, contains a potent reminder of the importance of the sermon: the white, ornately carved pulpit, crowned with a floating canopy, is not placed off to one side but is in the very center of the church, raised about six feet above the floor and reached by a curving staircase. The pulpit dominates the altar area and dramatically symbolizes the central role of the sermon in interpreting the Word of God for the faithful.

Apostolic clergy are open to new forms and new language in communicating the Christian message to the unchurched.

The forms and the language adopted by missionary outposts for their services and activities will depend on the unique needs of the unchurched who are in their particular areas. In the tradition of the early Church, the guiding principle that the clergy apostolate follows is to match the language and forms of communication to the characteristics of the unchurched: perhaps a seekers' worship service should be added, or a service in Spanish, or a contemporary service. In areas of changing demographics, the whole congregation may change culturally, or new kinds of music may be introduced. The clergy apostolate is open to these kinds of additions or changes in form and communication, as a prerequisite to making the Good News relevant and meaningful to the unchurched to whom it carries its message.

Apostolic clergy are committed to a comprehensive teaching of the "faith once delivered to the saints."

Christianity is a rich and complex religious tradition. In the mainline Church, simplicities are not valid substitutes for profound truths. In an era of growing biblical illiteracy, Christianity is a "new faith" even to many Christians; therefore, extensive education is necessary for newcomers as well as for members who want to become better disciples. The large, growing independent churches offer multiple instructional programs in Christianity. Willow Creek Community Church, for example, begins with a basic instruction course called "Christianity 101." St. Francis Episcopal Church, in College Station, has a course titled "Basics of the Faith."

If the Christian faith is to be appreciated in all its richness, its concepts and principles must be taught. Sermons are one way to teach the Christian faith, both in terms of content and in terms of referencing books and articles that the clergy believe the congregation may find helpful. Clergy who talk about what they have been reading encourage the congregation to read as well, thus deepening its understanding of Christianity.

The clergy apostolate understands that the education of disciples is essential to the work of the missionary church, and it does not underestimate (as the maintenance church does) the hunger for such instruction and knowledge. A program of education that begins with the basics and leads those who are interested into ever-greater depths of the Christian experience is rewarding for everyone, newcomers and disciples alike. Placher (1998, p. 994) reports on several such innovative classes in Christian education: in 1997, "Fifth Avenue Presbyterian Church in New York began a program of adult education, offering classes on topics as demanding and varied as 'The Nature of God the Father' and 'Renaissance and Reformation: The Formation of the Protestant Tradition'"; eighteen months later, the classes had enrolled fifteen hundred people, and this program had become "the single most effective way of attracting new members to the church. Courses in theology and Bible consistently draw the greatest interest." In the Diocese of Texas, Christ Church Cathedral in Houston began the Lay Academy of Theology, which attracted students from churches across the city. In its first semester, the academy attracted 150 students, a number that grew to 250 in the second semester, and future growth seems highly likely.

One aspect of America's spiritual quest is the desire to have life's great questions answered, or at least competently addressed. From its earliest times, Christianity has provided explanations for such mysteries as the existence of pain, the presence of evil, the inevitability of death, the hope of life after death, and the reason for existence. In addition to addressing such issues, the Church provides a practical program for daily living in response to the sometimes difficult events of the crucible of life.

14

JUDICATORY LEADERS IN
THE MISSIONARY CHURCH

All who believed were together and had all things in common.

—Acts 2:44

THIS CHAPTER DESCRIBES the apostolate of the judicatory leader in the denominations of the New Apostolic Age. Although the chapter is based on an example from the Episcopal Church, it has direct application to United Methodists, Evangelical Lutherans, and Roman Catholics because of their episcopal polity. For mainline denominations with congregational polity, the chapter provides an overview of how the judicatory can be used effectively as a coordinating body through which the congregations within its boundary can be transformed into missionary outposts of the "one church" of the judicatory. It also describes how the judicatory can be more effective in aligning and supporting congregational activities.

Characteristics of the Judicatory Apostolate

In the mainline churches with episcopal polity, the authority of the bishop is granted through a line of succession unbroken from the original apostles. By definition, the bishops or other judicatory leaders of the mainline denominations form an apostolate, and yet that function seems to have been lost in the maintenance church of the past century. For the most part, the bishop's primary role has switched to that of chief pastor to the clergy, who in turn serve as pastors to parishioners. Because the focus of the maintenance church is on maintaining itself, pastoral care of its current members is its major concern.

In the missionary church, the bishops or other judicatory leaders regain their role as chief missionaries of the judicatories and their congregations. As such, they symbolize the unity of the judicatory as one church, a role represented among the disciples by St. Paul. Scripture identifies St. Paul as an apostle—that is, as one sent out as a missionary, with authority to establish new churches and select appropriate leaders. In the missionary church, judicatory leaders establish a pastoral system that will allow them to concentrate on their missionary role.

In addition to being a pastor and evangelist, a judicatory leader serves as an administrator and teacher. As administrator, the judicatory leader serves the vision and keeps the judicatory functioning well. As a teacher, he or she goes into the field to instruct, to support the vision, and to remind the congregations of their missionary responsibilities.

The characteristics of the judicatory apostolate are rooted in the apostolic Church and defined by the missionary model. As chief executive of the judicatory, for example, the leader promotes the missionary vision and implements the model that supports it. Therefore, the judicatory apostolate has the characteristics described in the sections that follow. These characteristics reflect those characteristics of the model that were discussed in earlier chapters and that will be further explored in later chapters.

The perspective of the judicatory apostolate is holistic.

In the maintenance model, the perspective of the judicatory leader is reductionistic; that is, he or she is focused on the individual parts of the "great machine" that is the judicatory. The parts in question may be congregations, judicatory institutions, or issues considered apart from their relationships to other congregations, institutions, and issues. This preoccupation with components propels the leader from crisis to crisis, from tangential issue to tangential issue, from micromanaged event to micromanaged event. This perspective was more appropriate in an earlier era when the world was more stable and predictable, and when relationships among parts were more firmly established and clearly definable.

In the missionary model, the perspective of the judicatory leader is holistic. It is less mechanistic and more organic. It uses a systems approach rather than a focus on components. Rather than seeing the judicatory as a collection of congregations, the leader sees it as one church composed of a system of networked, complementary, and integrated missionary outposts dedicated to, and united by, a single vision. As I Corinthians 12:12

reminds us, "For just as the body is one and has many members and all the members of the body, though many, are one body, so it is with Christ." This postmodern perspective on the whole as one entity, consisting of an intricate, intimate, and ever-shifting set of relationships, provides the dynamic quality required to cope with the turbulent and unpredictable change of the new century.

When conceived as one church, the judiciary can bring significant resources to bear for the benefit of a single congregation, offering its members a plethora of opportunities to learn about and grow into a life in Christ. It can help each congregation customize what it can do best to meet the needs of seekers, newcomers, and disciples in its geographical area. Of course, the congregations are in fact one church already, but in the missionary church a common vision reflects the oneness of the judicatory, creating a culture that supports it and a structure that facilitates it. Judicatories may be considered liabilities in a maintenance culture, but they are powerful assets in a missionary culture.

The leadership style of the judicatory apostolate is participatory.

In the maintenance model of the mainline denominations with episcopal polity, the organizational chart is pyramidal, with the bishop at the top and everyone else below at levels of descending power and responsibility. In this autocratic model of functional silos, there is little interaction among departments or functions, and all decisions are made from the top down. The missionary church, by contrast, is based on the servant-leadership model of Robert Greenleaf, in which the bishop's role is primarily to serve the judicatory and its missionary outposts, which he or she does by leading them and acting as a resource for them. Jesus perfectly embodies the Christian model of servant-leadership.

In the missionary church, trust is a seminal goal. Trust develops when a judicatory serves the congregations, rather than vice versa, and when the word of the judicatory leader is kept. Trust is also built through delegation of responsibility and decision-making power to the individuals and entities who are most directly concerned with an area of ministry and who, by virtue of their familiarity with the situation, are most competent to make particular decisions. Missionary bishops empower staff members, clergy, and congregations by giving them authority to make more of the decisions that directly affect them. The vision and the success of the judicatory, as one church, are therefore owned by all the congregations and are not viewed as the province of the bishop alone.

The judicatory apostolate repositions the judicatory leadership and staff to serve as a resource for congregations.

In the missionary church, the function of the judicatory staff is to serve as a resource for the missionary outposts. Thus judicatory leaders and their staff members develop initiatives in concert with the congregations, rather than on their behalf. The judicatory apostolate understands that it works for the congregations, and not vice versa. To some degree, this change exemplifies the collaborative approach that is characteristic of the missionary church rather than the authoritative approach that characterizes the maintenance church. At the same time, this distinction between maintenance and mission flows from the fact that evangelism is effectively accomplished when it is centered in the congregations and supported by the judicatory. Staff members are on call to assist the missionary outposts, but they also take the initiative in visiting the congregations and working with them to develop new projects in support of the vision. Staff members act as a clearinghouse for congregational programs, initiatives, and projects that have wider applications. Staff members also assist the missionary outposts in networking among themselves.

The communication style of the judicatory apostolate is open, receptive, and listening-based.

In the maintenance model, communication is primarily top-down, with a tendency to dictate solutions rather than seek answers. Lecturing, whether in person or in writing, is the preferred method of communication, and feedback is discouraged through the nature of the process itself. In the missionary church, by contrast, communication is across a 360-degree field. Communication flows smoothly up and down reporting lines and across peer positions. As good leaders and good Christians, members of the judicatory apostolate search for alternatives by listening to those most affected by particular issues and decisions and to others whose counsel they trust. Rather than dictating predetermined solutions, members of the judicatory apostolate are open to changing their minds. Feedback related to performance, their own and that of others, is continually sought because one of the judicatory functions is to serve as a resource for the congregations. Improvement in these functions is a constant goal.

The judicatory apostolate chooses new clergy on the basis of the missionary vision.

In the missionary model, potential ordinands are chosen on the basis of their spiritual maturity, their leadership abilities, and their faithfulness to the vision. In selecting potential ordinands and in ordaining clergy, the bishop considers them in light of the requirements of the missionary church and the particular congregations to which they are called. Are they dedicated to making disciples? Are their leadership abilities commensurate with those required by a missionary church? Do they understand and support the missionary vision? Can they translate that vision into reality in their congregations? Do they have a passion for spreading the Good News and growing the Church? Such questions are not easy to answer, and they do complicate the selection of ordinands and the ordination of clergy, but they reflect the standards by which clergy are chosen in the missionary church.

With clergy selection, the judicatory leader suggests that the congregation conduct an analysis of its own potential with respect to the missionary vision, evaluating its missionary opportunity and the requisite talents of the clergy it needs. As in the maintenance model, the leader provides the congregation with the names of prospective clergy, and he or she gives the congregation the counsel it seeks, but in the context of mission and faithfulness to the vision.

When intervening in conflicted congregations, the judicatory apostolate addresses fundamental problems rather than treating symptoms.

For many different reasons, congregations in a denomination with episcopal polity may become conflicted and turn to their bishop for help. In the missionary model, the bishop does more than intervene to settle the immediate conflict. The bishop's perspective goes beyond the status quo, and the bishop's objective extends beyond merely protecting the existing community; therefore, members of the judicatory apostolate begin with a thorough analysis of the situation. They examine the case through the lens of mission, attempting to identify systemic problems in the congregation, problems of which the conflict is only a symptom. The judicatory leader's purpose is to build community in the congregation while preparing it for mission.

For example, congregational conflict in the Episcopal Church usually revolves around the rector, but the rector is seldom the whole problem. Therefore, the judicatory leader addresses the real cause of the congregation's problems. When a rector leaves after a conflict, more work frequently needs to be done to rectify systemic problems; otherwise, the next rector will inherit a dysfunctional system. In the Diocese of Texas, the bishop frequently uses a group of consultants to help congregations identify and address their dysfunctions. In general, problems are easier to identify and solve when there is a judicatory vision to serve as a guide. The absence of a vision can create serious misunderstandings about a congregation's goals.

The judicatory apostolate makes lay appointments on the basis of talent, expertise, and experience.

In the missionary church, the judicatory leader appoints lay leaders who are visionary and entrepreneurial and who are particularly suited to their positions because of their talents, skills, expertise, and experience. These criteria, rather than the candidate's length of tenure or the extent of his or her involvement as a church member, become the basis of an appointment. This shift from seniority to competence is crucial. Because each congregation and institution makes critical decisions in applying the vision, many highly talented leaders of demonstrated ability are required throughout the judicatory. By calling on such leaders, the judicatory takes advantage of the skills the laity have acquired in their business and civic endeavors.

A missionary church requires a much higher degree of leadership and managerial skill than the maintenance church does. Therefore, the governing principle is to use the best lay and clerical talent in the judicatory, seeking the most gifted individuals available. This commitment follows the biblical principle illustrated in the parable of the talents, wherein the master (representing Christ) calls together his servants (representing humankind). The master gives each servant a certain number of talents (a talent, in the ancient world, was a form of currency, but in this parable the talents represent the servants' spiritual, mental, and physical gifts, which include their intelligence, skills, abilities, and other characteristics). The master gives five talents to one servant, two talents to another, and one talent to a third. The master leaves after asking his servants to invest their talents. When he returns, he discovers that two of the servants have doubled their talents; therefore, these two have been equally faithful in putting their talents to good use. But the third servant has literally hidden his talent, refusing to invest it in the world. The master rewards the first two servants for being good and faithful. He gives them even more than they had before. But he punishes the third by taking away all the talents he was given. This parable teaches that Christians are expected to use their talents in service to Christ and to be equally faithful in their offerings regardless of the size of their talents. Those who are most talented are expected to do more, but all are expected to do something.

The judicatory apostolate delegates pastoral duties.

In the missionary model of denominations with episcopal polity, the bishop serves as chief pastor and chief missionary, but he or she delegates pastoral duties to a bishop suffragan or otherwise develops a system to deal effectively with pastoral concerns. This delegation of pastoral duties allows the judicatory leader to focus on evangelism. Even so, the bishop ensures that clergy members have access to every form of pastoral care they need, from self-evaluation to crisis support to continuing education to counseling and encouragement.

In the judicatory apostolate, budgeting and other financial decisions are made on the basis of the vision.

In the maintenance model, growth is not a driving factor in church decisions. Good, steady operation is the goal, and so the general procedure for developing the budget of a judicatory is to base it on the budget for the previous year. The proposed budget may reflect small changes related to increased or decreased contributions and to minor programmatic shifts. Commitments to subsidize certain congregations, even when such subsidies have continued for years without congregational growth, go unchallenged.

In the missionary church, by contrast, budgeting and other financial decisions are based on a set of criteria that flow from the vision. Here are some of the major budgeting principles of the missionary church:

○ The allocation of financial resources is analyzed annually in light of the vision, rather than in terms of the previous year's budget. Resources are allocated to proposed projects and activities that support the vision. Funding is increased, as necessary, for judicatory-based missionary projects that assist congregations and other judicatory institutions.

○ Accountability is an important consideration in the allocation of funds, which are invested where they will do the most good—that is, where the projected return will be highest in terms of making disciples, creating miraculous expectation and glorious transformation, and reaching the unchurched.

○ All allocations are considered in light of other allocations, with the goal of creating synergy among judicatory-based projects. As necessary, funds and projects may be reallocated, or programs may be redesigned.

○ Growing congregations and large churches are acknowledged, supported, and honored. Small congregations are assisted, and ways to develop their growth are planned. Often the judicatory can make a huge difference in the lives of smaller congregations (see Chapter Ten).

○ Declining or static congregations are not subsidized year after year, and alternative means of providing leadership are developed (again, see Chapter Ten).

In the judicatory apostolate, strategic planning is vision-based and extensive.

The term *planning,* in the maintenance church, usually refers to programmatic or maintenance planning aimed at tweaking the existing system. The vision of the maintenance church is the status quo, slightly improved;

therefore, the goals of the maintenance church are modest. Even so, usually there are no strategies to achieve the goals and no tactics to implement the strategies.

In the missionary church, by contrast, practical strategic planning is based on a compelling vision. The planning system is designed to meet the needs of a growing judicatory and its missionary outposts. With the vision as a guide, explicit goals are established, strategies are developed, and tactics are identified. In accordance with goal-setting theory, the goals of the missionary church are specific, challenging (that is, not easily achieved), reachable (but with effort and through miraculous expectation), embraced by congregational members of the judicatory, and monitored through feedback. Feedback is provided regularly to the clergy and the laity. Therefore, those who are in the missionary outposts, trying to achieve the goals established by the vision, know when they are succeeding, where they need to make improvements, and what more they have to do in order to be successful.

The judicatory apostolate reorients outreach programs, Christian education, and youth ministry throughout the judicatory toward living the vision and making disciples.

Outreach is that portion of the church's work that is conducted beyond its member community and that is primarily directed to people in extraordinary need (the poor, the sick, the disabled, the imprisoned, and the homeless). Many times, outreach is an indirect form of evangelism, as in an after-school program. It is a living out of the core Christian value to love. In the maintenance church, outreach grants are made and programs are developed without a strategic plan. As a result, the outreach program often consists of a group of uncoordinated projects. By contrast, in the missionary church, outreach programs are purposefully integrated to create synergy as part of a strategic plan that supports the vision. Congregations are intentionally networked by the judicatory, and good work and achievements are publicized and praised. Congregations are challenged, as one church, to implement the judicatory vision through their outreach programs.

In the maintenance church, judicatory-developed programs are generally either refinements of existing programs or new ventures that have been tried in other congregations or denominations. In the maintenance model of the Episcopal Church, for example, youth education centers on diocesan youth groups and chaplaincies in colleges. The congregational youth groups and the college chaplaincy in the maintenance model are primarily designed to serve Episcopalians. Youth are viewed as the "church of tomorrow," which means that young people are seen but not heard, and that they are present but not involved in any outwardly focused mission. At best, they may make mission trips to help others, but these trips are more like group pleasure excursions, with sponsors and a chaplain as leaders. No leadership for congregational mission is offered or expected.

In the judicatories of the missionary church, by contrast, programs are developed on the basis of a comprehensive analysis of judicatory and congregational needs and resources. Programs are designed to empower congregations to implement the vision and to make disciples. Christian education, for example, is expanded to include discipleship and mission. Youth ministry (rather than youth education) is reconstituted to train and deploy youth ministers throughout the congregations of the judicatory and to train youth for evangelism. Rather than serving only the students of their own denominations, university chaplains become missionaries to all students and faculty and attempt to train students and faculty to be missionaries. In the missionary church, youth are viewed as the "church of today," which means, in a practical sense, that they are actively engaged in the mission of the Church and have been commissioned for the task of making disciples. A youth program for high school or college students is not judged successful merely if a good number of the denomination's faithful attend; rather, a youth initiative is considered successful when the objective of making active disciples of the unchurched has been met. (Outreach, Christian education, and youth ministry in the missionary church are discussed in more detail in Chapter Sixteen.)

The judicatory apostolate understands the importance of communication in making disciples and uses communication to the greatest possible advantage.

In the maintenance model, the principal means of communication at the judicatory level is the judicatory newspaper, which generally functions either as a "meeting obituary" (recording events that have already occurred) or as a flyer for events to come. The newspaper's contents may not be effectively integrated, and the paper often records, in excruciating detail, events that are not newsworthy.

In the missionary church, the judicatory newspaper is only part of a comprehensive communication package that integrates print and electronic media to advance the vision. The newspaper is lively, readable, and informative. It supports the vision by regularly reporting news items about miraculous expectation, glorious transformation, and the development of initiatives to reach all sorts and conditions of people. The newspaper also reports on forthcoming events and activities that support the vision so that church members have time to plan their own participation, and it explains why these events are important. The newspaper is more than just an organ of the judicatory, however. It also reports on news, issues, and concerns that are of importance to all members of the judicatory community. The Diocese of Texas, for example, in addition to a newspaper, produces brochures, videos, and advertising campaigns for the diocese, as one church, and for its missionary outposts. The diocese also maintains a site on the World Wide Web that includes a diocesan chat room. (Such communications are covered in more detail in Chapter Fifteen.)

The judicatory apostolate sees congregational development as critical to the vision and work of the Church.

In the missionary church, congregational development is a central part of the vision and of the work carried out by the judicatory and its congregations. Congregational development has three goals: to plant new congregations, to grow existing congregations, and to reverse the trend in declining congregations. (Congregational development is discussed in more detail in Chapter Ten.)

In the missionary church, the purpose of the bishop's visitation is multifaceted and strategic.

The purposes of visitations by the bishop are to baptize, confirm, and/or receive, to consult with congregational leaders, and to meet with members of the vestry (the congregation's governing board). The purpose of the bishop's meetings with the vestry is to continue nurturing its members in understanding and supporting the vision, to assure them of continued diocesan support, and to solicit their input regarding the needs of their congregation. The bishop asks the vestry for a briefing on congregational activities, explores how the missionary outposts can further the vision, and, implicitly, raises issues of accountability and performance. The meeting also provides lay leaders with a splendid and timely opportunity to ask the bishop questions about the diocese and the larger Church beyond.

In mainline denominations with congregational polity, the same strategic function applies. Because the missionary model is vision-driven, the judicatory leader reinforces the vision across the congregations of the judicatory, meeting with lay leaders to emphasize the judicatory as one church and the congregations as its missionary outposts.

Choosing Judicatory Leaders

It would seem that those individuals most likely to be effective as bishops or other judicatory leaders in the missionary church are men and women who understand complex systems, who appreciate the focusing power of a well-articulated vision, and who are open to feedback and continuous learning. Working as rector or chief pastor of a resource church is one way to gain experience with complex systems. In a world of turbulent and unpredictable change, lifetime learning is a crucial component of effectiveness.

In addition to having an understanding of complex systems and a need for continuous learning, bishops or other judicatory leaders required by denominations in the New Apostolic Age should have the following characteristics:

○ They are guided by a vision and dedicated to mission.

○ They are committed to church growth and to welcoming seekers and newcomers as part of that growth.

○ They are willing to be held accountable, before the laity and the clergy of the judicatory and its missionary congregations, for the failure to grow.

○ They are effective as a change agent who can initiate or support the missionary model.

○ They are willing to take risks and fail.

○ They are capable of building a highly competent staff, both professional and volunteer, whose members have different abilities and perspectives and from whom honest input is sought.

○ They are able to identify and call forth extraordinarily capable laypeople to provide assistance at the judicatory and congregational levels.

○ They are willing and able to delegate.

○ They are able to use teams, to trust the staff, and to flatten the organization by moving decision-making authority downward. A judicatory leader cannot micromanage the vision. The vision is an overarching concept, not a detailed road map. It brings forth change, learning, and adaptation, all of which are enhanced when more people are empowered to participate.

○ They are dedicated to working very hard. The position of judicatory leader is not just a denominational honor or a career capstone. It is a strenuous, often difficult, and invariably time-consuming job in the missionary church.

As in the maintenance model, the leader of a judicatory in the missionary model must be spiritually grounded in a powerful way, as well as pastorally sensitive. Table 14.1 summarizes the different roles that the judicatory leader plays in the maintenance and missionary models of mainline

Table 14.1. Functions of Judicatory Leaders in the Maintenance Model and the Judicatory Apostolate in the Missionary Model.

Judicatory Leader's Function	Maintenance Model	Missionary Model
Primary role	Chief pastor	Chief missionary; chief teacher, evangelist, and vision communicator; chief pastor responsible for developing a pastoring system
Perspective	The judicatory as a collection of congregations; reductionistic	The judicatory as one church of networked missionary outposts united by a single missionary vision; systems-oriented; holistic
Leadership style	Hierarchical model; loyalty expected	Servant-leadership model; participatory; trust-driven
Communication style	Top-down; dictate; lecture; feedback not sought	Two-way; listen; teach; feedback solicited
Clergy performance standard	Loyalty to the judicatory leader	Clear performance objectives based on the vision; accountability for meeting performance objectives
Ordination of new clergy	Licensing professional clergy	Commissioning missionary leaders
Selecting potential ordinands	Select on the basis of spiritual maturity	Select on the basis of spiritual maturity, leadership abilities, and commitment to evangelism
Congregation in conflict	Intervene and settle immediate conflict	Resolve systemic causes rather than symptoms of conflict; provide a larger perspective related to community and mission; use outside consultants, when necessary, to resolve problems
Board appointments	Reward active, visible members with appointments, regardless of their skills or community leadership roles	Seek leaders who support the vision, are entrepreneurial, talented, experienced, and capable, and who are leaders in their communities

Table 14.1. Functions of Judicatory Leaders in the Maintenance
Model and the Judicatory Apostolate in the Missionary Model, Cont'd.

Judicatory Leader's Function	Maintenance Model	Missionary Model
Pastoral duties	Primary pastor to the clergy	Use delegation and a comprehensive system to address the pastoral needs of the clergy
Budgeting and finance	Develop a budget based on the previous year's; subsidize weaker congregations without a strategy for making them stronger	Analyze the allocation of financial resources; develop accountability for results; support growing congregations; develop strategies to assist weaker congregations; reallocate resources to support the vision; maximize return in accordance with the vision
Planning	Top-down, with little congregational input; usually programmatic or maintenance planning; no strategic or tactical planning	Solicit input from those to be served; initiate strategic planning; establish goals, strategies, and tactics for the judicatory
Clergy selection for congregations	Provide congregations with clergy names and counsel	Analyze the congregation from a missionary perspective and identify specific needs; gather external data and demographics; provide counsel and the names of clergy who are particularly well suited to congregations and their needs
Judicatory-based programs	Design programs to inform and challenge congregations and serve church members	Analyze all programs in terms of the vision and their effectiveness; design programs to inform but also to empower congregations to achieve the vision; serve church members and the unchurched

Table 14.1. Functions of Judicatory Leaders in the Maintenance Model and the Judicatory Apostolate in the Missionary Model, Cont'd.

Judicatory Leader's Function	Maintenance Model	Missionary Model
Christian education	Goals: Encouragement and knowledge	Goals: Discipleship; teach what evangelism is and how to accomplish it; stress spiritual formation
Youth	Program seen as youth education; youth viewed as church of tomorrow; judicatory youth groups; college chaplaincies primarily serve denominational students and faculty	Program seen as youth ministry; youth viewed as church of today; make disciples; train youth for evangelism; train and use youth ministers; appoint missionary college chaplains to serve all students and faculty
Communications	Judicatory newspaper (usually without a cohesive emphasis)	Judicatory newspaper that supports the vision and focuses on the miraculous; web page; e-mail; brochures and videos; advertising campaigns
Judicatory staff	Serve as chaplains; serve congregations in the greatest need	Serve as a resource to all the missionary outposts; solicit congregation's input
Outreach	Make outreach grants without a strategic plan	Develop a strategic plan for outreach funding; challenge congregations to achieve the vision; network congregations; highlight good work and achievement
Renewal	Develop programs to refresh the faithful	Develop programs to refresh the faithful and equip them for evangelism
Congregational development	Nonexistent, or only the judicatory leader is involved	Appoint a director of congregational development; analyze congregations according to type and provide resources accordingly; raise funds for congregational development

Table 14.1. Functions of Judicatory Leaders in the Maintenance Model and the Judicatory Apostolate in the Missionary Model, Cont'd.

Judicatory Leader's Function	Maintenance Model	Missionary Model
Financial development	Nonexistent, or only the judicatory leader is involved	Appoint a director of resource development; center fundraising efforts on evangelism in accordance with the vision; develop a system to increase financial resources and maximize their return in building new churches and in providing resources to diocesan institutions and congregations
Judicatory leader's visit to congregations	Minimal required functions (for example, in the Episcopal Church, baptism, confirmation, reception)	Baptism, confirmation, or reception; consultation with lay and clergy leaders to explore congregational goals, needs, expectations, and questions regarding the vision and other issues

denominations with episcopal polity. In denominations with congregational polity, some of the same functions will apply to the judicatory leader. In either case, the table illustrates the dramatic differences between judicatory leaders in the maintenance church and leaders in the judicatory apostolate of the missionary church.

PART FOUR

OUTREACH

15

COMMUNICATIONS
AND TECHNOLOGY

In the beginning was the Word.

—John 1:1

COMMUNICATION HAS BEEN an integral part of evangelism and the spread of Christianity since the time of Jesus. Imagine Christianity in the first century, or in the twenty-first century, without sermons, parables, or apostolic letters—all forms of communication. Try to imagine it without the word-of-mouth stories that circulated among pagans and the followers of Jesus, stories of many healings, of miracles performed, and of lives transformed. Word of mouth is still important, but new technology also plays a role. Television, radio, and the printed word have supplanted handwritten letters and eloquent speeches to large audiences by the sea. Not only has technology changed, but the audience receiving the words has also changed. Both the media through which the Christian message is delivered and the target of that message have shifted drastically in the last few decades. Both require a strategic reassessment of communication in the mainline churches.

Carol Barnwell joined the staff of the Bishop of Texas in 1992 as editor of the monthly diocesan newspaper, the *Texas Episcopalian*. With Bishop Payne's election, she became director of the diocesan Office of Communications. In light of the new diocesan vision and the shift from a maintenance-minded church to a mission-driven community of miraculous expectation, the Diocese of Texas was forced to redefine its communication effort. To be more specific, the diocese had to decide what the Episcopal Church had to offer its disciples and the unchurched, how the Episcopal Church in the Diocese of Texas would present itself, and how the diocese would communicate with its members and with the larger world. Out of this redefinition effort came a series of strategies developed by the Office of Communications:

○ Every diocesan communication reflects the vision and reinforces it, whether the communication channel is the diocesan Web site (www. epicenter.org), the weekly letter to the deans, or the monthly diocesan newspaper. The communication question is always "How does this story, or this action, or this statement relate to living the vision?"

○ The missionary focus of the Diocese of Texas is a commitment to making disciples, which means reaching the unchurched. Communications are prepared with the unchurched in mind.

○ In attempting to communicate with the unchurched, the diocese assumes no biblical literacy. It "unpacks" the church's language, discarding words that are incomprehensible to the unchurched or burdened with negative connotations. The guiding principle is to simplify the language; it is difficult to simplify too much.

○ Through every channel available, the missionary outposts of the diocese are helped to perceive themselves, along with the other congregations, as one church.

○ Each congregation is taught how to attract coverage from its local media by recognizing and promoting newsworthy stories. As Barnwell points out, "The unchurched are best reached by articles in neighborhood media vehicles."

○ The quality of all diocesan publications, from newspaper to brochures, has been raised in order to make them more effective. When special circumstances demand, outside design consultants are hired to improve the look of diocesan publications.

○ The gifts of the laity are being used. There is a wealth of talent in the pews, and there is a virtual army of people willing to help in communications if they are given the opportunity. For example, Barnwell recently noted a congregational newsletter that was especially well prepared. She called the rector of that congregation to congratulate her on its quality, and the rector said that a new member (of one month) had created the design and that another relatively new member had produced an entire series of pieces for the church's stewardship program, work that would have cost more than $15,000. The latter member ultimately became a member of the diocesan Communications Task Force. Another member of the task force, who owns an advertising agency in East Texas, has been instrumental in producing the diocesan advertising campaign and has donated an extraordinary amount of time and talent to the effort.

○ Communication in the Diocese of Texas is conceived to be broad and inclusive. It encompasses every statement made on behalf of the diocese, whether orally or in writing, and whether delivered from a pulpit or at a keyboard. Information and communications technology, properly exploited, make it possible to weave the diocesan congregations together and permit them to operate as one church.

Thus the single common characteristic of all diocesan communications is an endless reinforcement of the vision. The focused message—of one church of miraculous expectation and glorious transformation dedicated to making disciples—is repeated over and over in every medium available to the diocese. The Diocesan Bishop speaks in sixty pulpits a year and meets with as many vestries, always reminding the clergy and the parishioners of the vision. The Bishops Suffragan follow suit in their own visitations. This dedicated drumbeat is essential to change the entrenched mind-set of a maintenance church and to inculcate the missionary power of first-century Christianity in the congregations of the diocese.

Unpacking the Church's Language

"Unpacking the church's language" means simplifying the language in church publications and replacing Christian jargon so that the meaning of the articles can be understood by anyone, especially the unchurched and the biblically illiterate. Because the diocese intends to speak to the unchurched, it needs to do so in language that the unchurched can understand. For example, what would you make of the following passage?

> There's a major foam pit for "Aerial Nose Bleeds," and it's open to boards, blades, and BMX at the same time. A major wall ride and the famous, huge NISS starter ramp is set up for some major air over the first launch—right into the double spine with a connecting rail.

Are these astronaut John Glenn's journal entries? Not at all. They're taken from a story about in-line skaters and a new place to roller-blade; it is unlikely that the author cares much whether nonskaters understand what he or she has written. Those of us who are not in the market for in-line skates, or who are not looking for a good place to catch "some major air," probably do not care, either. But when it comes to reaching the unchurched, we should care a great deal. To the uninitiated, the language of the church can sound as strange as the phrases "major air" or "a connecting rail" sound to those unfamiliar with the sport of in-line skating. Moreover, "churchspeak" can carry negative connotations as well.

Missionary language is simple, understandable, open, and persuasive. It speaks easily and directly to people, in words that they can understand and on subjects that matter to them. The missionary church offers answers because seekers have questions. It offers comfort because seekers have fears. It offers hope because life without God is unsatisfactory and lonely. The language of the missionary church is filled with stories and metaphors that impart meaning, as the parables of Jesus do. It is devoid of complicated, esoteric phrases that confuse, bewilder, or alarm the unchurched. It is directed at teaching them about the Christian faith and the difference it can make in their lives.

The language of the maintenance church, whether it intends to do so or not, acts like a code that enables members to identify one another and exclude nonmembers. Therefore, it is exclusionary rather than inclusive. It erects barriers to the unchurched instead of removing barriers. It represents a mind-set that belongs to the Age of Christendom, one that is ineffective and counterproductive in the New Apostolic Age. The words of the past do not always speak to people in the present.

In order to explain the Episcopal Church to unchurched visitors, the diocese's Office of Communications "unpacked the language" in a series of five new brochures designed especially for seekers. Words and phrases like *Holy Eucharist* and even *Holy Communion, sacraments,* and *apocrypha* are not necessarily intelligible to or welcoming of the unchurched, and so they were eliminated. The office prepared very basic informational brochures and had them designed by a young graphic artist who was not an active churchgoer. If she had any question about the language, it was back to the keyboard for the writers. This set of brochures is intended to be a conversation starter. It is not intended to answer all the questions a visitor may have. The brochures are titled "Episcopalians," "The Sacraments," "Common Prayer," "Scripture, Tradition, and Reason," and "The Creeds." "Episcopalians" has been translated into Spanish, Chinese, Vietnamese, and Korean. Several of the clergy say that members of their congregations, many of whom are new Episcopalians themselves, use the brochures to tell their friends about the church. In the first nine months after their publication, the diocese sold more than thirty thousand of these brochures across the country.

The Judicatory Newspaper

As already mentioned, in the Diocese of Texas the judicatory newspaper is the *Texas Episcopalian,* a monthly that is 125 years old and is currently edited by Carol Barnwell. Before Bishop Payne's episcopate, it was an average of twelve pages long and consisted mostly of "meeting obituaries," reports of anniversary celebrations, and news of building dedications, with an occasional personal profile. The newspaper provided a good archival record, but its inward focus on events betrayed it as a publication of the maintenance church.

Today the paper averages twenty to twenty-four pages, with shorter articles, multiple authors, and contributions from the missionary outposts. The look of the paper has also changed. It carries the banner "A Community of Miraculous Expectation" to remind the faithful of the vision, and it features articles that exemplify how the vision is being carried out at the congregational level. An article in the May 1998 issue, for example, is titled, "Do We Really Expect the Miraculous?" Throughout the paper, the reader encounters the key words and phrases of the diocesan transformation from maintenance to mission: *community of miraculous expectation, transformation of lives, missionary outposts, the diocese as one church,* and *making disciples.* Stories are written to highlight aspects of the vision—for example, how an after-school program has "reached out to the unchurched" or "transformed lives." The paper is also a means of networking within the diocese because it carries contact names and phone numbers for programs or events that other missionary outposts may want to use.

One of the remarkable things about the vision is the accountability it fosters. The feature titled "Bishop Payne's Journal" is an excellent example of the chief missionary's accountability to his diocese. It recounts Bishop Payne's daily activities and offers a glimpse into his very busy schedule, but it also reveals a compassionate man profoundly involved in his diocese and deeply concerned about its welfare. Daily entries sometimes reflect stories that show the power, purpose, and fulfillment of the vision within the diocese. For example, on November 11, 1998, the bishop wrote, "I had the happy privilege of announcing to them [the members of the Church of the Advent] that on their own initiative and out of a tremendous concern for the Church of the Advent, the good people at Holy Comforter, Angleton, were sending them a check to be applied to their indebtedness. I later discovered that this check amounted to $5,000, a remarkably significant amount as a free-will offering from one missionary outpost to one of its sisters."

Another objective of the Office of Communications is to help communicators at the congregational level recognize the news in their congregations and work closely with neighborhood newspapers and other local media in publicizing it. For example, the communications chair of St. Mark's, in Houston, asked Barnwell to take a photograph of the bishop dedicating St. Mark's new youth building. Barnwell explained that the presence of the bishop did indeed provide an effective photo opportunity, but that the dedication was not the news St. Mark's wanted to communicate to the public, and that the diocesan newspaper was not the only available media vehicle. The more important news, perhaps, was that St. Mark's had even needed a new youth building. What was this missionary outpost doing, to attract so many new families with children? St. Mark's story, Barnwell assured the communications chair, was a story for the neighborhood. She encouraged the chair to invite the editor of the neighborhood newspaper to lunch and tell him or her the story of the new youth building. The chair followed up on the suggestion, and the *Houston Chronicle* ran the photo and the story on the front page of its neighborhood edition the following week.

In the communications arena, the role of the judiciary in serving as a resource to its congregations often takes the form of teaching and training. As in the preceding example, Barnwell spends a lot of time teaching people to recognize the news in their congregations and phrase it in a way that will attract media attention. She says, "I have 80,000 potential stringers out there for the diocesan paper and for the Episcopal Church. I've found many writers in our ranks and have even used a crayon drawing that a four-year-old put into the offering plate one Sunday. The drawing was a note to his grandpa who had recently died."

Three-quarters of the articles in the diocesan newspaper concern forthcoming events so that members of the diocese can become involved and participate; only one-quarter are about events that have already taken place. When articles are published about past events, however, they are not written as minutes of meetings but rather as stories about newsworthy happenings. They also include relevant telephone numbers so that readers can call for more information. Because 60 percent of the members of the Diocese of Texas did not grow up in the Episcopal Church, one of the newspaper's major objectives is to educate its readers about the Episcopal Church, about how it is organized, and about what it does. From time to time an article lays out the responsibilities of the congregation's governing body or explains the seasons of the Church.

Advertising the One Church of the Judicatory

In 1996, the Diocese of Texas began using the media, in a modest but effective way, to foster congregational development. Because unchurched people are most likely to attend worship services either at Christmas or at Easter, the diocese took out a full-page newspaper advertisement in eleven major markets throughout the diocese. The top third of the ad was an invitation to seekers to attend an Episcopal worship service. The bottom two-thirds of the ad listed all the congregations in the geographical region served by the particular newspaper, as well as their service times, addresses, and telephone numbers. The advertisements were intentionally placed in the main or entertainment section of each newspaper rather than in its religious section, in order to increase the likelihood of the ad's reaching the unchurched. The ads have also become a source of encouragement to members of the diocese and a symbol of the unity of the diocese as one church. The smallest congregations receive equal billing with the largest. As Barnwell says, "These advertisements were for our folks as well as for the unchurched. They were a way of saying, 'Look at how many of us there are; we're all part of a bigger church than our own congregation.'" The ads were run again in 1997 and 1998.

In 1997 and 1998, in the weeks just before Ash Wednesday, the diocese also conducted an advertising campaign that used newspapers, radio, and cable television. The purpose of the campaign was to encourage seekers to attend an Episcopal church at a time when many congregations were offering discovery classes. The campaign accomplished several objectives. It raised awareness of the Episcopal Church, interested those who had been thinking about going back to church, and opened conversations with seekers who had questions about faith or spirituality.

The advertisements solicited viewers' questions about the Episcopal Church and invited people who had once attended and those who had never attended to visit an Episcopal congregation. The advertisements provided a toll-free number and included the address of the diocesan Web site. The toll-free number was staffed by trained volunteers and operated twenty-four hours a day during the campaign.

The advertising campaign featured quotations from well-known individuals at the top of their professions, such as Colin Powell and Walter Cronkite, portraying them as people of faith and of the Episcopal faith in particular. Each year, the diocese received more than 150 calls during the three-week campaign period, and traffic on the diocesan home page increased fourfold, to 2,000 hits. In one congregation, a married couple showed up with two adolescent children and told the rector that they had driven by the church for eight years. They had seen the ad recently and, as the father said, "It just got us to thinking." Eight months later, the whole family was baptized and the parents were confirmed. The children are now active in the youth group.

Using the Internet

The diocesan Web site is designed for people who are unfamiliar with the Episcopal Church. The home page, which is warm, welcoming, and filled with pictures, carries this statement: "The Episcopal Church, in the Diocese of Texas, is one church of 156 mission-minded congregations, in the eastern quadrant of Texas, whose focus is on the unchurched. It is a community of miraculous expectation, under the leadership of Christ, welcoming all sorts and conditions of people."

The bishop's welcoming letter is addressed, "Dear Seeker." Subsequent pages attend to the spiritual needs of the cybervisitor by offering daily devotions, a weekly reflection, a sermon, and a place to e-mail prayer requests. Another page provides a glossary of terms and answers to frequently asked questions about the Episcopal Church. The listing of Episcopal churches and schools includes a mapping program that allows the visitor to print a map marking the route from his or her home address to the congregation of choice. Diocesan information and resources are also readily available, but the Web site speaks to the seeker first and is in line with the diocesan vision of making disciples.

The diocesan e-mail forum was one of the most active meetings on Ecunet (an ecumenical e-mail service provider) during the summer of 1998, ranking number five in the month of May out of hundreds of such meetings. Ecunet facilitates meaningful discussions among church members on a number of topics and makes it possible for them to meet many new acquaintances. Several hundred people participate in the meeting.

In combination, e-mail and the diocesan Web site serve a host of functions:

○ They permit rapid, efficient, interactive communication between the bishop and the clergy.
○ They permit rapid, efficient interactive communication between priests and their parishioners and among parishioners, making each congregation a closer community.
○ They allow the diocese to serve as a central resource to all congregations, permitting the smallest congregation to access the same information resources as the largest. Thus they enable congregations with limited funds to take advantage of the best available programmatic resources; rectors of small congregations do not have to reinvent the wheel.
○ They permit both priests and laity of different congregations to meet easily and efficiently in cyberspace, as members of the one church of the diocese, to discuss mutual problems and search for answers, new ideas, and "what works best."
○ They allow individual members of the congregation to study religion, the Bible, spirituality, the Episcopal Church, or almost any related field at any time of the day or night. Links to other sites provide additional resources.

Those who are interested can begin with the simplest lessons and work up to the most advanced.

○ They keep church members informed of the latest developments in the diocese.

Congregational Web sites, which exist for about one-third of the congregations in the Diocese of Texas, also alert members to the latest developments and allow them to comment on present and future issues of importance to the missionary outposts, the priests, and the bishop. Many of the congregations' Web sites were created by volunteers and cost little if anything to maintain. Indeed, as America becomes more and more oriented to the Internet as a primary communication system, the Diocese of Texas is well positioned to continue the conversation that began with the disciples on the shore of Galilee.

16

OUTREACH, CHRISTIAN EDUCATION, AND YOUTH MINISTRY

Like good stewards of the manifold grace of God, serve one another with whatever gift each of you has received.

—I Peter 4:10

OUTREACH IS A MAJOR FUNCTION of the missionary church, a living out of the core Christian value to love God and one's neighbor as oneself. It is a form of evangelism, although an indirect form, and may involve programs that are not designed primarily for evangelism, such as an after-school program or a mother's-day-out facility. In the Diocese of Texas, outreach is the responsibility of the Department of Ministry to Human Needs. The department is responsible for promoting the creation and maintenance of outreach ministries that engage congregations and individuals in service to those who are poor, sick, infirm, underprivileged, or troubled. The two primary functions of the department are to promote human-needs ministries by providing consultation, linkage, education, and recognition and to administer grants to agencies and programs in the diocese that actively engage church members in service delivery.

Outreach Programs

Many outreach programs in the Diocese of Texas are carried out by the missionary outposts, but several programs are creations of the diocese and are available throughout the diocese. These programs are of special interest because they exemplify the diocese in action as one church. Because the scope of such programs is beyond the ability of one congregation to handle, several congregations must come together on these projects, or the diocese itself must make resources available. The initiatives discussed in the following passages were developed through a coordinated, vision-based program of new ministries and expansions of existing ministries. They illustrate the broad range of outreach opportunities that blossom in the missionary church when congregations view themselves as one church, and when members live in miraculous expectation. Each is a powerful reflection of the missionary church and of the diocesan vision of miraculous expectation and glorious transformation. The particular initiatives described in this chapter either were begun after Bishop Payne's election as Bishop Coadjutor or were so dramatically transformed that they were virtually re-created in terms of their effect on the lives of the people they serve. Early in his episcopate, Bishop Payne saw the need for increased outreach as part of the vision and so undertook to bring it about. Of course, many outreach ministries have been developed in the diocese over the decades.

Each of the outreach programs described in this chapter was a result of the missionary vision of the Diocese of Texas. Three of the programs required substantial funding; two did not. Each meets a specific set of needs and was inspired by the vision of the diocese as one church. Miraculous expectation played a part in some of the funding, and glorious transformation played a part in all the results. Programs such as these can be developed in any judicatory of the mainline Church, whether that judicatory is wealthy or not. These kinds of programs are not fundamentally about money. They are about evangelism, the Great Commandment, and living in expectation that the Holy Sprit will inspire and enable the faithful to achieve the impossible—that is, the miraculous.

Episcopal Health Charities

On the day it was created, in 1997, Episcopal Health Charities (EHC) became the largest philanthropy in Houston devoted exclusively to assessing and enhancing community health. EHC was created to meet the diverse health needs of the diocese, especially the needs of indigent and underserved people, through needs assessment and grants. EHC's goal is to provide care for the ill and, more important, lifelong health and well-being. EHC was created through the restructuring of St. Luke's Episcopal Hospital (a diocesan institution, and home of the renowned Texas Heart Institute) into the St. Luke's Health System, of which EHC became one component. Income from $150 million in hospital reserve funds was allocated to the new charity, which was thereby provided with the equivalent of an endowment in the same amount. Through the new charity, it became possible to expand existing diocesan programs and to create new programs that were complementary to or synergistic with established programs. By encouraging applications for multicongregational projects, EHC has provided another incentive for congregations throughout the diocese to work together as one church. In 1998, about half of the EHC grants were to programs that involved the missionary outposts. Episcopal Health Charities is thus a highly visible arm of the unity of congregations in the Diocese of Texas. It is also a powerful symbol of the diocesan vision and of the missionary spirit that has infused the diocese. By reaching out to so many of the poor and underserved, EHC sends a powerful message of love and compassion, potentially recasting the public perception of the Episcopal Church in Texas.

Lord of the Streets Episcopal Church

Lord of the Streets Episcopal Church is another outreach ministry that exemplifies the power of the diocese as one church to transform human lives. This ministry was begun in 1990 by Trinity Church, in Houston, as an outreach program to help homeless people in the midtown area. In 1993, the Diocese of Texas recognized the ministry as a special evangelical mission of the diocese. In 1997, the ministry received a grant of $1.3 million from Episcopal Health Charities to renovate and convert an 18,000-square-foot building across from Trinity Church into a health care facility for the indigent and a recovery center for thirty-one homeless men. In a small meeting of homeless people at the recovery center, the men were asked, "What is your favorite verse from the Bible?" One of the men who had come off the street looked up and said, "When I was hungry, you fed me; when I was naked, you clothed me; when I was sick, you visited me."

Lord of the Streets is now supported by nine congregations in the diocese, whose volunteers take turns serving breakfast to more than 120 homeless people every Sunday. Services provided by the new center supplement those that were offered before. They include help with housing, with educational and occupational needs, with recovery, with psychological needs, with medical, dental, and health care, with spiritual issues, with legal needs, and with the needs of daily living.

Community of Hope

St. Luke's Community of Hope, established in 1994 by the Department of Pastoral Care and Education of St. Luke's Episcopal Hospital, trains volunteer lay chaplains to serve in health care settings, local congregations, and other places in the community. As lay chaplains, members of the Community of Hope extend caring to those in need and provide spiritual nourishment and encouragement during times of stress, change, and crisis. Through compassionate, empathetic listening, lay chaplains journey with those experiencing illness and recovery, helping them strengthen their faith and supporting them as they search for God's mercy, grace, love, and power. People of every faith are welcome to join the community.

This ministry is a source of glorious transformation for those who serve as lay chaplains as well as for those who are served. It confronts so directly and so intimately the great issues of life—pain, suffering, death, fear, love, faith, and hope—that one cannot participate in it and be unmoved. Spiritual resurrections are the province of such work, as are profound changes within the soul that are wonders to all who witness them: "I call upon you, O Lord; come quickly to me" (Psalm 141:1). Someone who is dying is miraculously cured; someone who is hating learns to forgive; someone who is broken is healed even though she dies. Courage and faith—their display and their acquisition—have made this ministry deeply rewarding to those in the Diocese of Texas whose commitment to Christ has led them in this special direction: "Jesus turned, and seeing her he said, 'Take heart, daughter; your faith has made you well'" (Matthew 9:22).

Camp Allen Expansion

Camp Allen, sixty miles northwest of Houston on eight hundred wooded acres, is a camp and conference center of the Diocese of Texas. Every year it hosts thirty-nine thousand guests, half of whom are unchurched. At a cost of $12.3 million, the diocese has instituted a three-phase renovation and expansion project, to be completed in 2004. The project will mean an expanded conference center, the new All Saints' Chapel, additional meeting rooms, 103 more guest rooms, an equestrian center, a new fitness center, a fourth camp site designed especially for handicapped and special-needs groups, "family" houses for small retreats and family gatherings, a seventy-five-acre lake for fishing and boating, a spiritual retreat center, and three quiet houses.

The House of Bishops of the Episcopal Church met at Camp Allen in the spring of 1999. "The entire expansion of Camp Allen is a broadening of ministry and is a result of the unfolding of the vision of one church reaching out to the unchurched," explains the Reverend David Thames, executive director. "We see our prime mission as being a gathering place for one church and as a port of entry for those guests who are not currently

attending church." A young mother and military officer who was participating in a U.S. Air Force organizational training event at Camp Allen
told Father Thames that neither she nor her husband had attended church
since their teens; after spending a week at the camp, however, it felt like
"holy ground" to her, she said. She and her husband plan to return to the
camp to have their nine-month-old baby baptized, and they have begun
to attend an Episcopal church near their home, in Arizona. "This could
not have happened without all the factors which are Camp Allen working together to create the atmosphere of sanctuary," the executive director believes.

The expansion of Camp Allen reflects the vision of the diocese in its
primary role of making disciples. Because it is relatively close to the geographical center of the diocese, the facility can function as a gathering
space for meetings of the "one church," including the annual Diocesan
Council. With expanded facilities and 150 guest rooms, it can accommodate secular conferences as well and can introduce those who are unchurched to a sense of the sacred that permeates the wooded site. But the
expansion of Camp Allen also reflects a financial reality. For years, the
camp had run at an annual deficit of approximately $250,000, which had
been compensated for by funds from other sources. With the new additions, Camp Allen will be able to host larger conferences and operate on
a year-round basis. It is projected to become self-funding two years after
the expansion, from revenues associated with the services and programs
that it provides.

Through a strategic alliance with an executive training firm, the camp
will offer executive retreats and corporate training for companies and will
include guided instruction through its Challenge Course. The traditional
summer camping programs are being expanded to run on a year-round
basis, and the summer program will include both family and elder hostel
programs. When the expansion is complete, Camp Allen is projected to
host eighty thousand visitors per year, or about double its present capacity. This also means that the Episcopal Church, as a denomination, will
have a facility large enough to host the major gatherings of its leaders,
(such as the House of Bishops) and of its lay leaders and clergy meeting
in convention or at conferences.

All Saints' Chapel, designed in the shape of a cross, was constructed in
1999. It seats approximately sixteen hundred people for worship services
and other gatherings and features an entire floor of meeting rooms below
its sanctuary, which is cantilevered over a hill. This compelling symbol of
the Christian faith is central to life at Camp Allen and communicates a
powerful sense of the sacred to all who visit. Towering and awe-inspiring,

All Saints' Chapel is a touchstone for people seeking to rediscover their faith or to find it for the first time.

Spiritual Development Program

The Committee for Diocesan Spiritual Development was created in 1995 as the Committee for Clergy Spiritual Development. The Gathering of the Diocese (see Chapter Six) revealed a great hunger among the laity for additional opportunities for spiritual formation, and so the committee was renamed and its work was expanded to include laity as well as clergy. Later it became the Division of Spiritual Formation, and as such it ministers directly to the spiritual needs of the faithful and the spiritual yearnings of the unchurched by providing educational opportunities in spirituality and spiritual formation as well as enhanced opportunities for reflection, prayer, and spiritual direction. The division offers a program known as Formation in Direction (FIND) to train spiritual directors and sponsors forums on spiritual development, retreats for clergy and laity, and quiet days in various locations. It also produces a directory of spiritual directors and will produce or sponsor programs related to its mission at the regional, convocational, and congregational levels.

Diocesan Outreach

The position of diocesan outreach coordinator was created in 1996 and filled by Sally Rutherford. Her primary responsibility is to act as a resource for congregations by serving as a clearinghouse for information on congregational outreach programs that could find wider application in the diocese. Under her direction, the first attempt in diocesan history to list and categorize all the outreach ministries of the diocese was undertaken. As a result, the *Directory of Outreach Ministries* was published, and a diocesan database was established. The diocesan outreach coordinator has the following responsibilities:

- Organizing, compiling, and updating information on the outreach ministries of the diocese
- Providing consultation to congregations, meetings of the Episcopal Church Women, outreach committees, clericus meetings, and interfaith coalitions
- Collecting and disseminating materials on outreach ministries
- Identifying possible funding for special programs from agencies outside the diocese

○ Educating the congregations about outreach grants that are available to them from the diocesan Department of Ministry to Human Needs

○ Working with members of Episcopal Church Women and with community groups to implement new initiatives, as directed by the Diocesan Council

○ Maintaining the *Directory of Outreach Ministries* as a resource for local congregations

○ Directing articles about outreach ministries to the *Texas Episcopalian*

○ Arranging for networking among the various missionary outposts so that they can participate as one church in large outreach projects exceeding the resources of any single congregation.

Christian Education

Christianity involves the heart, mind, and soul; it is intellectual, emotional, and spiritual. But it is primarily experiential. It is the experience of the living God in the life of believers that is mystical, miraculous, and ultimately transformational. The function of Christian education is to teach the richness and power of the Christian faith and how to apply its principles to daily life. Intelligent faith in God's power grows with an understanding of Scripture and tradition. Ignorance of Christian teachings, which is prevalent even among church members, is a serious drawback to experiencing the glorious promise of Christianity. It hampers Christians in their spiritual quest and frustrates them in their efforts to realize the full potential of their faith. The all-encompassing nature of Christianity and its power for personal transformation elude those who are not grounded in its principles. Inadequate knowledge also makes it difficult for mainline Christians to counter the simplistic pronouncements of proselytizing literalists because they lack the biblical understanding to do so. Many Christians are like people who are trying to put together a jigsaw puzzle, but with too many missing parts to make sense of the whole.

The missionary church has always been educational. From the beginning, it taught people about Jesus, about the Resurrection, and about life everlasting. Christian education is a major avenue through which the unchurched, as well as church members, find answers to their spiritual questions. An appreciation of the importance of Christian education among members of the Diocese of Texas was reflected in the results of the 1995 diocesan survey, *Shaping the Future*. That survey identified the three top priorities of diocesan members as evangelism, youth, and Christian education.

Christian education of adults and children is central to evangelism because it is part of the process by which new disciples are created and existing disciples grow in knowledge and commitment. Christian education is a central experience of Christian life and worship, not an adjunct experience. According to Arias and Johnson (1992, p. 20), it is "no less than the evangelization of each generation, learning together the way of the kingdom, in a community of disciples, at each stage in life and throughout all of the experiences of life, and in each particular context. Disciples are not born, they are made." It is often through small affinity groups—of Bible students, single mothers, senior high school students, recently divorced people—that a sense of community and belonging is most deeply felt in the congregation. From this sense of community and its accompanying spirituality, Christians find satisfaction for the spiritual longing of their souls.

With the casting of the new diocesan vision, the Division of Christian Education in the Diocese of Texas began an analytical process to determine what its unique role would be in support of that vision. In the process, it addressed three specific issues:

1. What were the basic functions of the division—in other words, how might it be defined?
2. What was the unique work that the division was called to do?
3. How could the division most productively and effectively serve the missionary outposts in support of the diocesan vision?

Kathy Barrow is the Christian education coordinator, the ministry staff person in charge of Christian education for the diocese. When she became coordinator, under Bishop Payne, she initiated scheduled visits to all the congregations in the diocese, something that had never been done before. Over a two-year period, she visited every missionary outpost to talk with Christian education leaders, solicit their advice, determine their needs, and explain the resources that the diocese could make available to them. Her goals were to find out what the missionary outposts needed and wanted from the diocese and to make the clergy, vestry, and church leaders aware of the diocese as a resource for their congregations.

After three years of study and analysis, the division determined that its mission was to train Christian educators, bring people and resources together, and develop educational training programs in support of the diocesan vision. The new brochure for the diocesan Division of Christian Education features these words on the cover: "The Division of Christian Education exists to serve you . . . members of the diocese."

The shift from maintenance to mission in Christian education required several significant changes:

o The Christian education coordinator became a member of the ministry staff, which afforded regular interaction with the bishop.

o A policymaking board, which previously had directed the Christian education coordinator, instead became a working board of lay and clergy who functioned as a think tank for the congregations and as a design team for various projects. By meeting with congregations in their geographical areas, board members extend the network of people who can train and provide resources to others.

o When the diocese is conceptualized as one church, whose function is to make disciples who make disciples, the role of Christian education becomes more focused. The division began to examine differences in needs related to Christian education among congregations of different sizes. It also began to develop a new strategic plan for Christian education.

The Coordinator continues to follow a three-year cycle of visits to every congregation, covering a total of thirty thousand miles per year, to stay in touch with diocesan needs. She is also present at every major diocesan function.

The objectives of the diocesan Christian education office clearly reflect the diocesan vision. They are as follows:

o Train Christian education leaders who can provide training and support for educators at the congregational level

o Develop new training resources

o Support and encourage directors of Christian education in their ministry of planning and teaching

o Consult with smaller congregations to revitalize static or declining Christian education programs

o Develop programs for faith formation and education of children and adults

o Conduct individual congregational training events

o Provide assistance to the congregations in identifying those in the Body of Christ who are called to teach

o Bring people together with people

o Bring people together with resources

The Division of Christian Education carries these objectives out in a variety of ways. For example, the division is actively engaged in designing training programs for leaders and teachers in the missionary outposts, programs that focus on the missionary nature of the diocese and on its critical need to equip disciples to make disciples. Because there is a turnover rate of approximately 50 percent annually among Sunday school teachers, extensive training is required each summer for the Sunday schools alone. During Bishop Payne's episcopate, the number of full- and part-time directors of Christian education in the missionary outposts has increased from twenty-seven to sixty-three, with six more congregations seeking people to fill vacant positions. Smaller missionary outposts are also discovering the importance of having highly skilled, well-qualified directors of Christian education and are being creative in financing those positions. Moreover, networking is a strategy that has proven to be one of the most effective ways of empowering the laity for ministry and strengthening the diocese as one church. A new diocesan directory of Christian education directors and youth ministers in the 156 missionary outposts makes it easier for Christian educators to interact with their counterparts when they have questions, concerns, or innovative ideas. The Division of Christian Education also operates a resource library that houses Christian education material, which can be checked out by the missionary outposts. It includes such resources as curriculum samples, sacramental materials, study aids, teacher training guides, vacation Bible school samples, arts-and-crafts idea books, and videos. Finally, in its role as a congregational resource, the Division of Christian Education also conducts numerous conferences and workshops, such as an educators' conference for the entire diocese, regional and convocational workshops, curriculum discovery workshops, spring and fall retreats for educational directors, and individual church training events.

In 1999, the division opened its new Christian Education Leadership Center. The center's purpose is to train Christian education leaders for every missionary outpost, regardless of size, and to certify directors of Christian education. Reallocation of training dollars will make possible a training cycle that begins in August and continues monthly through May. Training will be offered at the novice, intermediate, and advanced levels. In order to address the nationwide shortage of religious education directors, the facility will certify directors of Christian education through its yearlong, college-level certification program. There are only about fifty Christian education directors available in the United States at any given time (that is, there are only about fifty who are looking for new positions), and there are only thirty-seven paid Christian education directors in the diocese, a total that includes those at program-size and resource-size churches. The diocesan goal is to train enough leaders so that each congregation can have at least one who is competent and comfortable in the role of Christian educator.

Youth Ministry

In the maintenance model, youth education is a program, and young people are considered the church of tomorrow. In the missionary model, youth ministry is fundamental to the work of the diocese, and young people are viewed as the church of today.

Gay Stricklin is the youth ministry coordinator for the Diocese of Texas. In the maintenance model, the main functions of that position were to organize church lock-ins and big youth retreats. The coordinator was hired and directed by a board and had little interaction with the bishop or the rest of the diocesan staff.

With the change from maintenance to mission in the Diocese of Texas, the coordinator became a member of the diocesan ministry staff and so enjoys regular interaction with the bishop. She is responsible for coordinating all youth ministry events, including those for adults involved in youth ministry. She serves as a field resource for vestries, rectors, vicars, and youth committees who want to hire youth ministers or start up or improve youth programs. The responsibilities of the youth ministry advisory board have also been changed so that the board functions as a resource for the coordinator.

In the past, diocesan youth events were often in competition with congregational programs, or sometimes they were substitutes for them. Now events are vision-based and are designed to complement and encourage local youth ministry in every congregation. Before the vision, there were approximately twelve paid youth ministers in the diocese, and they received little support or pastoral care. Five years later, there were more than fifty paid youth ministers linked by a strong support network with deliberate programming for their training and pastoral support.

The mission statement of the Division of Youth is "Under the guidance of the Holy Spirit, the Division of Youth seeks to help young people and those adults who work with them to know Christ and make Him known in the world." The Division of Youth is committed to working with all missionary outposts in the diocese to support their efforts in youth ministry. To that end, the division conducts the following activities:

- o Provides discipleship, evangelism, leadership, and renewal opportunities for youth
- o Develops and implements skills and theological training, pastoral care, and professional development and support for all adults who work with youth

○ Offers print, video, and audio resources through the diocesan resource library that can be used for youth ministry programming,
education, and training

○ Networks and communicates with Province VII (a geographical
grouping of Episcopal dioceses that includes the Diocese of Texas)
and the national church to provide youth ministry information,
personnel, and programs

○ Through the office of the diocesan youth coordinator, offers professional consultation, programming, and support that seeks to
meet the needs of clergy and lay leaders of congregations throughout the diocese

○ Communicates with all people involved in youth ministry by producing publications, workshops, and networking opportunities

Two examples illustrate the kinds of changes that were made as a result of the comprehensive analysis of the Division of Youth's role in the
new diocesan vision. The Episcopal Youth Community (EYC) council was
an annual youth event that had been in place for more than twenty years.
It was primarily a discussion of issues in a legislative setting modeled after
the Diocesan Council. The Division of Youth checked this model against
its goals and its mission statement and found that there was not much discipleship, evangelism training, or leadership development going on at the
EYC council. As a result, the event was restructured to develop leadership
and evangelism skills, and it was renamed the Christian Leadership Conference. Eighteen youth and five adults from across the diocese, known as
the design team, now plan this week-long event, which has an annual
theme. The design team invites a speaker to do the teaching and recruits
some thirty college students and adults to lead workshops that provide
specific education and training on various subjects related to the theme.
The youth plan and execute all the daily worship services, fellowship activities, dorm arrangements, and pre-event publicity and recruitment. The
youth decided that it was important to them and to the diocese to have a
bishop present, and so they invited Bishop Suffragan Leopoldo Alard to
be an adult sponsor. The fact that the Bishop Suffragan agreed to come
for the week was indicative of the importance of the youth ministry to the
diocese.

The second example of a change in the Division of Youth that was driven by the vision is the new Center for Youth Ministry, which opened in
September 1998. The purpose of the center is to provide affordable, comprehensive, year-round skills training and theological education for all
adults in the diocese who work with youth. The center is open to paid

youth ministers, volunteer sponsors, parents, Sunday school teachers, acolyte wardens, junior Daughters of the King sponsors, and others involved with youth. It is a center without walls, a movable program currently housed in one of the smaller churches in the diocese. The center has a paid faculty composed of professional and volunteer youth ministers, college professors, and professionals in the field of adolescent psychology. The program includes training in four areas: adolescent psychology and spiritual development, youth ministry tools, the Bible and the Episcopal Church, and personal growth and development. Training is available at the beginner, intermediate, and professional levels.

The success of the Division of Youth in meeting the challenge of the missionary church can be attributed to four factors:

1. The bishop allowed the division the freedom it needed to try new initiatives, and he provided the support that the division needed in order to cope with failure as well as achieve success.

2. The vision provided a focus for the division in making its decisions and designing its activities.

3. Laypeople have been involved and empowered, and all programs are led by laity.

4. The bishop and the diocese have encouraged youth to come forward and participate actively in the life of the diocese and in the fulfillment of its vision.

EPILOGUE

Do not be afraid; from now on you will be catching people.

—Jesus Christ to Simon Peter (Luke 5:10)

AND SO LET US RECALL here how this book began, with a passage from the Gospel of Luke (5:1–10):

Once while Jesus was standing beside the lake of Gennesaret, and the crowd was pressing in on Him to hear the Word of God, He saw two boats there at the shore of the lake; the fishermen had gone out of them and were washing their nets. He got into one of the boats, the one belonging to Simon, and asked him to put out a little way from the shore. Then He sat down and taught the crowds from the boat. When He had finished speaking, He said to Simon, "Put out into the deep water and let down your nets for a catch." Simon answered, "Master, we have worked all night long but have caught nothing. Yet if You say so, I will let down the nets." When they had done this, they caught so many fish that their nets were beginning to break. So they signaled their partners in the other boat to come and help them. And they came and filled both boats, so that they began to sink. But when Simon Peter saw it, he fell down at Jesus' knees, saying, "Go away from me, Lord, for I am a sinful man!" For he and all who were with him were amazed at the catch of fish that they had taken; and so also were James and John, sons of Zebedee, who were partners with Simon. Then Jesus said to Simon, "Do not be afraid; from now on you will be catching people."

The story of Jesus and the miracle of the catch is profoundly relevant to the contemporary Church. It can be read as a metaphor that is both an explanation of and a call for what the denominations in the New Apostolic Age might be as a missionary church committed to "catching people." The parable begins with an example of inappropriate behavior. It says that the fishermen "had gone out of" their boats and, instead of fishing, "were washing their nets." In biblical times, washing nets was what fishermen did when they had nothing else to do. It was secondary to the job of catching fish and, when fish were still to be caught, was makework. The men had worked all night, had caught nothing, and had given up. Instead of going to sea the following day, they busied themselves with washing their nets. These fishermen can be said to represent the maintenance model of the mainline Church, whose members have left their boats (that is, have abandoned evangelism) and are busy washing their nets (that is, are lost in disputes over issues of internal concern) while the fish go uncaught. Like Simon Peter, the apostles of the maintenance church have given up on their real job. They have left their boats.

In the story, Jesus tells Simon Peter to "put out into the deep water." In other words, Jesus tells him to move the boat into waters away from the shore—into deep waters, where there are fish to be caught. Deep water is traditionally a symbol of uncertainty, the unknown, and danger. In exchanging the relative safety of the shore for deep water, fishermen invariably have put themselves in jeopardy, chancing unpredictable encounters with forces beyond their control. The missionary church is forever in deep water, always at risk, continually taking chances as it tries to carry the Gospel to the unchurched, in words and ways they can understand. It is the maintenance church that keeps its feet on the shore—unwilling to risk, unwilling to change, unwilling to encounter God in the deep water of the unchurched. Just washing its nets.

Simon Peter listens to the words of his Lord and obeys. Although filled with doubt, he does as he is told. The missionary church, in obedience to the Great Commission and the Great Commandment, and despite its doubt, enters into deep water in search of disciples. Like Simon Peter, the missionary church proclaims, "Yet if You say so, I will let down the nets." The maintenance church, consumed by itself and resistant to the challenge of growth, disobeys God and is left behind to wither, for the Lord is, metaphorically, in the boat from which the fish are to be caught, not on land, where the fish are not.

When Simon Peter obeys Christ's command by letting down the nets, he is rewarded with a great catch—not because he is a great fisherman but because God is with him, and because he has obeyed God's command. The apostolic Church in the first centuries of the faith put down its nets and harvested so many disciples that it filled the Roman Empire. What a beautiful metaphor for the mainline churches! How wonderful it would be if our nets were "beginning to break" from "so many fish" that our missionary efforts had brought forth! Could it actually be that way? Of course. The reward of earnest evangelism is always the winning of disciples. It was so in the early Church and it is so in the contemporary Church. It cannot be otherwise, for, as in the biblical story, the fish are the Lord's. They are caught at God's command and by God's power. Like Simon Peter, the missionary church is only the intermediary; disciples are made through the Holy Spirit. Yet, also like Simon Peter, the missionary church is called on to do the legwork. Making "disciples of all nations" requires us to be in our boats, in deep water.

In the story, so many fish are caught that another boat has to be called. The fishermen need help from their partners in the other boat to land the fish. The relevance of the metaphor to a judicatory or a denomination is clear: no missionary outpost is meant to fish alone. Each congregation needs the others in its judicatory—all the congregations as one church in miraculous expectation—to land the fish that the Holy Spirit makes available.

When Simon Peter sees what has happened, he falls down at Jesus' knees, for he has seen the wickedness of his disbelief. In the process of catching fish—of evangelizing—he is forced to see his own iniquities, to confront his own flaws, to accept his own sins. And he is ashamed. No wonder those in the maintenance church prefer debating issues to making disciples! Debating issues doesn't require them to confront their own sinfulness, only the perceived sinfulness of others.

But Jesus said, "Do not be afraid." In Christ we find forgiveness for our sins as well as the courage to confront them. God goes with us in our efforts to carry the Good News, providing help and comfort. The Bible is filled with passages that promise strength and courage to do God's will and walk in God's ways. "Do not be afraid." In the deep water of the missionary church, God is in the boat with us, leading us to great catches of fish, to the saving of human souls, to glorious transformation.

"From now on you will be catching people." Or, as Matthew records it, "Follow me, and I will make you fish for people" (Matthew 4:19). We belong in the missionary boat with God, not on the maintenance shore. We are called on to make disciples, to proclaim the good news to "the whole creation." It is our privilege and our obligation to do so. If the mainline Church is to survive, we must do so. And yet it is also in obedience to

God that human beings experience the profoundest joy of life. In abandoning the material safety of the shore for the spiritual life of deep water, we are touched by the awesome love of the Eternal God. In making disciples, we ourselves are remade.

Do not be afraid. Let down your nets.

REFERENCES

Arias, M., and Johnson, A. *The Great Commission: Biblical Models for Evangelism.* Nashville, Tenn.: Abingdon Press, 1992.

Armstrong, K. *A History of God: The 4000-Year Quest of Judaism, Christianity and Islam.* New York: Ballantine, 1993.

Barna, G. *Evangelism That Works.* Ventura, Calif.: Regal Books, 1995.

Barnwell, C. E. "Rice Farmer Turns Up the Heat in Matagorda." *Texas Episcopalian,* June 1998, p. 16.

Barnwell, C. E. "Bishop Griswold Dishes Up 'Soul Food' for Texas Clergy." *Texas Episcopalian,* June 1999, p. 15.

Broadway, B. "Poll Finds America 'As Churched as Ever.'" *Washington Post,* May 31, 1997, p. B7.

Dunnam, M. D. *Congregational Evangelism: A Pastor's View.* Nashville, Tenn.: Discipleship Resources, 1992.

Episcopal Diocese of Texas. *Episcopal Diocese of Texas Mission Opportunities Catalog.* Houston: Episcopal Diocese of Texas, 1999.

Fowler, J. W. "The Vocation of Faith Development Theory." In J. W. Fowler, K. E. Nipkow, and F. Schweitzer (eds.), *Stages of Faith and Religious Development: Implications for Church, Education, and Society.* New York: Crossroad, 1991.

Hadaway, C. K., and Roozen, D. A. *Rerouting the Protestant Mainstream: Sources of Growth and Opportunities for Change.* Nashville, Tenn.: Abingdon Press, 1995.

Hunter, G. G., III. *How to Reach Secular People.* Nashville, Tenn.: Abingdon Press, 1992.

Hunter, G. G., III. *Church for the Unchurched.* Nashville, Tenn.: Abingdon Press, 1996.

Hutchinson, M. "Lunch Feeds Deep Hunger." *Texas Episcopalian,* June 1998, p. 16.

Jones, J. "Doctors, Clergy Agree: Faith, Healing Go Together." *Houston Chronicle,* May 23, 1998, p. 8E.

Kew, R., and White, R. *Toward 2215: A Church Odyssey.* Boston: Cowley, 1997.

Kotter, J. P. *Leading Change.* Boston: Harvard Business School Press, 1996.

Lewin, K. "Group Decision and Social Change." In G. E. Swanson, T. M. New-come, and E. L. Hartley (eds.), *Readings in Social Psychology.* (2nd ed.) Austin, Tex.: Holt, Rinehart and Winston, 1952.

Martin, K. "Becoming One Church in Austin." *Texas Episcopalian,* June 1988, p. 4.

Mead, L. B. *The Once and Future Church.* Washington, D.C.: Alban Institute, 1991.

Novak, M. "The Most Religious Century." *New York Times,* May 24, 1998, sec. 4, p. 11.

Owen, H. *Leadership Is.* Potomac, Md.: Abbott Press, 1990.

Placher, W. C. "Helping Theology Matter: A Challenge for the Mainline." *Christian Century,* Oct. 28, 1998, p. 994.

Rothauge, A. J. *Sizing Up a Congregation for New Member Ministry.* New York: Episcopal Parish Services, 1986.

Schaller, L. E. *Tattered Trust: Is There Hope for Your Denomination?* Nashville, Tenn.: Abingdon Press, 1996.

Stark, R. *The Rise of Christianity: A Sociologist Reconsiders History.* Princeton, N.J.: Princeton University Press, 1996.

Trueheart, C. "Welcome to the Next Church." *Next from Leadership Network,* Dec. 1996, p. 1.

Vara, R. "A Home Built with Love." *Houston Chronicle,* Feb. 27, 1999, p. 1E.

Wuthnow, R. *Sharing the Journey: Support Groups and America's New Quest for Community.* New York: Free Press, 1994.

THE AUTHORS

THE RIGHT REVEREND CLAUDE E. PAYNE is the Seventh Bishop of Texas, having succeeded to the episcopate in February 1995 after serving sixteen months as Bishop Coadjutor (that is, as the elected successor to the diocesan bishop). Bishop Payne received his B.A. and B.S. degrees from Rice University (the latter degree in chemical engineering) and his M.Div. degree from Church Divinity School of the Pacific. He was awarded the D.D. degree in 1988 from the Church Divinity School of the Pacific and in 1995 from the University of the South.

Before his ordination, Bishop Payne was employed by Union Carbide Corporation, where he worked to shift the company's first production unit from operator-based to computer-based controls. During his six years with the company, he pioneered a more participatory management style in the production area. After his ordination, Bishop Payne served as assistant rector at the Church of the Epiphany and as Episcopal chaplain of Texas A&I University, in Kingsville, Texas. He later became rector of two resource-size Texas congregations—St. Mark's, in Beaumont, and St. Martin's, in Houston—positions that he held for twenty-five years. From 1973 to 1985 he served as assistant secretary of the House of Bishops.

Bishop Payne is chairman of the board of Episcopal High School (Houston), St. Stephen's School (Austin), Camp Allen Conference Center (Navasota), St. James' House (Baytown), St. Vincent's House (Galveston), El Buen Samaritano (Austin), and St. Luke's Episcopal Health System. This last institution includes St. Luke's Episcopal Hospital and the Texas Heart Institute (Houston). He has served on the boards of the Episcopal Seminary of the Southwest and the Church Divinity School of the Pacific, as well as on the board of the Presiding Bishop's Fund for World Relief. Bishop Payne is a trustee of the University of the South, a member of the board of the Baylor School of Medicine, a member of the board of Episcopal Health Charities, president of the American Friends of the Episcopal Diocese of Jerusalem, and a systems/management consultant to the Anglican Consultative Council in London. He is a recipient of Rice University's Distinguished Alumnus Award. Bishop Payne is married to the former Barbara King and is the father of two children, Elizabethe and Walter.

HAMILTON BEAZLEY is associate professor of administrative sciences at the George Washington University. He received his B.A. degree in psychology from Yale University, his M.B.A. degree in accounting from the Cox School of Business at Southern Methodist University, and his Ph.D. degree in organizational behavior from the George Washington University.

Before undertaking his academic career, Beazley served in various financial and strategic planning positions in the American oil industry. He was a founding member of the board of directors of DyChem International (UK) Ltd. and is founding chairman of the Oxy Houston Credit Union. He is also a former president of the National Council on Alcoholism and Drug Dependence. He is a member of the executive committee of Harvard Medical School's Division on Addictions, a member of the board of trustees of the Educational Advancement Foundation, a member of the advisory board of the Discovery Learning Project at the University of Texas at Austin, and a former member of the board of trustees of the Episcopal Radio-TV Foundation.

Beazley is cocreator of *Secrets Out,* a television series that aired on the BBC, London, during the 1984–1987 seasons. He is also the author or coauthor of numerous essays, which have been published in books and journals. His areas of professional expertise are servant-leadership, emotional intelligence, and spirituality in the leadership of organizations. He is a member of the American Psychological Association, the International Society of Simulation and Gaming, the Academy of Management, and the Organizational Behavior Teaching Society. He was born and raised in the Diocese of Texas.

Readers are welcome to contact the authors at the following addresses:

The Right Reverend Claude E. Payne, Bishop of Texas
The Diocesan Center
3203 West Alabama Street
Houston, TX 77098

Hamilton Beazley, Ph.D.
George Washington University
2136 Pennsylvania Avenue, NW, Suite 301
Washington, DC 20052

THE DIOCESE OF TEXAS

THE MISSION FIELD of the Diocese of Texas covers almost 50,000 square miles, or about 20 percent of the state. It includes the major cities of Houston, Austin, Galveston, Waco, Tyler, Beaumont, and Longview, as well as numerous small and medium-size towns. The diocese covers fifty-seven counties from Austin eastward to the Louisiana border and from below Dallas south to the Gulf of Mexico. It contains 45 percent of the state's population, or about seven million souls. The diocese has more than 80,000 members in 156 congregations. More than 40 percent of the people in the diocesan region are unchurched.

In the three years since Bishop Payne's election as Bishop Coadjutor, the Diocese of Texas has increased its membership by 10 percent, from 73,000 to more than 80,000. The number of people attending Sunday church services has risen from 23,000 per year to more than 28,000, an increase of nearly 22 percent. Confirmations have risen from an annual plateau of 1,800 to more than 2,000, an increase of 11 percent. The number of resource-size churches has grown from 14 to 16, an increase of 14 percent, and the number of program-size churches has grown from 19 to 29, an increase of 50 percent. Today the diocese contains 11 percent of the fastest-growing congregations in the Episcopal Church. It is the fourth-largest diocese in America but ranks first in church-school membership, in the number of children in parochial schools, in adult education, and in the number of members confirmed. These changes are a testament to the power of the missionary model implemented in the Diocese of Texas.

INDEX

A

Abraham, 44

Accountability, 78–79, 119; communication and, 223; in missionary versus maintenance model, 195; in resource allocation, 208

Acts, xii; 1:8, 126; 2:44, 202; 20:35, 151

Advertising, 224–225

African American congregations, 155, 161–162

African American membership, 59

Age of Christendom, 21, 22–23; dissolution of, 24–25; maintenance model and, 23–24

Alard, L., 66, 67, 160–161

All Saints' Chapel, Camp Allen, 231, 232–233

All Saints Church, Cameron, 159

All Saints Episcopal Church, Austin, 80

All Saints Episcopal Church, Crocket, 84

Altar call, 125

American Baptist Church: governance of, xvi, xvii; as mainline denomination, xiii

American Revolution, 21

American society: apostolic paradigm in, 21–22; belief in God in, 7; breakdown of support structures in, 50–51; diversity in, 58; lack of spirituality in, 7–8; mission field in, 190; secularization and, 24–25; spiritual hunger in, 5–13

Analysis: for change, 62; of Christian education needs, 235; of congregations, 142, 145, 146, 147–148, 152, 155, 206; demographic, 148; questions for, 72–73; of youth ministry needs, 239

Anchoring new approaches in the culture (change stage 8), 112–115

Anglican denominations: governance of, xvii; listed, xvii. *See also Episcopal headings;* Mainline denominations

Apocrypha, 222

Apostle, The, 198

Apostle(s): meaning of, 20; transformation of, 12–13

Apostolate, defined, 181, 192

Apostolate of the clergy, 192–201; characteristics of, 193–201; in missionary versus maintenance model, 192–193, 194–196. *See also* Clergy

Apostolate of the judicatory, 202–216; characteristics of, 202–211; in missionary versus maintenance model, 202–211. *See also Judicatory headings*

Apostolate of the laity, 181–191; clergy support for, 198; history and background of, 181, 182; lay responsibility for creating, 191; in missionary versus maintenance model, 183–191. *See also* Laity

Apostolic ages, 20–25

Apostolic paradigm, 20–22; postapostolic paradigm versus, 22–23

Apostolic succession, 29, 202

Apostolos, 20

Arias, M., 15, 235

Armstrong, K., 7

Asian ministry, 59, 162

Assimilation stage of evangelism, 139

Association, as term for judicatory unit, xvii. *See also* Judicatory

Assumptions, challenging, 72–73

Attraction, 128–134, 176; objects of, 128–130; process of, 132–134; seeker motivation and, 130–132

Austin Regional Planning Group, 79–80, 142, 144, 154–155

Authoritative approach, 205

I

Illness metaphor, 26–28, 31–32

Imagination, as vision gathering theme, 68

Impediments to implementation, 118–123

Implementation: analysis for, 62, 72–73; empowerment for, 103–108; financial resources for, 121–123; impediments to, 118–123; judicatory survey for, 64–65; of missionary vision, 62–73, 100–103; organic approach to, 62

Inauguration, as vision gathering theme, 69

Inclusivity: in communications, 221, 222; in missionary versus maintenance model, 49, 57–59, 117, 185, 196; multicultural congregational development for, 160–162; in vision gathering, 69

Incorporation, as vision gathering theme, 68–69

Individualism: secularization and, 24; spiritual, 6

Information, as vision gathering theme, 68

Information technology. See Technology

Initiation stage of evangelism, 139

In-line skating, 221–222

Innovation, encouragement of, 104, 105

Inquirers' classes, 136, 168. See also Discovery classes

Inspiration, as vision gathering theme, 68

Internal focus, in missionary versus maintenance model, 48, 50–53, 194

Internet, 225–227

Invitation, 133–134; lay responsibility for, 183, 185; to worship, 177

Isaiah 6:8, 182

Islands of health and wellness, 109

Issues, divisive, 32–36; focus on unifying vision versus, 32–36, 38, 72, 103, 106, 107–108; as wounds on Body of Christ, 33–36. See also Conflict

J

James Ministry, 175

Jeremiah, 103

Jesus: miracles of, 51; and the miraculous catch, 1–2, 241–244; servant leadership of, 75, 204; teaching and action of, 16; vision of, 43

John: 1:1, 219; 9:38, 124; 12:16, 141; 15:11, 9; 20:21–23, 16

John, Gospel of, on Great Commission, 14, 16

John the Baptist, 44

I John 4:7, 35

Johnson, A., 15, 235

Jones, J., 6

Joshua, 44

Joy, 47

Judicatory leaders, 202–216; accountability for performance of, 78–79; budgeting and financial decisions of, 208, 214; characteristics of, 211–212; clergy selection by, 205–206, 213, 214; communication style of, 205, 210–211, 213, 215; delegation of pastoral duties by, 207–208, 214; holistic versus reductionistic perspective of, 203–204; lay appointments by, 206–207; in missionary versus maintenance model, 202–211, 212–216; participatory versus autocratic leadership styles of, 204; as resources for congregations, 204–205, 215; role of, in addressing conflicted congregations, 206, 213; role of, in outreach and education, 209–210, 215; roles of, in missionary versus maintenance model, 212–216; selection of, 211–216; strategic planning by, 208–209, 214; terms for, by denomination, xvii; trust in, 89–90. See also Bishop

Judicatory organization. See Organizational structure

Judicatory staff: for congregational development, 143–145; education and training of, 99; lay contact with, 149; in missionary versus maintenance model, 215; as resource for congregations, 204–205, 215, 224, 237; role of, in spoke-and-wheel model, 76, 106, 109–110; teams of, 77–78

Judicator(y)ies: analysis of, 72–73, 142, 145, 147–148, 152; aposto-